Making It Together
as a Two-Career Couple

Making It Together as a Two-Career Couple

Marjorie Hansen Shaevitz

Morton H. Shaevitz

Houghton Mifflin Company
Boston 1980

Library of Congress Cataloging in Publication Data
Shaevitz, Morton H
    Making it together as a two-career couple.

    Bibliography: p.
    Includes index.
        1.   Married people—Employment—United States.
2.   Family life education.   I. Shaevitz, Marjorie
Hansen, joint author.   II. Title.
HQ536.S48 1980   301.42′7   79–20134
ISBN 0–395–28592–5

Printed in the United States of America

S 10 9 8 7 6 5 4 3 2 1

To our children:
Erica and *Jonathon*,
Geoffrey and *Marejka*,
and to
Cecilia Mary Theresa Hartmann,
the best damn child-care person in the world

Acknowledgments

First, we wish to thank our families and our many friends and colleagues who put up with us while we were writing this book.

Second, we wish to acknowledge the untiring efforts of Florence Friedman, who helped us with our research, who kept all the materials together, and who in her warm and friendly way goaded us when we slowed down, reprimanded us for unclear thinking, pushed us to finish on time, and even monitored some of our less than rational disagreements.

We want to pay tribute to David Hellyer, whose editorial guidance and sense of humor are evident throughout the book. Without his assistance, this book would still be in the file cabinet.

Finally, we express our special appreciation to David Harris, our editor at Houghton Mifflin; to our literary agents, Julian Bach and Linda Chester; and to Jacqueline Coolman, librarian at the University of California, San Diego.

Preface

This is a book *for* two-career couples, not about them; a book to help two-career couples be more effective and satisfied in their everyday lives. This is a book mostly about middle-class couples, the group with whom we have worked in private practice and about whom we have studied.

There are many popular psychology books now on the market that tell you what your problems are. They fall short, however, by not offering solutions to the problems described. This book is different. *Making It Together* describes what is happening today as relationships and roles change; it tells you what the problems are in dual-career relationships and why they are occurring, and it offers solutions or procedures to help you cope more effectively with these problems.

Making It Together is a guidebook to be used now and, as new issues emerge, to be used again. It can be read by you in a number of ways. First, if you are not in a hurry, each partner can read the entire book separately. We suggest that you set aside some time to talk with one another about what you've read and try your hand at some problem-solving. Second, if you have specific issues that you want to tackle right away, you may want to begin with those chapters which seem most relevant to you. Again, we urge that you discuss with one another what you have read and try solving the problems together. Third, if you both have the time, you may want to read it together, even reading sections aloud, so that reading, discussion, and problem-solving can take place at the same time.

Although there may be many solutions to your particular dual-career dilemmas, you may find that there are no specific answers to some of your questions. Through this book the authors want to encourage you, as a dual-career couple, to create solutions on your own that fit your circumstances. This book can't solve all of your problems, but we do hope to make your lives better. The very fact that you are now reading this is an indication of your interest in improving things.

There are two other points we want to note. First, in writing this book we were influenced by three eminent sociologists, Rhona and Robert Rapoport and Jessie Bernard. They are all wonderfully insightful, visionary, clear-thinking investigators and writers.

Second, the unattributed quotations in the book are taken from cases or combinations of cases from our professional work as clinicians, teachers, or seminar leaders. Fictitious names are used in order to respect the confidential nature of the professional relationship. The examples, however, are real.

Making It Together is also a celebration of the two-career couple, the new and revolutionary relationship that one writer has likened to "a symphony with two conductors." The potential for truly great music is there, but it takes exceptional measures of cooperation and teamwork to produce it.

Who are we, and why did we write this book?

First, we are a two-career couple with four children (two preschoolers, and two teen-agers from Morton Shaevitz's previous marriage). Our personal lives, therefore—at home and in the office—are the laboratory in which we are constructing and testing the ideas presented in this book.

In fact, if the truth be known, we were confronted with the subject of two-career couples in 1972, when we married. At that time both of us were involved in full-time careers at the University of California, San Diego (Morton Shaevitz as Dean and Director of Counseling and Psychological services; Marjorie Shaevitz as Director of Counseling and Registration Services, University Extension). We had no children living with us, but when we were home we found ourselves spending an inordinate amount of time discussing such important issues as who was going to take out the garbage!

Since we both come from the academic world, we decided to do what most academics do when they have a question for which they have no answers: we went to the literature. As you may guess, we could find no answers. What we did find was some preliminary research and writing about two-career couples that was descriptive in nature. That still didn't help us with our questions. It was then that we saw we had two choices: either we would wait for the literature and resources to develop, or we could produce them on our own. We chose the latter alternative. Over the past seven years we have been actively involved in doing research in the two-career area and in using the research of others as it has developed.

Second, we are professionals in the area of mental health and human relations. Morton Shaevitz is a practicing clinical psychologist with his Ph.D. from the University of California, Los Angeles. Marjorie Shaevitz is a mental-health counselor and consultant, with a master's degree from Stanford University, and is co-author of the recently published book *So You Want to Go Back to School: Facing the Realities of Re-Entry.*

We work with dual-career couples in private practice, offer educational seminars and workshops for and about dual-career couples at universities, and consult with business, industry, and government regarding family and work relationships.

The two-career phenomenon has increasingly occupied our thinking since 1972 to the point that now, personally and professionally, we are involved with it on almost a full-time basis. This book is the distillation of all our personal and professional experiences.

P.S. As to who took out the garbage, sometimes Morton did, sometimes Marjorie did. Now the teen-agers take it out. For an explanation of how we devised this solution, please read the book.

Contents

Acknowledgments   vii

Preface   ix

   I. The End—and the Beginning   1

  II. Two Careers: The New Game in Town   10

 III. Who Takes Out the Garbage?: Managing the Household   32

 IV. Two-Career Parenting   66

  V. The Other-Than-Mother Dilemma: Choosing Child Care   92

 VI. Dealing with Dollars   136

VII. Some Special Challenges: Launching, Role-Changing, New Opportunities, Similar Careers, and Successful Women   159

VIII. Choosing the "Right" Employer   214

 IX. "Help!": Coping with Overload   230

  X. The Couple Relationship: Some Final Touches   245

Reference Notes   257

Suggestions for Further Reading   269

Index   273

Making It Together
as a Two-Career Couple

CHAPTER I

The End-and the Beginning

It was only yesterday when life for most middle-class American men and women followed a predictable pattern. Men spent their youth learning a trade or becoming "educated," and then embarked on something called "work." Thereafter, through the long and often dreary years spent in an office, factory, or field, these men looked forward eagerly to that magical time called retirement, a time when they could—at last—do what they "really wanted to do"—travel, fish, or enjoy their grandchildren.

Women accepted without question that they would go to school (probably for fewer years than the men), fall in love, marry, and bear children. If they worked, their work was seen as an interim activity, to help launch the family. There was a "happy ever after" promise implied in this time-honored arrangement, but the promise was seldom fulfilled.

With rare exceptions, our grandparents lived out this scenario, and so did many of our parents. Even today, like father like son, like mother like daughter, thousands of American men and women follow, or assume they will follow, this classical model.

However, most of us now realize that storybook life

bears little resemblance to the real, everyday experience of the average American. Fewer and fewer men find mere "work" for work's sake fulfilling. More and more women feel short-changed, and yearn to add new dimensions to their lives. They no longer find satisfaction exclusively in their homemaker and mother roles, and are searching for new horizons.

The Roots of Change

The key word today is "change." People are changing. Roles are changing. Relationships are shifting. Expectations men and women have for themselves, and for one another, are being revised. In all probability, you too are changing . . . even though you may not yet be aware of it. You may even fear this change.

Do not be alarmed. You have plenty of company.

It is important, in the midst of all this upheaval, to understand how and why these profound alterations are taking place. Some of the answers lie in the past twenty years of American cultural history. The roots reach back into the early 1960s, to the beginnings of what became known as the women's liberation movement (which was, of course, a lineal descendant of the civil-rights foment of the 1950s and 1960s). "Women of America, arise, re-evaluate yourselves and your roles. Examine your options and exercise them." A major factor supporting this new self-awareness and the concept of options was the widespread use of birth control devices by women (the "pill" and the IUD), which gave them greater control over the choice of when or whether to have children.

The rationale for women's liberation was blunt and simple: *There is more to life for women than having babies and keeping house. Use your potential and your talents. Demand more out of life.*

One woman summed it up neatly:". . . It doesn't take

all I have to be a mommy—I have more potential than that. I've got more avenues to explore. I can work and still be a good mother."[1]

Worldwide propagandizing in favor of zero population growth, and increasing emphasis on what one researcher called "personhood," were among other social pressures responsible for the ferment and change.[2]

The Media Myths

The visible signs of change are all around us. Nearly every issue of every major consumer magazine includes an article or story about working wives or the "new elite," as *Time* recently labeled the two-career couple.[3] The media hype for the "new" woman or the "new" man is fairly consistent and quite clear. "House-husband" is becoming a part of the American vocabulary.

Magazine articles dealing with two-career phenomena tend to fall readily into one of two categories: either they describe very successful, attractive, energetic couples who seem to work twenty-four-hour days and who dispose of all their problems in superhuman fashion, or they depict those at the other extreme—the couples whose two-career marriages are falling apart. Neither of these categories gives a realistic insight into the day-to-day experiences of the average dual-career couple.

The media—print and broadcast alike—bombard us with perfect images, with "equal sharing" as the watchword. We are led to believe that the new two-career couples—bright, healthy-looking people in the prime of life, with happy, cooperative children—walk out of the house in the A.M. toward separate cars and separate careers. Then, on returning home in the P.M., the partners immediately share all the tasks. While he prepares dinner, she deals with the children. As she checks to see if the car needs lubricating or the fence needs painting, he takes care of the wash. Everything is beautiful, organized, calm, and efficient.

Do these media creations really mirror life? Our experience tells us otherwise; we believe that things are, in reality, much more complex and confusing. Indeed, as we look around us to see what is actually going on in the lives of dual-career couples, we find that in many instances there is little to distinguish their lifestyles from those of "conventional" couples. A Cornell University study revealed that, to a measurable extent, women in two-career relationships still bear the major responsibility for household management and child care.[4] The study found, further, that, even though there has been some increased participation by the men, in the main the woman's workday simply grows longer when she enters the job market. In other words, while assuming additional work responsibilities outside the home, women also keep many of the household and child-raising tasks they performed before they took on a career.

The Vanishing American Paycheck

By the late 1970s, the average cost of a home in the United States, nationwide, exceeded $60,000.[5] The Volkswagen "bug," which, in 1966, sold for $1800, became a rabbit and soared to $5200. Shoes once ticketed at $20 to $30 a pair were priced at $50 and $60, and more for designer brands. Gasoline prices zoomed ahead, and the $1.00 gallon—yesterday unthinkable—became reality.

These and other indices clearly show that it is no longer possible for most middle-class families to depend exclusively on the income of one wage-earner, especially if the wage-earner does not moonlight. For example, the U.S. Bureau of Labor Statistics reports that as of 1977, the average salary earned by a full-time worker in the United States was $12,679.[6] However, it was estimated that a family of four needed $17,106 in 1977 to maintain an intermediate standard of living.[7]

It's obvious that we can't survive on Jim's salary alone. After taxes, withholding, and so on, our combined salaries are $1200 a month (and Jim is doing well and moving up in the organization). While we had originally planned for me to work until we had our first child, now we find that it's my work that allows us to go on vacations, to eat out, to do the kinds of things that we'd always hoped to do.

Middle-class families today are caught in the same bind that gripped only lower-class families a mere fifteen years ago. In the early sixties, the model middle-class American family was one in which the man earned a salary that was adequate to care for all his family's needs. This historical "truth" has gone the way of other myths about couples, marriage, and the middle-class family.

So, quite apart from any philosophical reasons she may have for moving into the job market, the middle-class American woman today is motivated by cold economic reality to seek employment, or to upgrade her employability by returning to the classroom. She also may be urged forward by *Ms.* magazine, consciousness-raising groups, or her career-oriented friends, but she is *first* and *foremost* acutely mindful of the month-end avalanche of bills.

Since inflation continues to average in excess of 10 percent a year, with no end of the spiral in sight, the trend toward more and greater participation by women in the nation's job market seems firmly established.

Second Thoughts in Midcareer

I'm not really sure that I like being a dermatologist. In fact, I'm not even sure that I like being a doctor. I make a lot of money . . . but when I think of how I spend my time every day, and

I think of the kinds of satisfaction I get out of my work, I begin to have some serious reservations.

But then I can't really think of something else that I could get into that wouldn't take me another five years to prepare for. I really don't want to start from scratch again. But when I think of myself and my life, and I think of doing this for the next twenty years, it really gets depressing.

It may be that physicians in the fifties had similar misgivings and concerns about their work. But twenty years ago there was not much support for changing careers in midstream. The concept of the "midlife crisis" is still rather new.[8]

We are no longer afraid, though, to admit that some work may be boring. The alleged excitement that was supposed to go hand in hand with a career in business or industry has been demystified and in most cases found to be hollow and spurious. A new generation of men and women who have achieved early success in one enterprise or another are now asking themselves serious questions about what they have achieved, and whether they want to continue along the same time-worn route (or rut).

Middle-level managers no longer see themselves as committed with single-minded devotion to the organization that hired them. At a recent conference in the Midwest, four directors of personnel agreed that they looked with some suspicion on any person whose file indicated no job changes over a five- to ten-year period.

I was a firehorse—was willing to jump through hoops. People aren't like that anymore.[9]

So the word is out: It's okay to change jobs. It's okay to change careers. It's okay to do whatever you think you should be doing, and it's even okay to do it if other people don't like the idea. Work exists not only to bring in money; it should also have meaning and satisfaction and should bring you fulfillment. Management consultant Sharon Connelly has noted:

Quality of life is becoming as important a concern to people as their career progress or their financial standing.[10]

Today, no one can count on anything. Women can no longer count on seeing their men continue on a given career path. Men can no longer count on women's historic commitment to the home.

Whatever were the rules no longer are. In fact, no one really knows what the new rules are.

Marriage, Contemporary Style

JUDGE: Friends and neighbors, Bob and Marilyn are glad that you are able to be here with them today. As you know, they've been together for three years, and now they've decided to marry.

So they come together before you to share this experience and my job is to make their marriage official.

Do you, Bob, accept Marilyn as your wife, and contract to stay with her so long as you love her, and so long as you are both growing in the same way? Do you, Marilyn, accept Bob as your husband, so long as you love him, and so long as you both see your relationship as a growing one?

If so, I now officially declare you married.

Lament its passing though we may, "until death do us part" is out of style for a great many people. Many men and women approaching marriage do so with caution and reserve. They are willing to live together for a period of time, but they also want an option to sever the relationship "if it doesn't work out." Prenuptial agreements, once exclusively the instruments of the multimarried wealthy, are now becoming commonplace, particularly for those in their twenties.

In those states with no-fault divorce laws, the rate of dissolution today parallels the rate of marriage. Obviously, there are innumerable couples who have decided they are not "growing together." Given this as a reality, it is no longer possible for men and women—and women in particular—to view the marital relationship as a guarantee of personal or economic stability, *even if they wanted to.*

The reality today is that men and women alike are pushing for a life in which they can, if necessary, take care of themselves. Any career counselor who now encourages women to do anything less than maximize their economic potential is counseling for an era long since gone. Like it or not, the need today is for everyone, man or woman, to develop the capacity to function independently, alone. Harold Frank, a management consultant, has said:

Until recently, both husband and wife concentrated their combined efforts on the husband's career. The wife of a career-oriented executive usually worked as many as 70 or 80 hours a week at managing a household. She cooked and cleaned, looked after her husband, reared their children, and participated in church and community affairs. In short, she did everything necessary to make the family function as a unit.

The wife's occupation inside the home made marriage relationship interdependent: the husband was free to work at his career more than full time only because the wife shouldered all the familial responsibilities.

This *modus operandi* is impossible in a two-career marriage. When both the husband and wife are pursuing professional lives outside the home, they're not interdependent; in fact, they often end up being counterdependent—or resisting dependence on each other. They may find they cannot meet each other's needs and still maintain their independence.[11]

Yes, it's a confusing period in our history. Everything appears to be up for grabs. Relationships are impermanent. Everybody has to work. Nobody has to be committed to a job. Do your own thing. Men are supposed to *care* more. Women are encouraged to *do* more. Couples are implored to *be* more.

For a long while, nobody really knew what it all meant. But now, at last, we are beginning to read the signs, to interpret, to define, and to understand.

We see individuals emerging as more than unidimensional stick figures. Men and women alike are finding that they have parts and potentials they never knew existed. Men are enjoying some heretofore buried emotional part of themselves. As fathers, they are becoming more and more involved with parenting functions that used to be left exclusively to mothers, grandmothers, and other female caretakers. Women are seeing new strengths in themselves. They are finding not only that they can be supportive and caring, but that they can also be assertive and intellectual, and effective leaders. Couples are experimenting with new kinds of communication, going beyond stereotyped ways of relating. Families are seen as a powerful stabilizing unit within which new roles for men and women are emerging.

We are beginning to comprehend that, though all this ferment may mark the end of an era many of us thought would never end, it also may signal the beginning of a new and better era for multitudes of Americans.

CHAPTER II

Two Careers:
The New Game in Town

Believe me when I tell you it is possible to have a marriage where neither mate is the boss but where both are partners. This makes for a harmonious home, helps keep both spouses' blood pressure normal, ulcers from forming, and heart attacks from occurring.[1]

This is a book for working couples, couples like Jim and Jodi Michaels. Both were deeply concerned about their failure to adjust to the special demands of a relationship in which both partners were committed to careers *and* to making their marriage a success. They were finding these two goals difficult to achieve simultaneously.

JIM: It all began about seven months ago when Jodi got involved in this Zero Population Growth movement. At first there was just a couple of hours a day and maybe a phone call or two in the evening. But now it's gotten out of control. She's spending every afternoon away. Nothing's getting done around the house. The phone begins ringing at seven in the morning, and almost every evening there's a meeting of some kind. I know she's having a lot of fun and it's very exciting for her, but things are just falling apart around the house. Whenever I try to talk with Jodi about it she tells me that I'm being selfish and that if I have my work, why can't she be doing something for herself. So I feel angry and guilty at the same time. And it's beginning to affect our relationship. Our sex life has deteriorated. Half the time she's so damn tired by the time she gets home that even when we do have an evening together, she's usually asleep by nine o'clock. I've had it.

Jim and Jodi are not alone. They, and thousands of other contemporary couples, are struggling—often without help—as they try to solve their dual-career problems. Much of the time they feel anxious and isolated, confused, guilty. They tend to view their problems as unique. Typically, the parties to these quarrels see their spouses as uncaring and unsupportive. There is much blaming and large doses of raw anger, and often there is total breakdown in communication. Each member of the team resents any infringement (real or imagined) on his or her autonomy, and each is angry at what is viewed as a lack of understanding on the part of the other.

JODI: I'm finally beginning to feel good about myself. I worked for the first three years after we got married, and then when the kids came along I really wanted to spend time at home. But now it's different. Timmy is six, Ruth is nine, and I've had it with lunches and P.T.A. and the rest. I could go back to work, but Jim's making good money and besides, somebody has to become involved in these kinds of things. I've always been ecologically minded, so when the opportunity came to work on the Zero Population Growth thing I jumped at it. The project grew faster than I thought it would, but that doesn't make any difference. For the first time in years, I feel *alive* and *excited* . . . and I'm turned on by the people I'm working with, and the chance for learning. Sure, I do feel upset about leaving the children and the housework, but I'm trying as hard as I can to make sure the kids are taken care of. *I'm* the one who's still available when they're sick. *I'm* the one who does the babysitting arrangements. Frankly, my beef is not so much with the children as with Jim. He just doesn't seem to understand. He's angry most of the time, and doesn't want to participate with me in any of the things I'm doing. He seemed interested at first, but as I became more involved and turned on, he seemed to resent things, and me, and everything I'm doing. It seems as though I must either stay home and be unhappy myself, or do what I'm doing and make him unhappy with me and me with him. I don't get it. Right now we're at war, and neither of us seems to know what to do about it.

A "Symphony Led By Two Conductors"?[2]

What is a two-career relationship? Earlier writers have defined it as one in which both partners are involved in full-time careers. We find this definition too narrow, and prefer a more contemporary description, which reflects the changes taking place in our society:

A two-career relationship is one in which both partners have a significant commitment, full time or part time, to a role outside the home.

If one party is working full time while the other is studying toward a degree on a part-time basis, this would qualify as a two-career marriage. If one partner is involved ten to fifteen hours a week as a volunteer, acquiring new skills in anticipation of taking a paying job, this could also be termed a two-career relationship. The distinguishing characteristic of a two-career couple is their commitment to their respective pursuits outside the home. The commitment may or may not involve compensation. Commitment, as we mean it, implies responsibility; it is not play or a hobby or something one dabbles in.

The term "career" in the traditional sense has come to imply full-time, demanding job activity. We give the word a broader meaning, because we think that the time-honored concept of "career" is outdated. We are convinced, after many years of counseling, teaching, and lecturing in this subject area, that men and women in today's America no longer blindly accept the definition conventionally applied in business and corporate circles.

Society can no longer afford careers that imperil or destroy the family. Instead, we need to develop careers that better meet our personal realities, that allow for work outside the home while, at the same time, leaving time for individual and family needs and responsibilities. We must acknowledge and plan for that new world of multiple careers described in Alvin Toffler's *Future Shock.*

"Under conditions prevailing at the beginning of the 1960's . . . the average twenty-year-old man in the work force could be expected to change jobs about six or seven times." Thus instead of thinking in terms of a "career" the citizen of super-industrial society will think in terms of "serial careers."[3]

Each of us may, at one time or another, feel a need to return to the classroom to stretch the mind or the spirit. Many of us may want to volunteer for some worthy activity. Others may elect a career involving work for compensation. Each of us needs to realize that these options exist and that we can exercise them.

Career, as we have defined it, allows for these natural alterations, options, and cycles.

If you are to cope with whatever problems you may encounter in a two-career relationship, it is imperative that you understand that *the dual-career phenomenon is probably the most important social change of the twentieth century.* Jessie Bernard, a well-known sociologist, compares this change, in magnitude, to the domestication of animals, the move from an agrarian to an industrial society, and the Industrial Revolution itself.[4]

So American society, in common with societies in many other nations of the world, is in the midst of a social revolution. Involved are 55.6 percent of all American husband-wife families who already are living as two-career couples, and their number is increasing geometrically.[5] (This, of course, does not even take into account unmarried two-career couples.)

Much of the change we are describing has taken place since the late 1960s and early 1970s. The change has occurred with such lightning speed that most of us were (and some still are) entirely unaware of it. In contrast, other great shifts in the social order, such as the Industrial Revolution, occurred at a much slower pace, giving men and women time to adjust to the alterations.

In the two-career phenomenon, then, we are dealing not only with radical change itself, but also with change at a vastly accelerated rate, which exacerbates the problem.

Two-career relationships are not for everyone, and we clearly do not advocate the mode for all couples. Experiences and statistics have shown us, however, that countless thousands of couples already are embarked on a two-career relationship or are contemplating one. The following are typical categories:

1. Couples in which both partners are highly skilled, well-educated professionals. The pressing question here is not whether to become a dual-career couple, but how to cope with the problems that can arise from such a relationship. If one partner becomes more "successful" than the other, how do both adjust? What happens when one partner is offered a better position in another community? Does the entire family relocate? Does one partner commute?

2. Young couples just beginning their respective careers. Where should they locate so that both will find

first-rate jobs at the outset? Should they have children? When, and how many? At what intervals? How are the responsibilities of household management shared?

3. "Traditional" couples who, for a period of years, have maintained a relationship in which the man has "gone to work," and the woman has "kept house." They agree to change this pattern, usually at the wife's suggestion. What effect will her absence have on the children? Who will "keep house"? What will be done with "her" money if she finds a paying job?

4. Middle-aged couples whose careers are out of sync. We know, for example, of a number of instances in which the husband is "gearing down" to a more leisurely pace after a long, high-pressured corporate career. Simultaneously, the wife is "gearing up" to a new career, or perhaps studying for an advanced degree after many years of housekeeping and family-rearing. The possibilities for stress and strain in such relationships are legion.

Do Your Own Thing

> I do my thing, and you do your thing.
> I am not in this world to live up to your
> expectations
> And you are not in this world to live up to mine.
> You are you, and I am I,
> And if by chance, we find each other, it's beautiful.
> If not, it can't be helped.[6]

Fritz Perls's famous maxim of the sixties was accepted without much question by countless thousands of young adults in their twenties and thirties. Esalen, Synanon, sensitivity training, the human-relations movement, and encounter groups—all seemed to impart the same message:

"Do your own thing. It's your turn now. Take care of yourself. Meet your own needs. Take care of number one."

A forty-two-year-old woman with two teen-age children reviews what she's been doing for the last twenty years, and says, "I've been taking care of my husband, I've been taking care of my kids, I've been taking care of the P.T.A., and my parents, and everyone else for so long. And now I am being told I can take care of myself, and I'm damn well going to do that."

This middle-aged housewife is probably the best example of the "do your own thing" era, which in some particulars is a narcissistic view of the world. We sympathize strongly with those who are concerned primarily with their own growth and development. We are convinced, however, that merely doing your own thing with little regard for the rights and needs of others is inappropriate for couples and has disastrous implications for the family unit.

Though the era of narcissism is still with us, we see evidence of renewed interest in family life in America. We sincerely support this trend. On the basis of personal experience with our own two-career marriage, and of our hundreds of contacts with two-career couples, we agree wholeheartedly with the views of Shephard G. Aronson, of the New York University School of Medicine:

As the husband of a liberated woman and the father of two bright, liberated children, let me put to you *my* conviction, that no other institution on earth can sustain and delight two human beings as fully and for as long a period as a modern, loving, sharing monogamous marriage.[7]

It cannot be denied, however, that the institution of marriage is in deep trouble in America, and that restoring the family to its rightful place will take more than wishful thinking. It will take hard work, the kind of work not mentioned in an article in one of the country's leading magazines.[8] This piece, described on the periodical's cover as dealing with two-career crises, discussed the ways in which several glamorous, successful celebrity couples were handling such issues as competition and privacy. There was no mention of arguments at eight in the morning, dirty diapers, sinks overflowing with egg-encrusted plates, split-second schedules, dead-tired people, and cantankerous kids. All their problems—in this rosy-hued article—seemed to be thoroughly and enthusiastically discussed, pro and con. Nobody yelled. Nobody pouted or walked away in a huff.

Were these real people—people like Donna and Hal?

DONNA: We seem to be fighting all the time, and when I get home at the end of the day I'm really bushed. But I still seem to be the food machine. After putting in ten hours listening to other people's problems, I need some time for myself. But there just doesn't seem to be any. The kids are waiting to be fed. The babysitter wants to escape. And I seem to have turned into a yeller . . . I yell at the kids, I yell at the cat, and I yell at Hal. And when I hear myself yelling, even I get turned off with me.

Hal doesn't seem really to give a damn. He's so caught up in his new job—he seems to be coming home later and later —and the minute he walks in the door the phone begins ringing. For *him.* He's such a damn chauvinist, to try to get him to help is like pulling teeth. He's always talking about how he brings home most of the income, and because of that we're able to have lots of help. He doesn't want to spend his free time vacuuming or washing dishes. But damn it, if he doesn't do it, guess who does? Me.

HAL: Donna has become impossible. I admire and support her for having an important and responsible job. She makes almost as much money as I do. But the price we pay is too high. I'm concerned most that we have almost lost one another, and that she's much more interested in her work and the house and the kids than she is in me. This "individual development" stuff is okay, I guess. But frankly, I think she's become a narcissistic bitch.

Since Donna and Hal—and Jim and Jodi—lack information about what is normal in two-career problem areas, they tend to view what's happening to them as unhealthy and abnormal. Labels come easily: she's *selfish,* he's *chauvinistic;* he *doesn't give a damn,* she's *narcissistic.* The more sophisticated the partners, the more sophisticated their attacks: he's *neurotically involved in his work;* she's into a *late adolescent, self-gratification phase.*

Sometimes they don't blame one another; they begin to think their marriage is falling apart. "After all, responsible, loving, caring adults should be able to work out their problems. And since everybody else seems to be working out theirs, what's the matter with us?"

Nothing. Probably nothing at all is the matter. The fact is that most two-career couples have sets of predictable problems to deal with. And problems are not necessarily and inevitably indicative of a bad marriage or of unhealthy, abnormal behavior by either party. Such problems are simply indicators of a real, hard fact: two-career relationships are very, very difficult to pull off. Particularly during the beginning phases, there are certain to be many issues to deal with, a moderate degree of conflict, and some inevitable arguments.

As one observer expressed it, "I find the bustle and strain of the couples' lives created an infectious exhaustion."[9]

If you will accept as Basic Fact Number One the inevitability of "infectious exhaustion," you are on your way to becoming a more successful, happier two-career couple.

One of the reasons that things are so difficult right now for two-career couples is that, in a very real sense, they are breaking ground for those who will follow. They are the pioneers—and so are you—and that means that often you will be forced to work out your own solutions to inevitable problems.

Statistically, two-career couples *are a majority.* [10] But they are really *treated like the minority* in the sense that they are discriminated against by institutions, tend to be looked down on by their traditional friends, and often are faced with defending their lifestyle to their families.

Though there are a few support systems available to dual-career couples (and we will identify these later), most couples have to make it on their own at first. Even though armed with information and skills, the new working couple will face a series of impressive hurdles before achieving the harmonious relationship that both partners desire and deserve.

Society in general has not adjusted to the phenomenon any better than the couples have themselves. If, for example, the dishwasher breaks and you call a repair shop for help, you will be told that "somebody will be there on Tuesday." When you try to set a more definite time and date, you are quickly struck by the realization that service businesses always assume there will be someone at home who will wait for the repair person to arrive. It is only by valiant effort that one can change this mental set.

School activities provide another example. In most instances, activities involving parents are planned on the assumption that women will be available to take part in them during the working day. Lamentably, if both parents are working full time, they cannot become involved in school activities. Parents, children, and school systems alike suffer the consequences.

What all of this means is that, to a large extent, there is a significant gap between the picture we are given in the media and the actual behavioral changes that have thus far occurred. What is more, there is an implication that in two-career families, there is equal role-sharing and minimum resentment, there is support and understanding, and that decisions are reached on the basis of calm, rational discussion and negotiation.

The mere fact that one has made a commitment to the dual-career idea does not necessarily mean that one will have the skills and knowledge to carry out such a commitment, nor—and this is even more important—that one's emotional reactions will be consistent with one's intellectual commitment. The discrepancy between the emotional and the intellectual is typified by the behavior of those men who are intellectually committed to seeing their wives in careers or returning to school, that is, spending time doing "meaningful, significant things," but who at the same time don't want their lives altered. They still want the children taken care of and the dinner on the table at 6:00 P.M.

The discrepancy is typified also by those women who yearn for a complete change in lifestyle but are unwilling to surrender a whole range of presumptions that conventionally have been associated with the woman's role. They don't want to give up well-prepared, homemade meals. They don't want to do without freshly ironed, spotless clothes with all the buttons and zippers in working order. Though they are committed to activity outside the home, they want to maintain that gracious aspect of their lives that has been inculcated into them by early social training.

In addition, not knowing the problems that are inherent in this evolving kind of relationship, some two-career couples wind up looking for external causes to which to ascribe the confusion that is, in reality, normal—albeit painful. Imagine what it would be like (and many women have had this experience) to go through childbirth without knowing that certain kinds of discomfort are both normal and predictable. Not to know what a labor pain is.

To be mystified by the breaking of water. Not to understand that those strange contractions are part of the process all women in labor must experience.

Although the comparison may be a bit grim, it is true that dual-career relationships have certain built-in phases and problems. Being able to understand and anticipate them doesn't necessarily make the pain go away, but at least the foreknowledge helps one to distinguish what is normal from what is abnormal and unhealthy in human behavior.

Communication Breakdown

You're always inconsiderate. You've never been interested in my career, and now that I finally have an opportunity to get some real training, you're putting it down. I'm astounded that a mature man could be so stubborn, infantile, and pigheaded. I've explained that the training program will last for only two weeks, and that's surely not a great sacrifice. You'd think the world was coming to an end.

Blame, attack, criticism, name-calling. These are what couples frequently resort to when they become entangled in differences and don't know how to extricate themselves. In the example cited, she feels blocked in her progress toward a goal that, to her, is very important. She sees her husband's intransigence as something to be overcome, lashes out at him, and is determined to win at any cost. The husband sees it somewhat differently:

Whenever I try to get into it with her, she won't respond. She gets hurt. She acts hurt, closes the door, and won't talk to me. It drives me absolutely wild. And frankly, when she does that, I get even angrier. I start out with a positive resolve. I try to approach her in a way that seems reasonable. But as soon as I raise my voice a few decibels—which is my way of being emphatic—there are those tears, and that stoic look on her brow, and it's clear to me that the conversation is over. So what do I do? Raise my voice five *more* decibels. And even as I'm going out of control, I watch her go farther and farther away.

Silence, fear of confrontation, unwillingness to face up to differences and deal with them—these kinds of behavior seem to go hand in hand. Blaming increases as responses decrease. People withdraw as they feel themselves under attack.

Many couples, two-career or not, lack the skills essential to communicate effectively and to work out problems. Somehow, if there is enough time to deal with them, the tensions may not prove too great. A drink, a comfortable meal, an evening of leisurely lovemaking, time for reflection, and above all a sense of humor will work wonders. The danger is that many two-career couples are eternally pressed for time. They have few spare moments to deal with even the normal and the usual, let alone with the unconventional and unexpected. Hence, lacking time to confront and dispose of problems, they may shunt them aside by ceasing to communicate.

Assume, in the case of the couples cited above, that they suddenly become enlightened. They come to understand that problems are normal and usual to dual-career relationships. They have become enthusiastic participants in a group-counseling program called Effective Couples Communication, and are able to level with one another, speak clearly and without passion, disagree openly, forego attacks and name-calling, and avoid withdrawal. They should now be able to deal effectively with any problems or issues that can possibly arise.

Right?

Wrong!

Real Change Is Difficult

Even when armed with the requisite information and guided by a clear set of identifiable, "usual" problem areas, people find that change comes very hard indeed.

Why?

Here are some of the considerations that make change so difficult in a two-career relationship:

Male/Female Identity Tension Lines

HE: I don't have any difficulty taking out the garbage, checking the gutters, making sure the cars are in tune. Frankly, I don't even mind clearing the table now and then, particularly if it's a family dinner. But when we have guests, I'm just not about to do an apron scene. I know I should, but when I get up and begin moving, I feel dumb, like everybody's looking. And embarrassed. And damn it, I don't want to feel embarrassed.

One concept that women find most difficult to accept is that men are reluctant to perform certain tasks they are clearly capable of performing, in the physical sense, but resist because of preconditioned notions of what is masculine. A historic, unconscious set of imprints tells them—and their spouses—what are the tasks that may appropriately be called "men's work," and what may be properly termed "women's."

Al . . . says that there are some basic things he feels are the "wife's part of the business." He is not, he says, "going to be programmed or scheduled to vacuum or do the laundry or—"

Thelma objects: "But you do those things all the time. You help with the laundry, you clean—"

"Sure I do," he comes back, working to make just the right distinction, "and I will continue to do them. But the point is, I'm not going to be scheduled. It doesn't fit me."

The reason it doesn't fit Al Johnson, and a lot of other men, has to do with being a man. The role boundaries are blurring; accepting a formal share of "woman's work" might erase those boundaries altogether. *Men know what is fair; they balk at making it official.* (Emphasis added.)[11]

Even when recreation is involved, these unconscious resistances are at work.

SHE: He got me this bicycle, and it was really beautiful except for one thing: it had those turned-over handlebars. And when I got on it, I felt like a jock. I know that riding is better that way, and I can really get more distance with less fatigue. But whenever I catch a glimpse of myself, hunched over, I just don't feel like a lady. It's irrational, it's illogical . . . but that's how I *feel.*

Rhona and Robert Rapoport began exploring this issue when, in the early seventies, they wrote about two-career couples in England. They said that "identity dilemmas stemmed from discontinuities between internalized early experiences and current wishes . . . [that] produced doubts about being a good person."[12] Our professional experience in dealing with two-career problems is that the matter of Male/Female Identity Tension Lines is a major problem that most two-career couples must deal with, and about which most of them know little or nothing.

What is an identity tension line? It is a very personal, internalized set of images, values, feelings, and behaviors. If the person departs from these internal "norms," he or she becomes uncomfortable. The line varies with the individual and is conditioned by his or her upbringing. It is powerful; it is unknown to the individual; and—fortunately—the line can be altered or adjusted by the individual.

Most men do not mind doing the traditional "male"

chores around the house: lawn care, repairs to the plumbing or electrical systems, painting. They may not object to clearing the table or vacuuming or sweeping—usually the latter in private. But how about sewing? Or making a bed? Or ironing clothes, especially if there are other men around?

At some point in performing such chores, many men begin to feel some discomfort. Not recognizing that their discomfort is due to conflict between what they *believe* and what they *internally feel,* they begin to blame and get angry with their spouses instead of dealing with their own feelings. Women, on the other hand, tend to become infuriated by what they view as their spouses' stubbornness or obtuseness, until they have an example that helps clarify things.

I didn't really believe him when he said that he didn't see the papers in the middle of the living room. It used to infuriate me when he would walk by and even walk around his own clutter. Each time I pointed it out to him, he was apologetic and helpful, but kept telling me that he just didn't see it.

Then one day we walked out to the garage. We had just gotten a new car, and suddenly he was yelling, "Where did that dent come from?" Dent? What dent? I said. "Right there, on the fender," he said. I looked and looked, and I didn't see any dent. Then he walked over and pointed, and he was right, but I hadn't seen it. Then it struck me: it's not that I wasn't capable of seeing, and it wasn't that I had any visual problems. It was just that I never looked for those kinds of things. It also explained why I could never hear when the car was hissing, never noticed when the oil pressure was low. Once when Jim took my car—fortunately he was alert—he put *four quarts* of oil in it. If he hadn't, the mechanic told us the car would have—whatever happens to a car when it doesn't have any oil in it.

We are in no way supporting the concept of "men's work" versus "women's work." We do believe, however

—and there is more about this in Chapter III, Who Takes Out the Garbage?—*that greater equity is needed in the distribution of "role" responsibilities and tasks.*

Inertia

After a series of disastrous experiences with child-care help, we spent almost six weeks looking for someone to take care of the children. Finally, we thought we were going about it the right way. We had put an ad in the paper, interviewed people, and finally made a decision. Mathilda seemed competent, pleasant, and responsible. During the first month, everything went well. She took marvelous care of the baby, she charmed two-year-old Peter, and seemed to be getting along well with Joey, who's eleven. Still, over a period of time, we began to feel a strange apprehension.

The two-year-old would cry when I left the house. My husband, Dan, said that Mathilda yelled at Peter all the time. And whenever we came home, things didn't seem quite right— there was a kind of tension. I felt more uncomfortable about leaving the house, and kept complaining to Dan about my concerns.

See, we knew it wasn't right. But at the same time, we had spent so much time finding her that we were reluctant to change. Besides, who knew if we could find someone better? We were uncomfortable with the situation, but not uncomfortable enough to do anything about it.

Inertia is a powerful force. It makes change difficult, particularly if you've taken a great deal of time to find the new housekeeper, hire the new secretary, accept the new position, or work out an appropriate relationship with a child-care person.

Oh, Lord! Upset the apple cart? Start all over again?

The same force, inertia, operates in all phases of the two-career relationship. You've spent a year working out a model that would compensate for his going back to school while she was increasing her workload from half to three-quarter time. The housekeeper who was the key to the model has become unreliable. The house is beginning to decline; the laundry is overflowing. Yet you are reluctant to look for a replacement housekeeper.

Resistance to change. Inertia. An unwillingness to work out a *new* solution, the amount of unwillingness being directly proportional to the amount of energy you spent in arriving at the *old* solution.

It has been our observation, in dealing with two-career relationships over a long period, that if a situation becomes uncomfortable and remains that way for an extended time, change is necessary. You must be willing to overcome the inertia, and make the change. Often it does mean tearing down in order to rebuild; but waiting for things to get better simply will not work.

The Payoff Can Be High

We've painted the picture somewhat starkly because we want to be realistic. But for those couples who are able to "make it together," there are several rewards. These should be remembered whenever the stresses and strains seem overwhelming.

Here are some of the rewards:

1. Women often are enriched by a commitment outside the home. As a result, they become more stimulating partners and better parents. Men often are enriched by deeper involvement in the family and the home. They thus become more concerned parents and better husbands.

2. When a wife works, or—even more significant—when the husband scales down his career drives, the statistical chances for a happy marriage increase greatly.[13]

3. The children of working parents—assuming the children are given good to excellent care—tend to have

higher educational and career aspirations, especially the girls. They also develop greater independence and resourcefulness. And there is less risk that they will become the parents' sole or primary sources of satisfaction.

4. Working couples tend to be closer as intellectual companions than do couples whose lives are separated into "his" world of work and "her" world of the house. Many researchers agree that true companionship is the most important expressed aspect of marriage.[14]

5. In nearly every instance, there will be an eventual increase in net income when there are two wage earners. The increase often can make a real difference in the family's standard of living.

6. When both partners are wage-earners, each has greater flexibility in terms of changing jobs or careers, doing part-time work, returning to school, or taking time off for rest or self-improvement.

7. The economic impact of a long-term illness or of a death will not be as great in a dual-career relationship as in the traditional one wage-earner family.

8. It is generally agreed that women who work enjoy better mental health than those who remain at home.[15] Unless they have prepared themselves by cultivating interests other than those that are related to their children, women are especially vulnerable to depression and related maladies when the "empty nest" stage is reached.

9. Two careers can bring added knowledge, skills, and competence to all members of the family.

10. Two-career couples bring themselves and their families a potentially wider range of social and business relationships and friendships.

Most Two-Career Couples Need Help

There is no one around to tell us how to do things or show us what's wrong. There are plenty of people around who tell us what we're doing *wrong,* but scarcely anyone who can tell us how to do it *right!*

With all of the intellectual excitement found in dual-career relationships, those actually involved in such marriages are finding them emotionally painful. No one prepared American men and women for the changes that would occur when wives went back to work or returned to school. Couples who are struggling to make such relationships work are handicapped by the absence of role models for these relationships. There are no pictures of how to do it, because most of us have never seen anyone doing it before. Certainly we are unprepared for the strong feelings that will be aroused when, for example, a man is informed by his wife that she is leaving town for a few days on a business trip and that he will be responsible for the children in her absence. Or when a woman returns from such a trip to a home that looks like a disaster area.

Printed matter devoted to the *working woman* and her problems is abundant. *Ms.* magazine, *Working Woman,* and *Woman's Day,* among current periodicals, focus on issues from the point of view of women. But where does the *two-career couple* turn for help?

We were struck by the need for direct, pragmatic help during a recent seminar at Stanford University. We had spent a long evening before an audience of some 300 men and women, discussing the two-career phenomenon and describing in some detail the research literature on the subject. One person in the audience, obviously exasperated by all this pedagogy, stood up and said, "Who the hell cares about all that theory? What we want to know is *how to do it!*"

So that's what this book is all about: how to do it. How to cope with the problems of a two-career relationship.

How to make a two-career marriage work. How to make it all happen together.

What to Expect

First, we will identify the predictable issues and problems that are inherent in this kind of relationship. It is important that you understand that these problems are normal in two-career marriages. Couples who do not understand this tend to view their problems as the result of *his* being crazy, *her* being crazy, or their having a bad marriage.

1. How Will Household Tasks Be Assigned?

Who is going to do what? How will decisions be made? Whose standards will be followed? In sum, who takes out the garbage?

2. Two-Career Parenting.

How can working couples be effective parents and have successful careers at the same time? Who will be responsible for the care of the children? Who will be available in emergencies?

3. The Other-Than-Mother Dilemma.

What are the realistic child-care alternatives? How do you choose high-quality child care? When is it time to change?

4. Dealing with Dollars.

Where does the money go? Who has control when both are contributing to the bank account? Will there be "his" and "her" accounts? What are the rights of each in regard to spending the money?

5. Some Special Challenges.

What happens when two careers take divergent paths? Example: a transfer to Texas for her, a promotion in New York for him. Should they commute? What happens when one party is dramatically more successful than the other? How does a couple make fair and intelligent decisions on such issues?

6. Choosing the "Right" Employer.

How should your two-career marriage influence your job choices or the selection of the organizations you will work for? What are the things to look for? What do you do when your employer ignores your two-career status?

7. "Help!": Coping with Overload.

How do you know when you're in trouble? When does a couple get burned out? What can you do to help?

8. The Couple Relationship.

What are the specific things that dual-career couples can do to enhance their relationship? How can they reap the rewards, once the problems have been dealt with?

As we discuss the issues, we shall present a series of processes or techniques that we think can, if employed appropriately, yield significant benefits. These include problem-solving, decision-making, and negotiation. Finally, we shall describe various solutions that other dual-career couples have utilized in dealing with their problems.

CHAPTER III

Who Takes Out the Garbage?: Managing the Household

". . . and a good cleaning lady never hurt."[1]

It is 5:27 P.M. Meg has just come home after "one of those days" at the bank. She is greeted by the sight of newspapers strewn over the living room floor, dishes piled in the sink, an unmade bed, and clothes draped carelessly over Wes's wooden valet in the bedroom.

Her glance also takes in Wes, comfortably ensconced in his lounger chair, a waterfall of newspapers cascading from his lap. Wes is watching the five o'clock news.

Meg pauses at the dining room mirror to study herself and—reflected behind her—the clutter.

I'm furious about the way this house looks. I can't accomplish one single thing until it's straightened out. I can't cook, or talk, or be pleasant, or do anything at all until this house is brought into order . . .

Meg doesn't *like* having such thoughts. But she feels good when all is in order, when clothes and dishes are put away. When things are chaotic, she feels anxious, unsettled, angry. Though she loves Wes, his disorder and messiness make her feel confused and angry . . . and a bit guilty.

I really respect Wes. I love the way he thinks, the way he looks . . . but the more I have to deal with this side of him, the more resentful and confused and angry I get. I feel so helpless . . .

As Meg strides into the living room, Wes winces inwardly.

My God, she's at it again.

He watches from the corner of his eye as Meg crisscrosses the room, picking up and folding newspapers. She passes between him and Walter Cronkite without a word, but with "that look" on her face. She finishes—still ominously silent—and stalks from the room. Over the newscast, Wes can hear the clatter of dishes in the kitchen and the slamming of doors and drawers.

Wes's feelings are a compound of annoyance, guilt, and a kind of will-it never-end despair. He and Meg have tried various solutions to this household problem, including "let's straighten up together, in the mornings." But nothing has worked. Nothing (Wes tells himself) seems good enough for Meg. Wes is not terribly distressed about clutter. He's willing to help Meg pull things together, but he'll be damned if the first thing he's concerned with on coming home is whether the bed is made.

Basically I'm somewhat relaxed about these things. Personal hygiene is important to me—I shave twice a day, wear clean underwear, and all that stuff. But when I read the paper, it seems silly to have to fold up each section as I read it. My office is full of clutter and it doesn't bother me. I know it bothers Meg, but what am I supposed to do? Turn into Mr. Clean?

Meg and Wes have no children. Married for two years, in their late twenties, they both hold full-time, demanding jobs. Obviously, the housekeeping issue is a major problem for each of them, individually and as a member of a couple. They find themselves adversaries every evening, and they leave the house every morning angry and resentful. Open fighting is frequent and bitter, and a communication breakdown appears imminent.

Household Management Is a Big Deal

Among working couples, Wes and Meg are not at all atypical. Of all the areas of potential strain that face working couples, the most troublesome is household management. Who's going to do what? When? How? Will it be done carefully or in slapdash fashion?

It's no secret to anyone who has lived in a household that enormous quantities of energy and time must be devoted to the simple—and sometimes complex—chores that keep the household functioning. The tasks are imposing enough when merely two people are involved. But add two, three, or more children or stepchildren, parents, grandparents, in-laws, dogs, cats, fish, hamsters—and the array of chores to be performed becomes monumental.

Most one-breadwinner families include a "wife," who traditionally has been responsible for many or most of these services. But the time-honored formula is outmoded for today's working couples. How, then, does a two-career couple solve the dilemmas of household management?

There are, of course, no universal answers that will apply in all cases. Each family is different, and each has to arrive at its own custom-tailored solutions. However, most of the problems that arise in working-couple relationships are common to them all. We will describe some of the more important of these problems, and the actions and interactions that frequently arise from them. More important, we will describe several solutions to these time-and-resources dilemmas so that working couples can shop among these solutions for the ones that may prove most helpful to them.

Why is keeping a household intact and operating such a big deal for working couples? First of all, let's get one thing clear: it *is* a big deal! Most women are acutely aware of the enormous number of details involved in living with and caring for a family. They also know that these details are generally ignored by others in the family *unless they are not taken care of.*

When a house is in order, when food is in place and prepared, one is not very conscious of it. It is only when there is no food, when the house is dirty, when buttons are not sewn on and clothing not ironed, that one becomes aware by its absence of the routine work that goes on in a household.[2]

More specifically,
•Who notices a *clean* living room? Nobody.
•Who notices a *messy* living room? Everybody!
•Who sees an empty trash box? Nobody.
•Who stumbles into the overflowing trash container? Everybody.
•When clothes are clean, folded, and neatly in drawers, who notices? Nobody. But when there is no clean underwear, and the suit or dress that is going to be worn to that special meeting is still wrinkled and spotted—who notices? You, your boss, your colleagues—everybody.

The point here is, of course, that our lives are cluttered with details. Someone has to organize all these nitty little chores, because the alternative is chaos. Someone has to develop a system for dealing with the host of mundane tasks and services on a day-to-day basis, and to set up a parallel system for handling now-and-then emergencies. As Lyn Tornabene puts it: "Behavioral scientists have clearly demonstrated that humans need order in their lives to function at their best. The order of our days in many ways gives us our image of ourselves."[3]

A Woman's Place: Myth versus Media

The rash of articles and commentaries in the media since the upsurge of the feminist movement in the late 1960s and early 1970s might lead one to believe that household management more and more is being shared by couples. News and feature-story headlines tell us that WORKING PARENTS SHARE CHORES,[4] and HOW WORKING COUPLES WORK IT OUT.[5] Even from the sociologists and psychologists on college campuses comes increasing talk about the "egalitarian American family."

The implication is that, somehow, working husbands and wives are sharing equally the tasks and services required to keep a household together. Yet the couples with whom we have worked in our practice tell us that it is not true for them, even though they may have a vague feeling that *other* couples are sharing the work at home.

What is really happening? A few couples, mainly young and without children, are beginning to share housekeeping chores as part of their general "togetherness." Harvard Medical School psychiatrists Theodore Nadelson and Leon Eisenberg report one case where a workable formula was devised.

That couple decided, not without some anguish, to contract on alternate months for one and then the other to take full responsibility for the household, including shopping for, and cooking, meals for guests. At follow-up, three years later, the plan is working remarkably well; the husband now boasts, to the considerable discomfort of his male colleagues, of his success in his new role.[6]

But the overwhelming evidence, based on current studies, is that women still bear the major *responsibility* for domestic chores, regardless of their workload or their careers outside the home.[7] A U.S. Department of Agriculture study demonstrates this graphically. (See the chart on page 38.) Of course, this does not mean that men are not "helping" in varying degrees. But it is the woman who usually knows what must be done and sees to it that the chore is executed, with or without help.

Media coverage and the general "feel" of what is happening on the family scene certainly reflect the American public's changing notion of what is appropriate sex-role behavior for women. A growing number of men and women appear to agree that there *should* be equality of opportunity for women in the work place. More and more also appear to be endorsing the need for equal division of labor at home. The crux of the problem is, however, that such endorsements are verbal, and are rarely translated into true behavioral changes.

Margaret Mead long ago pointed out that one of civilization's recurring problems is the need to define adequately the role of the male in society.[8]

Rhona and Robert Rapoport have noted: "In today's nuclear family, the role the father plays is a key to its stability. And all the evidence now seems to point to fathers participating more in household activities."[9]

Recent studies demonstrate that "household tasks are still highly sex-stratified, with wives generally taking major responsibility for washing dishes, cooking, and child care, while men service the car and do the lawn work or move the heavy furniture."[10] It is the women who "accommodate their schedules to family and homemaking demands."[11]

An especially dramatic example of this stratification came to light during one of our workshops. One husky

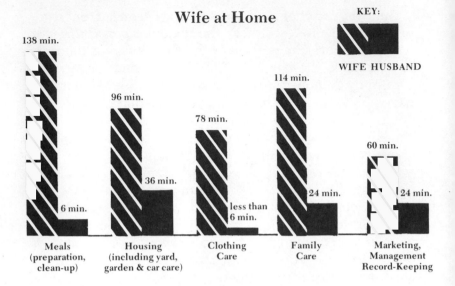

Wife at Home

KEY:

WIFE HUSBAND

138 min. / 6 min. — Meals (preparation, clean-up)

96 min. / 36 min. — Housing (including yard, garden & car care)

78 min. / less than 6 min. — Clothing Care

114 min. / 24 min. — Family Care

60 min. / 24 min. — Marketing, Management Record-Keeping

How the Man in the House Shares the Work

Working Wife

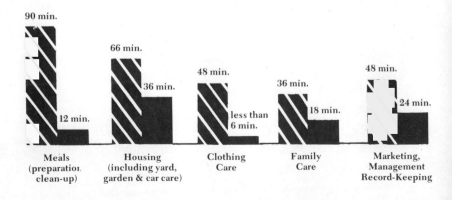

90 min. / 12 min. — Meals (preparation, clean-up)

66 min. / 36 min. — Housing (including yard, garden & car care)

48 min. / less than 6 min. — Clothing Care

36 min. / 18 min. — Family Care

48 min. / 24 min. — Marketing, Management Record-Keeping

man—who turned out to be a former FBI agent—was involved in a discussion about men doing housework.

I just feel silly doing dishes or vacuuming—men don't do those kinds of things. I know that she can't do it all, and I'm willing to hire someone to come in and help her, but it's not worth it to me to feel like a fool, running around with an apron and broom.

Men appear to be giving lip service to the new equality, though in practice they are behaving much as men did five, ten, or twenty years ago. Women respond with anger, because their expectations of help and sensitivity from the men are not being satisfied; that is, men are not delivering the goods. At the same time, women may feel guilty about needing help or about making demands, and they may behave in ways that would not be considered appropriate by their mothers or even their older sisters.

Some women contribute to their own household-management dilemmas. It must be remembered that most American middle-class women have been raised in an environment that puts a major premium on certain standards of housekeeping. Therefore, some women are unwilling to change their standards and to accept changes in the styles to which they have grown accustomed. Yes, homemade desserts are wonderful, but—in a two-career family—a good frozen pie may prove more practical. Certainly one should use fresh vegetables, but frozen ones take just minutes to prepare after a hard day on the job. Does the bathroom really need cleaning as often as in the past? How fluffy do the pillows really need to be?

What is the difference between what is desirable, what is appropriate, and what is manageable?

For many women, especially those who have worked primarily as homemakers for a significant period of time, the surrendering of household responsibility and the al-tering or lowering of standards often proves extremely difficult. We have observed, for example, that women returning to school or work sometimes spend hours trying to make sure that nothing changes, for them or for their families. They thus create part of their own overload. These same women—some of them perfectionists—may respond with criticism rather than with words of support when their husbands begin to perform tasks that are unfamiliar to them and that may make the husbands uncomfortable. In such cases, the wife is in a terrible quandary: on the one hand, she really needs and wants the help; on the other, she has a certain way she likes things done and is unhappy when they are done any other way.

"George! Don't you even know enough to clean the sink when you're finished with the dishes?"

"Bill, the dining room table has fingerprints all over it."

"Peter! For God's sake, if you don't take the clothes out of the dryer right after it turns off, they'll be wrinkled beyond recognition. They *are* wrinkled beyond recognition!"

"Fred, a part of cleaning the kitchen after dinner is sweeping the floor and mopping sticky areas! And putting *all* the dishes away. And cleaning the broiler, not leaving it dirty in the oven!"

The Woman's Dilemma

Women sometimes resist the idea of hiring outside help for household chores. When women resist this alternative, they tend to do so for one or more of the following reasons:

First, they feel an emotional commitment to their homes, and therefore oppose the idea of an outsider coming in to perform tasks they feel responsible for and probably can perform better than most outsiders.

Second, a woman may be troubled when the appearance of her home does not meet the standard *she* has set for herself. Helen provides a good example of this syndrome. She is a highly paid executive, respected by her colleagues as an effective administrator, and regarded by both women and men as a leader in the business world. Helen's image of herself is that of a competent businesswoman. Yet when she leaves work and steps into her home, she doesn't feel nearly as good about herself if her home is not as neat as her standards require.

A woman's identity is determined, partially at least, by how she perceives her home and children being cared for, and by how *others* judge her in these areas. Any lessening of her standards here translates into a lessening of self.

Third (a motivation that is often overlooked), some women may reject a solution that will allow their husbands to "escape" tasks and responsibilities which they, the husbands, historically have found unpleasant. As one woman said to us, "I've been making beds for ten goddam years. Now it's his turn."

The Man's Dilemma

Men also are caught in their own personal conflicts, most of which derive from their macho image. In most cases, men were raised in traditional homes, where they learned to do the things men traditionally do: cut the lawn, change a tire, paint the fence. For such men, undertaking new household-maintenance tasks means learning a whole new set of skills, all with a very low or zero payoff. It is no more gratifying for men *than for women* to make a bed, wash a window, or clean a countertop, especially when they are asked to begin doing these things at the age of twenty-five, thirty-eight, or fifty.

What is more, in most instances a man already works full time outside the home. (There are very few families where, by choice, men work only part time or not at all.)

Now he is being asked to assume added responsibilities in the home.

Men's resistance comes from the internal discomfort of having to assume tasks that they dislike, and for the performance of which they may be criticized by their spouses, if not by their male friends or colleagues. Is it surprising, then, that we are living in times when men are verbally committed to equality but behaviorally resistant to any major change in their household chores?

Taking Inventory

If asked, could you name all the tasks and services involved in the management of your household? Most women have detailed household-management maps in their heads. But many men, and most children, haven't the faintest idea of what is really involved.

For those already in the know, what follows will be merely review. But for those who never gave the matter much thought, the list of tasks and services that follows should be a revealing documentation of what is truly involved in running a household.

As we use the term, "household management" includes all those responsibilities, tasks, and services required to maintain a couple and their dependents in a home. The list that follows classifies these items under various basic headings (Housecleaning, House Maintenance, Meals and Food, and so forth). Although it is a comprehensive list, you may want to add items that are specific to your household, or cross out entries that do not apply in your case.

Household Management

Housecleaning
Cleaning house regularly (tidying, dusting, vacuuming, washing floors)

Picking up in house every day
Organizing and cleaning special areas (garage, closets, laundry room)

House Maintenance

Organizing long-term improvements and repairs (painting, fence-building, patio construction, etc.)
Executing or organizing immediate house or household-appliance repairs (broken washing machine, leaky toilet)
Taking appliances to shops for repair

*Children-related Activities**

Preparing children for school
Transporting children to and from child-care centers or school
Supervising older children after school
Taking care of children during school vacations and weekends
Attending school functions
Disciplining children
Chauffeuring children to afterschool activities
Arranging visits with friends
Preparing children for bed
Organizing children's chores
Meeting everyday needs of babies and young children
Getting up at night with young children

Meals and Food

Routine menu-planning and shopping
Preparing breakfast, lunch, and dinner
Preparing special meals for guests
Clean-up after meals

---

*Chapter V, on child care, will deal with issues of children, parenting, and schooling.

Clothing

Washing, drying, ironing, folding, putting away clothes
Mending clothes
Taking clothes to cleaner and picking them up
Purchasing clothes for family
Helping family members select clothing

Yard and Plants (Indoor and Outdoor)

Gardening (planting, fertilizing, mowing lawn, raking, weeding)
Watering yard and plants regularly
Maintaining sidewalks and patio areas

Automobiles

Maintaining car (including gas, oil, water, tires)
Washing and waxing car
Executing or organizing car repairs
Keeping licenses current

Finances

Purchasing special household items (furniture and equipment)
Budget-planning
Organizing and paying bills
Record-keeping, including medical insurance and other forms

Health-related Activities

Scheduling physical and dental checkups
Taking care of sick children
Taking sick children to the doctor
Organizing physical-fitness activities for individual family members

Family and Social Relationships and Events

Arranging visits with relatives and friends

Planning and executing social occasions
Planning for and organizing special events
Remembering birthdays, anniversaries
Helping friends or family when need arises

Vacation-related Activities
Planning and organizing family vacations (including travel arrangements, child-care arrangements, house care while gone)

Religious Activities
Organizing attendance of religious services
Preparing for special religious observances (Christmas, Passover)

Family Pets
Feeding, watering, walking family pets
Cleaning animals or animal areas
Veterinary appointments

Emergencies
Taking care of children or other dependent-related emergencies
Taking care of house-related emergencies

Deciding on Standards

With this imposing list before you (perhaps modified to meet your special case), can you and your partner agree on what chores and services really need to be performed? What standard of housekeeping you would really accept as satisfactory? Most couples *have* standards, but would be hard-pressed to define them precisely. In fact, few couples ever talk about their respective standards for housekeeping. Again, as pointed out earlier, the topic usually comes up only when something is not done, or when something is done inadequately according to someone's criteria. "This is the way mother did it (or didn't do it)" may be one criterion.

Even though couples may share similar cultural, racial, or economic backgrounds, they probably do not share similar experiences in terms of the way their parental households were run. When nonworking wives were home to keep house, standards were automatically set, or at least they evolved over a period of time. With both spouses working, this is not an issue that can be taken for granted. Both partners need to agree on a standard of living so that they can decide which chores and services really need to be done, how well or extensively they should be done, and—of course—who should do them.

Being specific about what needs to be done in your household is the first step. "Nothing in a dual-career marriage can be taken for granted," says Pauline Bart, professor of sociology in psychiatry at the University of Illinois Medical School. "Everything from career opportunities to household responsibilities is subject to negotiation. Who stays home with a sick child? You can't look it up in Dr. Spock."[12] The partners, first individually, and then together, should spell out what standard of living they want. Using the household list as a guide, select those items which you need or insist upon as components of your standard of living, *making selections without regard to who does what.* It is critical, at this point, not to get hung up on assigning tasks. Simply agree on the *what.*

After you have agreed on *what* needs to be done, then specify *how well* things should be accomplished. Again, go through your household list and begin to talk about your individual expectations with regard to each category. After you have exchanged impressions, try to devise some complementary standards acceptable to both of you. Take meal preparation as an example. Ask yourselves what kind of meals you can expect. Are breakfasts sit-down affairs? Or are they hot coffee and cold cereal events? What is realistic and will meet your needs? Are dinners to be formal and candlelit? Or do you both want a more informal atmosphere? How many times a week can you expect to eat out? How much money are you going to budget for eating out or for bringing home take-out food? What kinds of foods do you prefer? How much preparation is involved in the kinds of foods you like?

In making your selections about how well things should be done, be aware that the way you are doing things *now* may not necessarily be the best way. Are your standards too high? Are they too low? (They rarely are too low, but often are too high.)

Be aware, also, that individuals and families are highly resistant to change, for no special reason other than that they are resistant to change.

Once you have determined *what* you want done, and how well you want it done, the next and most important step is to determine who should have primary *responsibility* for a given area, and who should execute the tasks or services in that area. Responsibility is an emotional-intellectual commitment for which one feels accountable. Traditionally, women in our culture have been responsible for household management, with family members or hired outsiders "helping" with the chores. But being a "helper" does not necessarily involve responsibility. Therefore, as you designate *who* does *what* in your home, it is most important that everyone understands who is responsible, and acts accordingly.

The All-Important Who

In approaching the question of *who* shall do what, it is vital to agree that *no one person in your household should become a sacrificial lamb.* Every couple should strive for a balance of responsibility and task assignment so that *neither the wife nor the husband feels unjustly treated.*

Researchers in two-career family relationships have noted that many couples appear to be able to go just so far toward equal sharing before one or the other feels uncomfortable. At this point, a man may say: "This is as far as I can go" . . . "Don't press me any further" . . . "I can't tolerate any more change." These limits are the identity tension lines we described in Chapter II.

Assigning the Who

How is the *who* assigned, in two-career families?

Our professional experience and the findings of others in this field indicate that there are five major options for the division of household responsibilities. Here they are, with some of the pros and cons for each:

1. One partner takes total responsibility for management and completion of household tasks and services, with occasional help from others in the family.

In this model, there is little confusion about who does what: the person in charge does it all. This approach may work well for a two-person family with a small home and no children, but it is flawed in many respects as a model for more complex family systems. First, the one in charge must enjoy excellent health and abundant energy in order to accomplish everything at home in addition to his or her work outside the home. Second, the one in charge cannot avoid feeling resentful about having "to do it all." Resentfulness can engender temper outbursts, but more often than not the resentment merely smolders inside. And smothered feelings can cause such psychosomatic symptoms as migraine headaches, back pain, hypertension, and other common maladies. Third, the person having two jobs (one at work, one at home) will have little time or energy for contacts with friends or—even more important—with others in the family.

So, assigning housework in this model is not "making it together." In a sense, everybody loses. The family that permits one member to do everything tends to be less appreciative of one another and to have less sense of community in the home.

2. Either partner accepts major responsibility for household tasks and services, with the help of one or more cooperating couples.

Many working couples are exchanging tasks and services with other couples, both working and traditional. Although the motivation for this model is economic (it is cheaper in most instances), it is also a feasible choice that is well worth mentioning.

The degree of exchange ranges widely, including such simple swaps as evening babysitting and school car pools. At a more complicated level, we see couples organizing food-shopping co-ops, exchanging monthly housecleaning service for yard care, and pooling financial, babysitter, and housekeeper resources for vacations.

The major advantage of this model is that it makes available a pool of people for the provision of services. A disadvantage is that more organization and communication are required to coordinate all these people.

This model should be approached experimentally, because, with so many complex interactions implicit in such a system, the failure potential is high. Working couples who live close to one another and have similar standards of living seem to adapt best to this model. They work together as peers, and proximity reduces the need for involved communication and organization.

3. The man or the woman accepts major responsibility for household tasks and services with the aid of full-time help.

(a) Live-in help. Live-in help includes those who live in the home five, six, or seven days a week, with certain set working hours, and receive room, board, and wages.

Families choosing this model are lucky if they can find and *keep* a good live-in person. A good housekeeper can, to say the least, make the difference, for working couples, between chaos and controlled disorder. A certain amount of disorder is inevitable, even in the best-run households. Psychiatrists Nadelson and Eisenberg have said:

What is essential to a workable arrangement is a "good wife" for both spouses—the luxury of a competent and caring housekeeper who not only does the household tasks but helps in the planning . . . That such a person is difficult to find hardly needs mention. Those who do find one feel blessed.[13]

The major advantage of a live-in person is that the work, whatever it is, gets done. Another advantage is that housekeeping standards usually become more flexible, that is, less demanding, if the person responsible is not actually doing the housework. This phenomenon is especially true for the women involved in these families. One wife admitted that she can ignore dust balls in the corner if they result from her housekeeper's carelessness, but not if they result from her own. A third advantage is that the presence of a live-in person, night and day, means that household emergencies are more easily handled. Finally, some help in the child-care area is possible. However, do not confuse housekeeping with child care, as they not only are different functions, but are often incompatible (see Chapter V).

The greatest disadvantage in the live-in arrangement is, simply, that there aren't many people who are willing to live in and work, and to do the job with a smile, with reasonable standards, for a long period of time. High turnover rates, low standards, and grumpy dispositions seem these days to be the norms. Live-in helpers also tend to be newly arrived immigrants, or even undocumented workers, whose reliance on native tongues requires their employers to learn Spanish, Portuguese, Vietnamese, or some other foreign language. Finally, some couples find it irritating to have an outsider always in the house, "under foot."

(b) Live-out help. Another choice is to find a full-time, live-out housekeeper, a person who works regular hours, coming in the morning and leaving at the end of your workday. There usually are more people available to do live-out housekeeping than to live in. By requiring that they be able to drive a car (either theirs or yours), you will vastly increase the potential usefulness of such employees. In addition to keeping a house clean, doing the laundry, and preparing meals, a live-out housekeeper who drives can also be assigned to a whole array of errands, including ferrying children to and from school, buying groceries, and picking up out-of-town guests at the airport.

The major disadvantage of this set-up is, of course, that it will cost a fair amount of money. In general, dual-career couples should expect to pay minimum wages, to grant two weeks' paid vacation, to make provisions for sick leave, and to provide for social security and unemployment benefits. In fact, if you expect to hire a really good person, you should be willing to pay a dollar more than the minimum hourly wage at least. With live-in or live-out help, the old adage that "you get what you pay for" is especially true.

4. Either partner accepts major responsibility for household management, and hires part-time people or agencies to complete household tasks and services.

Among the part-time "hired-out" personnel used by couples are once- or twice-a-week housekeepers, cleaning services, gardeners, cooks, miscellaneous repair people, students who perform a variety of tasks and services, and interior designers.

Meg and Wes, the couple mentioned at the opening of

this chapter, relieved much of their distress by hiring a part-time helper. After reviewing a long list of proposed behavior changes (Meg tried to ignore Wes's messiness, Wes tried desperately to be neater, and both failed), Wes finally suggested a very creative solution. They found a high school girl to come in at some time during the day for half an hour or an hour *after* they left for work and *before* either returned home. The girl made the beds, picked up the clutter, emptied and filled the dishwasher, and generally put things in order. The results surprised and delighted them both. Not only did Wes and Meg have a neat house to greet them, but they stopped arguing. In fact, with the pressure off, both of them changed subtly as time went by. Meg became a little less order-oriented, and Wes even began to pick up after himself and to clean up after dinner.

Larry and Delia are another couple who decided to use part-time help in a number of ways. They found that their kitchen, which was perfectly adequate for them when they were childless, became a problem when children arrived. No more than two could be seated for a meal without causing major congestion and arm-bumping. They hired an interior designer to lay out an eating nook that would fit into the kitchen at a price they could afford. The designer arranged for a built-in seating arrangement for four people. She also helped them to rearrange shelves and drawers so that meal preparations were more convenient and efficient. Delia and Larry also hire college students from a local student-employment office to wash and wax their cars, help with parties, water the yard, and haul away trash.

Such services can be expensive, but they need not be, if used selectively. Most working couples utilize some of them. The major advantage is, of course, that whatever needs to be done is *done*. (Or sort of!) The standards of service people often are not the standards of the people who hire them. It's sometimes a major hassle to find the kind of service people you need, communicate your needs to them, and get them to do work that even approximates your standards.

5. The partners share responsibility for household management and for the completion of tasks and services.

Couples who share these responsibilities, and thus spread the workload between two persons, are generally less fatigued, more energetic, happier people. Furthermore, partners who care together for themselves and their home appear to have more appreciation for one another's contribution to the upkeep of the house. If you clean the kitchen regularly, for example, you are less likely to leave it in a real mess when you and your partner share the work because you know from experience how much work is involved when someone leaves a mess for *you.*

Some couples run into trouble with this sharing concept if either of two things happens: first, if one partner does not carry through his or her assignments, there's trouble; second, in striving for a "perfect sharing" of chores, a couple may make a travesty of the whole idea. A partner may be so concerned about doing only his or her share, or making sure that the other partner does his or her exact share, that more problems are created than are solved.

No one member of the family should ever feel overloaded with household requirements, although this is bound to occur from time to time.

A HELPFUL FORMULA

One couple, Marilyn and Steve, have developed a formula that helps them to decide who does what. They set up three criteria, "availability," "skill," and "enjoyment" on a scale of 1 (the negative end) to 10 (the positive end). Here's how it works for two different types of meal-preparation problems:

Problem 1: Who should prepare breakfast for Marilyn and Steve and their two children, ages one and three? This is how Marilyn and Steve approached the breakfast problem. Each took a piece of paper and graded the criteria. Steve completed his worksheet as follows:

Availability   1 2 3 4 5 6 7 8 (9) 10
Since he doesn't have to be at his office until 9:00 A.M., he is generally available to make breakfast. He therefore has circled 9 as his score.

Skill   1 2 3 4 5 6 7 8 9 (10)
Steve and Marilyn have decided that, although they want to have breakfast (clearly a choice), they prefer to have it in its simplest terms—juice, milk (or coffee), and cold cereal or the equivalent. The skill required is minimal, so Steve has marked 10 as his score on this criterion.

Enjoyment   1 2 3 4 (5) 6 7 8 9 10
Steve doesn't really enjoy the preparation of food, but he does like being with the children early in the morning. Preparing the breakfast and sitting with the children are fairly enjoyable to him; therefore he gives enjoyment a score of 5.

Marilyn completed her worksheet in the following manner:

Availability   1 2 (3) 4 5 6 7 8 9 10
Marilyn has to be at work by 8:00 A.M. So, although she is "available" earlier in the morning, the children sleep at least until 7:00, which means she would have to put together breakfast in a few minutes if she did it. She gives herself a score of 3.

Skill   1 2 3 4 5 6 7 8 9 (10)
Clearly, Marilyn has the skill to prepare their agreed-upon kind of breakfast. She gives herself a 10 for skill.

Enjoyment   1 (2) 3 4 5 6 7 8 9 10
The morning is a time when Marilyn feels pushed the most. She is not one of those "bushy-tailed," energetic, early-morning enthusiasts. Getting breakfast ready is a pain for her. Although Marilyn loves her children, even seeing them in the early A.M. is not really enjoyable. She gives herself a 2.

Put together the scores of Marilyn and Steve to see who should prepare the morning breakfast:

	Steve	*Marilyn*
Availability	9	3
Skill	10	10
Enjoyment	5	2
Total	24	15

The individual with the highest total score is the one who should accept the task. Steve's score of 24 far outranks Marilyn's 15, so Steve is "elected." Of course, if the circumstances of their lives should change, they may reevaluate the situation and prepare another worksheet. They use this formula though they know that nothing is forever.

Another meal-preparation decision faces the Loves:
Problem 2: Who should prepare a formal dinner for eight people on a Saturday evening?
Jonathan Love begins the process with his criteria and scores as follows:

Availability   1 2 3 4 5 6 7 8 9 ⑩

Jonathan is available that particular Saturday night. He gives himself a score of 10.

Skill   1 2 ③ 4 5 6 7 8 9 10

Jonathan is not a seasoned cook. He feels that he could put together something in a pinch, but neither he nor his wife, Evelyn, would be satisfied with the outcome. He gives himself a score of 3. (By the way, he notes down that he will be very willing to help Evelyn with preparation, particularly by caring for the children while she cooks.)

Enjoyment   1 ② 3 4 5 6 7 8 9 10

Because he is not very good at cooking, Jonathan wouldn't enjoy preparing a formal dinner at all (although he likes to barbecue). He circles 2.

    Evelyn scores herself as follows:

Availability   1 2 3 4 5 6 7 8 9 ⑩

Evelyn is available; therefore she marks 10.

Skill   1 2 3 4 5 6 7 8 ⑨ 10

Evelyn is an excellent cook, fully prepared to produce a fine formal dinner. A 9 here.

Enjoyment   1 2 3 4 5 6 ⑦ 8 9 10

Evelyn truly enjoys cooking. She likes to prepare meals of the kind they are thinking about, although it isn't easy to fit it into a busy schedule. She marks 7.

    Comparing Jonathan's and Evelyn's scores:

	Jonathan	*Evelyn*
Availability	10	10
Skill	3	9

| Enjoyment | 2 | 7 |
| Total | 15 | 26 |

Evelyn clearly "wins." So she agrees to prepare the Saturday evening meal, with Jonathan's help.

This formula is only one of many imaginative solutions to the problems of household management. At the end of this chapter is a list of other household- and time-management tips. Select and try out a few of the solutions you think may work for you, remembering that managing a household is a very personal, highly individualistic business. A system that may work for one couple may fail miserably for you, and vice versa.

6. Having your children take some responsibility for household tasks and services.

Using your own children in household management is important for many reasons, some of them obvious. First, children thus acquire competence in a variety of practical life situations. Second, by contributing to the smooth running of the family, children gain a sense of appreciation for the work that needs to be done and, in addition, learn to work together for a common cause. Third, by having male and female children perform a variety of household tasks, you are helping to break down the time-honored, sex-stratified "this is what men do; this is what women do" myths. Finally, with the children's help, the work gets done, which is the point of the whole exercise.

And there are bonus advantages you may not have considered.

Because everyone contributes instead of leaving it to mama, say many corporate mothers, their children get a fringe benefit: They grow up independent and dependable. "They rise to the occasion," says Barbara Cella, a personal banking manager at Continental Illinois Bank and the mother of eight.[14]

As we have indicated, of all the areas that dual-career couples fight about, household management is number one. If you are not arguing over who is going to take out the garbage, then you are probably debating the real or symbolic issue of "how clean is clean."

It is confusing. It is nagging. It can drive you crazy. Most two-career couples face major conflicts over this emotion-laden area. But there are ways of improving your situation. This chapter has outlined some. You, no doubt, have some of your own. The push to resolving the household-management dilemma should be toward bringing organization, routine, and order to this usually chaotic area of your life.

Some Nitties and a Few Gritties

Because two-career couples need to be better organized and more creative than most people about using their time and other resources, we offer the following suggestions.

Managing Your Time

The resource in shortest supply for working couples is *time*. There never seems to be enough of it, for anybody, or for anything . . . and, least of all, for yourselves. What little time you *do* have, therefore, should be managed efficiently and guarded zealously.

Many good books on time management are now on the market. Two of them are Alan Lakein's *How to Get Control of Your Time and Your Life*[15] and Donna Goldfein's *Everywoman's Guide to Time Management.*[16] Both cover the subject in great detail.

The following tips have been gleaned both from our personal and professional experience and from current literature on time management.

1. Yearly Calendars.

One practical way to keep on top of your joint and separate commitments, both at home and at work, is to buy three generous-sized wall calendars: one for his office, one for her's, and one for the home message center (see number 3). A wide variety of sizes and styles can usually be found in any well-stocked stationer's. Note all important dates on these, including both professional and social events—and don't forget vacations.

2. Weekly Meetings.

Once a week—Monday evening is a good time—schedule an informal family meeting for all hands living in the house, including older children, live-in help, parents or other relatives who may live with you. On this occasion, have a weekly calendar (for the upcoming week) on hand, and mark important events on it for each person in the family. Examples: evening meetings, doctors' appointments, social events, school activities. Also mark down household-task assignments, with the names of those responsible for doing them.

3. Message Center.

If you don't already have a message center in your home, set one up now. A free wall space near the kitchen phone is a good place. Here you can post your weekly and your year-long calendars, along with a permanent memo pad and a pencil or pen. Three lists of phone numbers should be posted at the center: a list of emergency numbers (doctors, police, fire, a relative or relatives), especially important if one or both parents are to be away for extended periods; a second, for personal numbers frequently called; and a third, for services, such as plumbers, caterers, electricians, and the like. Ready access to these numbers will save an astonishing amount of time and could even save a life.

4. Invitations.

Consult with each other on all invitations either of you

receives. When invited to any social event, do not accept immediately. Say, instead, that you will have to check with your spouse. You will thus gain time to think it through and to decide whether you really want to accept, at the same time making sure there are no time conflicts. By doing so, you will winnow out the marginal ones and accept only those in which you both are genuinely interested.

5. Information Bank.

Create a personal information bank in which to keep appliance instruction and maintenance manuals; credit card numbers; phone numbers of reliable services, shops, and businesses; personal medical information (blood types for all members of the family, their inoculation records, and so on); an inventory of your household and personal valuables; warranties and guarantees for your cars and appliances; clothing sizes for all members of the family, close relatives, and perhaps a few close friends; plant-watering instructions—in other words, the thousand and one little bits and pieces of information you may need at any moment and haven't the time or energy to dig up when you need them.

6. Doctors, Dentists.

Try to select doctors and dentists with offices convenient to your home (where children are involved) or your offices or both. And it doesn't hurt to let such professional people know that both parents are working and that neither has time to spend endless hours in a waiting room. This message comes across with extra force if the mother and father alternate in taking the kids to the doctor or dentist.

7. Time-Wasters.

Take a critical look at your daily schedules. Are there any obvious time-wasters there? Is that commute to work too long? Would it be feasible and desirable to pick up and move to a residence closer to your work? If moving is not a realistic alternative, is there some way to use your commuting time better? Can you dictate memos, ideas, letters, or other matter to a tape recorder or dictating machine in the car or on the train? Or do you prefer to keep this time alone, private and inviolate? What about lunch times? Are they often wasted, or do you find them important as "battery-charger" periods, when you can be alone? Maybe the lunch break would be a good time for a brisk walk, a jog in the park, or a visit to a nearby library. We all suffer those irritating waiting periods in doctors' or dentists' offices; make those moments count by taking along a memo pad, letter-writing supplies, or a good book (as an alternative to the year-old copies of *Time* and *Newsweek*). Whatever you can do to avoid the gross waste of precious minutes or hours will be a step well worth taking.

Managing Your Home More Efficiently

If we were challenged to propose a slogan for working couples that would inspire them to manage their homes and their affairs more efficiently, we would without hesitation propose the following three words: SIMPLIFY YOUR LIFE.

Simplify your lives in as many ways as possible. In your house, for example:

1. Buy labor-saving appliances, such as trash compactors, dishwashers, ice-makers for your refrigerators, food processors, large freezers, and automatic garage-door openers.

2. In buying a home, look for easy-care features in the carpeting and other floor coverings. Whenever possible, choose a home that will need the minimum of painting— exterior and interior.

3. Look for homes with low- or no-care yards (unless you get your relaxation in yard care and gardening). If watering is essential, install a watering system with a timer. Lots

of these—some of them very sophisticated—are available today, and most of them can be installed by the owner in a weekend or two.

4. Use Scotchgard on all your upholstered furniture.

5. Organize your home so that everything has its place. Keep things that will be needed for specific jobs in one location: correspondence (paper, pens, stamps, envelopes, address books, typewriter); bill-paying (checkbooks, staples, paper clips, calculator); manicure and pedicure materials; shoeshine equipment; car-washing and -waxing supplies; and so on.

6. Develop some sort of system for storing mail, packages, and other clutter out of sight until it can be sorted, stored, or tossed. If you don't, every flat surface in the house will always look like Monday morning at Coney Island.

7. Schedule periodic raids on clutter: weekly, for mail (especially junk mail), newspapers, magazines; every six months for clothes, toys, dishes, and other stuff you no longer need or want. Offer usable items to a church or charity thrift shop, or some organization that holds rummage sales. You may want to consider an occasional garage sale, yard sale, or "estate sale" of your own, but probably won't have the time needed to organize and execute one.

Saving Time on Meals

1. Nutritionists generally seem to agree that it is healthiest to eat a heavy breakfast, a medium-sized lunch, and a light dinner. If you both return home from work in the late afternoon or early evenings, try to avoid elaborate meals. Concentrate on simple fare, like soups, salads, cold cuts, and the like.

2. When you invite others to your home in the evening

—especially on week nights—invite them for dessert rather than for dinner.

3. Eat out as often as practical and convenient. To economize, you can share a meal and order an extra salad. (Most restaurants don't object to this practice, particularly when you're regular patrons.)

4. Plan ahead before going to the grocery store. Buy in bulk; often it's much cheaper. Avoid impulse buying; it takes both time and money.

5. When you cook, try to double or triple the recipe, and freeze the surplus for another time. This works, of course, with some foods and not with others. (It's great for lasagna, for example, but not so good for certain desserts.)

6. Buy convenience products (not junk foods). Examine the choices carefully. Many frozen foods can be as nutritious and as attractive as their fresh counterparts.

Your Clothes

1. Buy wash-and-wear, no-iron clothing, especially for children.

2. Hire someone to do the laundry who not only washes, irons, and folds clothes, but will look out for torn hems, missing buttons, wayward zippers, and similar disasters. Or use a laundry service that performs all these minor miracles.

3. Coordinate your clothes so that nearly everything goes with nearly everything else. This will save you time when dressing and rushing for the 7:58 commuter train, and time when buying your clothes.

Miscellanea

1. Use the telephone or the mail service as much as possible for personal business. Write or call for tickets; call libraries to renew overdue books, and return them when

it is convenient for you; order items by mail or phone whenever possible.

2. Keep a supply of small gifts and cards on hand for those important birthdays, anniversaries, and other predictable dates. This way you'll avoid those last-minute dashes to gift shops, supermarkets, or drug stores.

3. Develop checklists of things to be done before you leave on trips or vacations. Examples: notify the paper boy to stop deliveries until such-and-such a date; stop milk deliveries; arrange with a neighbor's youngster to empty your mail box (if you have home delivery); inform your closest neighbors you will be away; leave some inside lights on automatic switches, and perhaps some exterior lights on sensors; put your phone on vacation standby service if you will be gone long enough.

4. If you must choose between "personal" and "impersonal" tasks, retain the personal and delegate the impersonal. Although almost anyone can clean, wash, water, and repair, the parents would certainly prefer to be with their children.

Spending Money to Save Time—and Energy

1. Use Professionals.

Many people are gifted with talents for architecture, interior decorating, or landscaping (for example). If you have such talents, and the time as well, you may enjoy designing, decorating, and landscaping your home or your office.

Our observation is, however, that few people have both the time and the talent for such tasks, and that most two-career couples have neither. Most couples will, in the long run, save both time and money by hiring people with these talents.

We have also noted, in our own experience and that of our friends and associates, that "cut-rate" services are seldom a real economy. In the long run, such services cost more than they save, because their providers so often botch the job.

The moral to this story is: When you have a chore that needs to be done, and you cannot or will not do it yourselves, *get the best, and pay for it.*

2. Parking.

If parking is a continuous hassle and convenient paid parking is available, save wear and tear on your nervous system by contracting for paid space.

3. Service People.

Establish personal, working relationships with a plumber, electrician, grocer, service-station attendant or owner, car mechanic, bank teller, and so forth. You will get more service, and you will get it faster, if you are able to ask for "Herman the plumber" or "Mac the mechanic." These contacts, and your consistent patronage of them, will save you much time and grief.

4. Drive-ins.

When possible (if you are on wheels), use drive-in banks, drive-in laundries, and other services that cater to people in their cars. Sometimes it's worth the money to have laundry, milk, prescription drugs, groceries, and other goods delivered rather than using the time, gasoline, and energy needed to pick them up.

5. Catering Services.

If you are entertaining more than just a couple, or if you are entertaining formally and don't have the time to prepare an elaborate meal, you may find a caterer to be a boon. Sometimes they wind up being less expensive than doing-it-yourself, believe it or not. Consider hiring, for a few hours, someone to help with cocktails or serving the dinner or cooking or cleaning up afterward. For parties requiring equipment you would seldom use, rent it and have it delivered. Then you don't have to put things away when the party's over.

CHAPTER IV

Two-Career Parenting

All of a sudden, it seems young American couples have stopped wondering, "What shall we name the baby?" and started asking, "Should there be a baby at all?" and if so, when and how many? Gone are the days when the teething ring was the inevitable successor to the wedding ring.[1]

Shall we have children?

No other decision a two-career couple must make will have greater impact on their separate and collective lives than their response to this question.

For traditional couples, the decision is also a major one. But for working couples, the issues involved are much more complicated, and some of them are special to the two-career relationship.

Time was—and that until very recently—when couples brought children into the world with little if any serious thought about the consequences. There was minimal soul-searching, and decisions were dictated largely by biological imperatives. In American society, at all levels, having babies has been simply the thing to do.

Today, the more enlightened couples at all levels are looking for answers beyond the myths in which folklore and custom have swaddled babies. One myth, venerated by generations of acceptance, is that all babies are "bundles of joy." Another, somewhat more cynical, insists that babies are a "drag," with fragrant diapers their predominant feature.

But as babies are neither joy-bundles *all* the time, nor drags even *most* of the time, today's couples are trying to face the baby issue maturely and intelligently. Since this enlightened approach is relatively new, little charting of the terrain has been done, and there are few precedents to guide new parents.

On one point, most forward-thinking couples will agree: the decision to have, or not to have, offspring should be much more than a matter of chemistry. Involved is a whole gamut of personal and interpersonal considerations, including:

•the respective career commitments of the partners;

•their physical and mental health;

•pressure from family and friends;

•their respective childhoods and—perhaps most important—

•the honest inner feelings of each about having, or not having, children.

We agree with Constance Rosenblum's assessment that "it's the hardest of all personal decisions to make because it's so completely irrevocable. People change jobs, mates, homes, and neighborhoods, but nobody trades in a child."[2]

To Be or Not to Be (Parents)

There is, of course, no sure-fire way to avoid mistakes in making such a crucial decision. However, there are certain steps you can take that may help you with the decision. They are the following:

1. Talk.

Don't sidestep the issue. Begin by talking candidly with your partner, discussing your innermost feelings about having a baby. Set aside a special, relaxed time when you can do this. Do *not* try, at this point, to persuade, exhort, or convince—that comes later. Step 1 is strictly an information-sharing experience. First one of you, then the other, should open up. Talk about your hopes, images, fears, preconceptions, and fantasies about babies and having babies.

In your imagination, what is parenthood like? How do you see yourself, in your mind's eye, as a father or mother?

How do you see your spouse, in your mind, as a parent? (Experience has shown that, quite often, partners have mental "scenarios" in which their spouses act out parental roles. One partner may merely daydream these scenarios, never discussing them with the other. Then, when the baby comes, and the true-life actions of the partner do not match the daydream, disappointments and frustrations are inevitable. In the end, there may be anger and tension, and communication may break down.)

If the prospect of parenthood frightens you, what are the roots of your fears?

Think beyond the bundle-of-joy image to the time when the baby becomes a person. Talk about that.

Many couples fail to go beyond the impasse reached by Tom and Christina in the following dialogue:

TOM: I really *want* to have a kid!

CHRISTINA: Well, I don't. It's easy enough for you to say—you're not the one who will be pregnant, have the baby, nurse it, and change its diapers.

TOM: (Silence. He is thinking, but not saying, that he doesn't understand why Christina is so selfish. He's always wanted to have children—and not just one child. He's enchanted by the prospect of a family around the table at meal times, and children playing in parks and playgrounds. Tom sees himself as a genuine father figure, very active in his role as a parent.)

CHRISTINA: (Silence. She has a lot on her mind, but voices none of it. In truth, she is admitting to herself that childbirth frightens her. She's heard other women discuss it, and it all sounds rather grim. She's also worried about having to quit work to have a baby and to care for it—and she doesn't want to quit working.)

Most couples are Toms and Christinas, talking around the issue, never really facing reality, because to do so would stir up a lot of emotion. So they never reveal their deepest thoughts and feelings. In sum, they never really *communicate*.

So, *talk*. You may find—to your happy surprise—that you are agreed on most points without even knowing it. You may, for example, both be "thinking" that you would like to have a child *in a few years*. But if you were forced to answer the question "Shall we have a baby?" right this instant, without discussion, you might be forced to say no.

It is quite probable that you will agree on many or most of the questions about having babies. But how will you ever know, if you don't bring the subject out into the open?

Before the practical decisions about child care and the assignment of responsibilities can be arranged, a husband and wife should discuss their individual and mutual expectations of life, marriage and each other. Ideally such discussion should take place even before a couple gets married.[3]

If you have difficulty warming up to the discussion, you may find some help in the lists of the *rewards* and *costs* of parenthood that were developed by Linda Beckman, a psychologist at the University of California at Los Angeles.[4] (See pages 70–71).

Rewards of Parenthood

1. Watching child's growth and development
2. Relationship with the child (getting and giving love)
3. Enjoying children's activities (being in touch with youth)
4. Teaching role (helping and guiding growth and development)
5. Having a family
6. Self-development and growth (makes me more mature, a better person)
7. Fulfillment (biological fulfillment for the woman)
8. Helps marital relationship (an expression of love)
9. Companionship (child may be a companion; may keep me from being lonely)
10. Comfort in old age (child may provide companionship and financial security)
11. Immortality (a part of me lives on; child carries on the family name)
12. Nurturing (taking care of dependent human being; giving something to someone else)
13. Challenge, achievement, creativity
14. Social expectation (parents or friends or society expect it; affects positively relationship with parent)
15. Keeps me young (see things through a child's eyes)
16. Social contribution (creating a good person)
17. Other (for example, income tax deduction)

Costs of Parenthood

1. Economic
2. Noise, hassle, frustration
3. Restriction of freedom, opportunity, privacy, or mobility (may have to forego opportunities)
4. Great responsibility
5. Interferes with relationship or time with husband

6. Interferes with career (problem of two full-time roles)
7. Other time factors (less time for own interests and activities)
8. Worry (regarding social problems or the child's health and development)
9. Doubts about my adequacy as a parent
10. Too much work
11. Child-care problems (problems finding adequate help; problems regarding disciplining of children)
12. Guilt or conflict (concerning behavior toward children or too much time away from children)
13. Boredom, drudgery (of child-care tasks; being stuck at home)
14. Contributing to overpopulation
15. Other (for example, afraid children will not live up to ideals; pregnancy unpleasant)

As you talk, questions may arise that you cannot answer; questions, for example, about childbirth and child care. This takes you to Step 2.

2. List Your Questions.

There are a number of ways to find the answers.

Reference books: Below, many of the better reference tools are listed, together with names and addresses of organizations from which you may request publications and information. Buy or borrow the publications you need; read them carefully.

References

Books

Bernard, Jessie. *The Future of Motherhood.* New York: Dial Press, 1974.
Boston Women's Health Book Collective. *Our Bodies,*

Ourselves. New York: Simon and Schuster, 1976.

Boston Women's Health Book Collective. *Ourselves and Our Children.* New York: Random House, 1978.

Peck, Ellen. *The Baby Trap.* Los Angeles: Pinnacle Books, 1976.

Peck, Ellen, and William Granzig. *The Parent Test.* New York: G. P. Putnam, 1978.

Price, Jane. *You're Not Too Old To Have A Baby.* New York: Penguin Books, 1978.

Rapoport, Rhona and Robert N., and Ziona Strelitz. *Fathers, Mothers and Society.* New York: Basic Books, 1977.

Whelan, Elizabeth. *A Baby?... Maybe.* New York: Bobbs-Merrill, 1975.

Organizations

A Baby?... Maybe Services   165 West End Avenue, New York, NY 10023

National Organization for Non-Parents   806 Reistertown Road, Baltimore, MD 21208

Parenting by Choice   110 West 86 Street, New York, NY 10024

Planned Parenthood Federation of America   810 Seventh Avenue, New York, NY 10019

Pondering Parenthood   405 West 118 Street, New York, NY 10027

Zero Population Growth   1346 Connecticut Avenue, N.W., Washington, D.C. 20036

Classes: Check to see if seminars or courses related to parenting are offered through the continuing-education or extension departments of nearby universities or community colleges, designed for couples confronting the challenges of parenthood. Such classes can arm you with useful information and counsel. They will also let you mix with others facing the same dilemmas. Joining a peer group is usually a good idea, because you learn from one another, and can empathize with your peers.

3. Practice Parenting.

You may decide, before having your own children, to get some firsthand experience with the children of others. Margaret Mead once said she thought couples should experience "trial parenthood."[5] Try this by spending time with the children of friends or relatives. Offer to babysit for a couple over a weekend. Develop a special relationship with a favorite niece or nephew or young cousin. Join Big Sisters or Big Brothers. Practice mother-and-dad-ing not only with little kids, but also with some school-agers and teen-agers.

Talk with couples who are already parents. Be sure to question them about both the rewards *and* the problems.

These experiences cannot, of course, duplicate all the circumstances of real parenthood, but they may help you to decide whether or not parenting is for you. And—who knows?—you may make some rewarding friendships in the process.

4. Name Your Conditions.

Each partner should specify the conditions he or she hopes will be met before saying yes to the question "Should we have a child?" Remember Tom and Christina. He did and she didn't. Let's see where they are now.

TOM: I *still* want to have a child. But I think, now, that it would be a good idea to have a house that will fit the three of us beforehand. And maybe a house with enough room for a live-in babysitter. [Pause.] Come to think of it, I'd like to work for a couple of years before we do it so that I will be in a better position to spend time with the baby.

CHRISTINA: I guess I really do want to have a child, too. But first, I want to find a really good pediatrician who's used to working with thirty-year-old mothers. And I'd like both of us to go through a Lamaze class together. Also, even after the baby comes, I'd like to be able to work part time.

It is important to be specific about your conditions. Indicate clearly the who, what, where, when, and why—and how much. In the Tom-Christina scenario, for example, Tom should have in mind

•a good idea of the house he wants—number of bedrooms, bathrooms, and so on;

•how much he and Christina want to pay (and *can* pay);

•where—the neighborhood, town or city, tract;

•by what date;

•who takes responsibility for the search and the details of the purchase.

What does Tom mean by being in "a better position" at work? Is this a realistic expectation?

How much time does he think he wants to spend with the baby?

Christina will also have a set of conditions that she should specify. What does she mean by a "really good pediatrician?" By what or whose criteria? How does one find a good pediatrician? What qualities does one look for?

Once you and your partner have agreed on conditions, you may wish to write these down for a permanent record. If you cannot seem to agree at this point on conditions, you have several other possible actions open to you, including the following:

(a) Set the question aside for the time being. Agree on a date to revive the discussion, and mark it on the calendar.

(b) Seek help from a skilled third party as a negotiator. This party could be a well-informed friend or relative whose judgment you trust. Or the person could be a professional—psychologist, psychiatrist, marriage-and-family counselor, or social worker.

(c) Negotiate a change in your individual attitude, on your own.

It goes almost without saying that good faith, by both parties, is imperative. Neither of you should try to sabotage the whole issue by imposing so many conditions, or such difficult conditions, that the goal can never be reached. If either partner really does not *want* to have a baby, he or she should be brave and honest enough to say so flatly and unequivocally. At least both partners then will know exactly where they stand.

Step 5 in the whether-or-not process returns full circle to Step 1:

5. Keep Talking.

We stress this step again because experience has demonstrated clearly that people tend to avoid unpleasant and difficult topics like the plague.

The mere act of talking—as opposed to thinking about or postponing—usually brings an issue to resolution. If you can't make it on your own, call in some help. There are trained specialists available in nearly any community of any size who can and will render such aid, either free (public agencies) or for a fee (private professionals).

Enjoying children is not the same as parenting them. The conceiving, bearing, and rearing of offspring gives much joy to some, much grief to others. You cannot afford to make a mistake on this key decision. Children are for keeps.

If It's Yes, Then When, How Many, How Far Apart?

If your joint decision is no, this discussion will be purely academic and can be skipped. If it is affirmative, you may profit from close attention to several related questions.

Before we had Amy, I was really uncertain about this baby business. But now that she's part of the family, I can't imagine life without her. Question is, should we have another? Mom and Dad say yes, some of my friends say absolutely no. We just don't know. We think we'd resent any other child moving in on Amy's time, yet we also think it might be good for her to have a brother or sister to play with. Amy's nine months old now, so I suppose we should make a decision soon. Because we think it would be best to have them close together. Or would it?

Couples who elect not to have children still make up a very tiny minority in America. For most couples, the question is not *whether,* but *when* and *how many.*

On these questions, there are some suggestions for working couples. Examine the guidelines that follow, and decide for yourselves what course you should take, based on your own special circumstances. And remember, what may be right for one couple may be an absolute bomb for another.

Studies, by experts, of working couples indicate the following:

1. Waiting until you are in your thirties is probably a good idea. The authors of *The Parent Test* (see page 72) extend their professional necks by saying that "people under 25 should not have children." They state further that, according to their research, the most satisfied parents are those who had their first child after they were thirty-five, because the delay allowed both partners to "grow up" before having kids.[6]

Thousands of couples now in their twenties are saying, "No kids, under *any* circumstances." Many of these couples, however—if history repeats itself—will reverse fields in their thirties when the "biological imperative" and other pressures make themselves felt. Some in their thirties, and even in their forties, are now saying yes, and, in some cases, are going to extremes (such as reversing vasectomies or tubal ligations) to make conception possible.

2. Couples who postpone parenting until both are firmly established in careers usually have (a) higher incomes with which to underwrite quality child care and other services; (b) more flexible work schedules; and (c) more job privileges (leave time, longer vacations, and so forth).

3. Small families tend to be happier than large ones. "An inverse relationship exists between marital adjustment and family size—the more children, the less adjustment . . ."[7] There is widespread denigration of the one-child family, which is not supported either by common sense or by fact. With the addition of each successive child to a family, there is an increased burden in household and caretaking tasks, not to mention the added financial load. One researcher[8] cites a nationwide study which found that a mother's housework load may double with the arrival of her first child. The same study found that mothers of preschool children spend some fifty to sixty hours a week on household chores. Other research in the same field came up with these findings:

•If there are no children, 1000 hours of housework are required per year (an average of 2.74 hours per day, 365 days per year).

•If there are no children under the age of six, 1500 hours of housework are necessary (an average of 4.11 hours per day, 365 days per year).

•Where there are children under six, 2000 hours of housework are performed[9] (an average of 5.48 hours per day, 365 days per year)—and it *seems* much more.

Finally, other studies have shown that "even taking into account differences in social class . . . intelligence measures [of children] progressively decline with family size."[10]

Having made a case for the one-child family, we should

note that Lois Hoffman and Jean Manis, in a recent study of why couples choose parenthood, found that most couples want *two* children.[11]

4. Couples who have children in close succession will lessen the total number of years devoted to the heavy demands of babies and young children. (Research studies indicate that this appears to be the pattern followed by the better-educated, higher-income families.) Though the immediate load may be greater on parents who elect to have children in close succession, in the long run there is a net gain, because the years needed for intensive child care are telescoped into a few. This leaves more relatively free time in which the parents may pursue careers or other activities.

5. There is evidence that siblings help one another in rough, stressful situations. If two children are enrolled in a child-care center, for example, the stress on both will usually be less than on a single child. Children also are company for one another in the parents' absence (working, vacations, business trips).

What, Really, Is Parenting?

To paraphrase Helen Rowland,[12] "Parenting is like twirling a baton, turning handsprings or eating with chopsticks. It looks easy until you try it."

If you can't define "parenting," don't feel put down. *Webster's* can't (or doesn't), either. The best that *Webster's* can do is define the noun "parent" as "one that begets or brings forth offspring"—something most of us have known since we were six years old.

Dr. Fitzhugh Dodson, an expert on the subject, says "to parent" is "to use, with tender loving care, all the information science has accumulated about child psychology in order to raise happy and intelligent human beings."[13]

Note that Dodson attaches no father or mother labels to the verb "to parent." Neither do we.

A couple's parenting "style" is usually a compound of influences from many sources. Because all of us have been "parented" as children, most of us start with the memories of our own childhood and the impact (negative or positive) made on us by our own parents. Many of us want to raise our children just as we were raised. Many others want to make sure that our children are raised quite differently! Two-career couples are handicapped, in a sense, if they look to their parents as models, since most of their parents were traditional mom-at-home, pop-at-the-shop stereotypes, in the conventional American mold.

Well-educated, middle-class mothers and fathers of today are acutely aware that times have changed since they were kids. They are looking for expert counsel and for guidelines. And there are plenty of sources for advice —Dr. Spock, Parent Effectiveness Training (PET), TA (Transactional Analysis), and Fitzhugh Dodson, to mention a few. But few contemporary experts have much to say that will specifically help the two-career couple. Most of their advice still is based on the conventional model. And even among the experts, there is no clear consensus on the one best way to raise kids (because there is no such way).

Most working couples, in the end, develop their own parenting styles through experience, through observation of the behavior and experiences of others, and by doing the best they can.

Making Time for Your Children

If both parents work all day every day, how do they find time to spend with the kids?

That kind of time doesn't just happen. It is *made* to happen.

Here are some of the ways two-career couples have solved this riddle:

1. Part-Time Work.

A variation of this solution is to find work that can be done at home, such as processing forms, selling or writing, and so forth. If workload and family demands clash too heavily, this arrangement may not prove satisfactory. But part-time work outside the home often becomes a very practical answer to the problem, particularly if the job allows the part-time worker at least 50 percent of his or her time at home with the children.

2. Job-Sharing.

In the academic world and in some public sectors and in some private businesses (in particular, when a couple owns their own enterprise), couples may share one job while also sharing the child-care tasks at home.

3. Taking the Kids Along.

Although this option may sound a bit wild, some parents actually are taking their infants or young kids to work with them. The women of *Ms.* magazine provide one example. We also know of a high-ranking woman administrator at a West Coast medical school who, soon after giving birth to her son, took the infant with her on cross-country trips to Washington, D.C., and New York. She was able to continue breast-feeding on schedule while keeping her appointments and maintaining a full workload. In the process, she delighted many of her colleagues with her creative and courageous solution to the problem of "spending time with the baby." A few large industrial plants have attempted to sponsor in-plant day-care facilities for the children of employees so that they can—in a sense—take the kids along. Some of these have succeeded, but others have been shut down because of the parents' lack of interest in using them.

Time: Quality versus Quantity

"How much time should I spend with my child?"

Parents who ask this question usually follow it with another: "What should I be *doing* all that time I'm with my child?"

There is no magic formula, of course, to determine how much time should be spent with one's child, but at least quantity can be defined in terms of hours, minutes, and seconds. *Quality,* as applied to time, eludes such measurement.

Over and over, we read—and hear—that "it's not how *much* time, but the *quality* of that time with children that counts." But *never* do we read—or hear—quality defined in that context, nor the amount of high-quality time specified.

Some students of the subject believe quantity *and* quality are better than just quality.[14]

Quality may, on one occasion and with one parent and child, involve a hugging session lasting just a few seconds. On another, an hour of uninterrupted chatting may be insufficient.

Wrestling with the problem of defining "high quality," we came up with the following:

1. High-quality time is being with *and interacting with* a child. Self-evident? Not really. Some parents think that merely being "at home" with their child is the same as high-quality time. The key element is interaction. Mere physical presence is not, in this context, enough.

2. High-quality time is *child-initiated* or *child-sanctioned* activity. Successful interaction, and the establishment of true rapport, often means the parent's doing what the *child* wants to do. Although doing what the *parent* wants to do and the child does not may at times be appropriate, that cannot be considered high-quality

time with the child (even if what you are doing is "for the child's sake"). If your two-year-old asks you to play blocks on the floor with her, and you do, that's child-initiated activity. If you ask your two-year-old to go to the grocery store with you, and she responds enthusiastically, that's child-sanctioned activity.

3. High-quality time is demonstrating, through words or actions or both, that you love the child. Some children want to be hugged and kissed and held. Others want, simply, to be near the parent. Be sensitive to what they want *from* you and to what they want to give *to* you.

4. High-quality time spent with your child immediately after you return home (even if you stay only a few minutes) is probably more important than any other time spent with the child. How easy it is for tired working parents to walk into the house and immediately sort through the mail or read a newspaper or mix a drink or start cooking a meal, without paying more than passing attention to the child hovering nearby. We recommend that your first activity, immediately on entering the house, should be to spend a few minutes of high-quality time with your child. You will probably find—as many parents have found—that once the child's immediate needs for attention have been met, the child will be satisfied to go on with whatever he or she was doing before your arrival.

5. High-quality time involves active participation by the parent. Talking to, playing or working with, or in some way being personally and fully involved in a child's activity, is extremely important. Merely watching your son play in the patio or backyard is not high-quality time. Talking on the phone to a neighbor or friend while playing with your nine-month-old daughter is not high-quality time.

Having made our point, we quickly admit that giving a

child high-quality time is not always easy, and on occasions may be impossible. One New England businessman, writing in *American Home*, [15] expressed his cynicism this way:

Don't tell me quality is better than quantity. That's what she told me. It goes this way: It's not the amount of time you devote to your children but the degree of giving that takes place during that time. That's another specious hype invented by writers who have never lived through the situation. What happens in real life is that my wife comes home from work tired and grumpy. She snaps at the children. The quality of that time is awful. Weekends are better, but that is also when we play tennis, run errands, and spend time with each other. In other words, the quality is better then, but the quantity is so limited that I wonder if the sparse, part-time parenting makes up for all the lost time.

This writer and his wife (who had a $14,000-per-year job) had two children—aged two and four—and a $10,000-per-year housekeeper.

The writer's argument is persuasive. But it does not cancel out the logic of the theme under discussion: there is no substitution for the precious minutes and hours shared by parent and child. Those minutes and hours are investments in the future of another human being; they will pay rich dividends for that person's entire lifetime.

What Children Really Need—and Don't Need

Apart from their basic survival requirements, children must be supplied with an imposing variety of spiritual, social, and intellectual nutrients.

Central among these is the child's need for love. Urie Bronfenbrenner, professor of human development and family structure at Cornell University, put it engagingly:

. . . There has to be at least one person who has an irrational involvement with that child, someone who thinks that kid is more important than other people's kids, someone who's in love with him and whom he loves in return.[16]

What follows is a list of a child's psychosocial needs, originally developed by Nathan Talbot and Kellmer Pringle:

1. to be wanted and needed;
2. to be cared for, protected and attended to;
3. to be valued, accepted, and given a sense of belonging;
4. to be guided, educated, stimulated toward social capability and subject to limits of socially acceptable behavior;
5. to be given opportunities to gain satisfaction in life and feel responsible through new experiences, useful work, and creative recreational activities;
6. to be praised and recognized.

Talbot and Pringle also point out what children do *not* need, as follows:

1. being shunned or considered superfluous;
2. being neglected or abused (psychologically);
3. being maliciously belittled, hated, rejected, spurned;
4. being indulged;
5. being denied responsibility or opportunities for independent thought and action; having everything done for one.[17]

Fathering: A Learned Skill

The authors of most child-care manuals, with remarkable tunnel vision, simply ignore fathers. And many pediatricians turn a bit nervous whenever a father comes into the office. The father, in short, has customarily been regarded as some sort of organism who just happened to be around at the laying of the keel.

The truth is that when it comes to the rearing of children, there are only two acts a woman can perform that cannot be performed equally well by a man: childbearing, and breast-feeding.[18] The fact that men have not, until now, taken a more active role in rearing their children is not attributable to any law of nature. It is merely that, in America's work-oriented society, the man has been *expected* to concentrate on his job and the woman has been *expected* to concentrate on the home.

Parenting is a *learned skill.* One is not born with this talent; it is not transmitted in the genes to either parent. Mothering, or fathering, derives from learning and practice. This is an elemental fact, long since established by research.[19]

Obviously, then, to be *good* at parenting, both parents need to learn how to parent. The learning is accomplished by trial and error, by observation, and by study.

Three Steps to Effective Fatherhood

Most fathers truly believe they are good fathers; that is to say, effective fathers. If you were to ask them, most fathers would reply that they spend a *lot* of time with their kids. But Bronfenbrenner, who made a study of the subject, concluded that "middle-class fathers thought they averaged 15 or 20 minutes a day playing with their year-old infants, when actually the average number of interactions per day was only 2.7 and the average duration of the interactions [was] less than a minute—37.7 seconds."[20]

There are certain steps fathers may take to become more effective parents. And, in the process, to become better partners in a dual-career relationship.

Step 1. Spend "Early" Time.

Fathers should consciously plan to spend early time with a newborn infant. Ideally, a father should become involved in the birth itself by enrolling, with the mother, in an instruction course, such as Lamaze.

Psychologists established years ago that a mother's intimate feelings toward her child result from two influences —the biological changes that take place in the mother during gestation, and her early experience with the infant. It is also known that mothers who are separated from their newborn during the babies' first days of life tend to have less desire to continue mothering those infants than do mothers who remain with their newborn continuously.

Said another way, mothers become "hooked" as a result of this early intimacy. In psychology, this is known as "bonding."

The same phenomenon can occur with fathers. Fathers who are intimately linked to their newborn infants, especially during the babies' first three months of life, become hooked. Bonding occurs. Thus, to increase the father's participation in parenting, there should be *early-time* bonding between father and child.

(There is a grim corollary that should be noted. Children who are separated from their mothers in the early-time phase sometimes do not develop normally—clear evidence of the enormous importance of intimate parent-infant ties in this critical period of growth.)

Early-time involvement, then, is the first of three steps to effective fatherhood.

Step 2. Schedule Specific Time.

The natural and historic tendency, in our society, is for fathers to put work first and families second. Step 2 requires a 180-degree turn in thinking, reversing the priorities by putting family first, work second. This will require fathers to schedule *specific* time to be devoted to their kids.

We have all heard parents lamenting, later in their

lives, that they had not spent more time with their young and growing children. Such laments usually come from lonely couples whose grown offspring show little if any affection for their parents and pay little if any attention to them as the parents grow older. In these instances, it is probable that there was little or no bonding when the children were infants and during their formative years.

Scheduling time for one's children means precisely that: scheduling. We see nothing unusual about scheduling time for an appearance at the first tee on the golf course or for a game of bridge with friends. Yet how many of us block off chunks of our time to devote exclusively to our kids? Fathers, to become effective and useful parents, should reserve specific days and hours for their youngsters. The casual "now and then, if and when I have time" approach simply will not work.

Step 3. Plan Activities.

Just *being* with a child is commendable. And with very young infants-in-arms, the mere being with, the holding, the feeding, the diaper-changing—these *are,* at that stage, activities. But as the child grows, and its needs become more sophisticated, there should be planned activity. As noted in the earlier discussion of good-quality time, much of this activity may be proposed by the child, or at least endorsed by him or her.

In sum, the three steps to effective fatherhood are:

1. Get involved *early,* preferably from the child's birth on.

2. Schedule *specific* time for the child.

3. Plan *activities.*

Tomorrow's Fathers Are Already Here

Evidence is mounting that more and more fathers are rejecting the time-honored formula that puts work first and families second. A large measure of the antiestablishment feeling evidenced in the sixties and seventies was a rebellion against the "work first" equation and a call for greater stress on family.

One federal bureaucrat left the government after less than three months in a high-echelon job because of the dehumanizing influence of his work. David Breneman, former deputy assistant secretary for education policy in the Department of Health, Education, and Welfare, resigned to return to the Brookings Institution because "the hectic, adrenalin-powered world of top bureaucrats and presidential assistants was no place for a man with a family."[21]

Finally, fathers—and mothers, too—should learn to *enjoy* their kids, and the kids to enjoy their parents. There should be a lot of laughs and a barrel of fun in family living. Kids who remember home as a happy, fun-and-games place never miss a chance to return to the family hearth for a visit. In their parents' senior years, such offspring manifest their early and continuing love by heading home for the holidays, bringing the grandchildren, and thus enriching the "sunset years" for their aging fathers and mothers.

Bonding with one's offspring, therefore, not only helps assure the normal and wholesome development of the child; it yields priceless benefits to the bonded parent by creating a happy home environment while the child is growing up and many years of satisfying companionship in later life.

In Closing, Some Random Suggestions . . .

Do your kids know where you go and what you do at work?

Do you and your children really have time to talk about problems, successes, plans?

Are you taking part in the kids' important activities?

If your answers are no or maybe to any or all of these queries, you may find the following suggestions—drawn from the real-life experiences of working couples—of some help.

1. Explain to your kids what you do at work. Tell them what your job title is, and describe your duties. Otherwise, your young one may be like the five-year-old who "couldn't understand why her mother needed to spend a full working week doing 'the laundry.' It took a lot of gentle probing before it was discovered that the child had 'laundry' mixed up with 'library,' where her mother did work full time."[22]

Another mother, with five kids under seven years of age, "made sure . . . that the children were prepared for my new job. I took them to the office so that they could picture where Mommy was 'wooking.' "[23]

If possible, take your children to your work place or office. Show them your desk. Let them sit in your chair. Show them where you eat your lunch. Introduce them to your colleagues or associates. Demonstrate what you do in your job. This will give the children a mental picture of how you keep busy and where you are while they are at home, in school, or at a day-care center.

If you can, plan to leave home and return at more or less set times. Be sure to tell them—especially the preschoolers—when you will return. Even if they don't understand time, they will be reassured that you are returning, and this reassurance is what is important.

2. Because a dual-career schedule leaves very few extra moments for interaction with the kids, we suggest that you arrange for family meeting times, perhaps once a week. These can be started even when children are very young. Set aside a regular period—perhaps fifteen to thirty minutes—when all hands gather to discuss the coming week's events, appointments, or the special needs of any member of the family in the period ahead. Example:

"Mother will be working extra hard next week, so let's all try to help her by not asking her for any special favors." Or, "My school's having a field trip next week to the tide pools, and we need some parents to drive. I wish one of you could come. Could you?"

These "town meeting" sessions can also serve for the airing of feelings, disagreements, and conflicts. But to keep them from degenerating chronically into gripe sessions, make sure to say something positive at each meeting about every member of the family. A game can be made of this by challenging all present to finish such sentences as

"I really like you because . . ."

"I like the way . . ."

"One of the things that you do best is . . ."

This finish-the-sentence game is a good way to end meetings on an upbeat note.

A family bulletin board is also a good idea as a communications center. Calendars of events can be posted there, messages and reminders can be thumbtacked, and schoolwork can be displayed.

3. Try to find out from your kids what events, programs, and other occasions are really important to them. Working parents will drive themselves crazy if they try to take part in *every* activity involving their children. Hence the necessity of filtering out the relatively trivial from what the child considers the truly important.

A suggestion: as you participate in, for example, school events as parents, explain to school officials your special problems, as two-career parents, in terms of time schedules. Schools still organize most of their parent-involved activities on the premise that mom is at home all the time, and dad is always at the office. Point out that schools, by scheduling events at more reasonable hours, will ensure greater parental participation.

Working couples are uniquely challenged in their dual

roles of worker and parent. Although some may question the compatibility of these roles, many dual-career couples are living examples that it can be done well. As one parent has said:

It takes more of just about everything—planning, money, concentration, sensitivity, talking with one another, and a whole lot of love! But the reward is having a family in which there is a balance in meeting parents' and children's needs. We all give and we all receive. Isn't that what family life is all about?

CHAPTER V

The Other-Than-Mother
Dilemma: Choosing Child Care

Five million American children under the age of 13 now spend
30 hours or more a week in the care of someone other than their
parents or their school teachers.[1]

No decision facing a two-career couple is more charged
with potential trauma than the choice of child care for
their children. The younger the offspring, the more agonizing—and critical—the choice.

There is no single "best" answer to the other-than-
mother question. This chapter explores the various child-
care options available today, and suggests some guidelines
for selecting the one best suited to your children.

One reason that the child-care problem in contemporary America is so acute lies in our national history. Until
barely yesterday—certainly not more than a generation
·ago—it was a given that a mother's place was in the home
with the kids. Period. On a national scale, as a society, we
had not worked out answers to the problems of child care
because, in the main, there were no real problems. Child
care simply·has not been, until recently, a burning issue.
The writer Ellen Goodman has said:

We all observed that the changes of the 1960s were disruptive; Vietnam, Watergate, the sexual revolution. The biggest change, however, was the advent of working mothers.[2]

Within the lifetime of all readers of this book, the old order has changed. Ellen Goodman also noted:

It is ironic, paradoxical, that the ideal family to many Americans is one that has two children, the mother at home and the father at work. *Only 10 percent of the families today meet that description.* (Emphasis added.)[3]

Child care has gone, in scarcely two decades, from no issue at all to Burning Issue Number One, as far as two-career parents are concerned. So rapidly has it zoomed to its present status that we have been caught, sociologically speaking, with our pants down.

Many other nations of the world where child care has been an issue have long since grappled with the problem, with varying degrees of success and by using a variety of approaches. The British "nanny" has been a respected institution in upper-class England for generations. There are schools for nannies, and special employment agencies for nannies. Most important, however, is the fact that to be a nanny is to be respected as a professional. And, by British economic standards, to be well paid.

Across the Channel, another child-care institution has long thrived: the *au pair* girl. *Au pairs* are young women, with different levels of education and from a broad range of backgrounds, who seek employment with a family in a country other than their own. Often, their primary motive is to learn a foreign language. The arrangement usually calls for the *au pair* girl to exchange child-care services for room and board, plus a small salary. Because the *au pair* may have no special training for this occupation, the quality of the service may vary widely. But here again, the important fact is that, in Europe, it is traditional and socially acceptable for young women to engage in this kind of employment—in fact, to *seek* it.

There is no such tradition, no such social seal of approval, on child care in the United States. Most young American women would never consider giving child-care services of the kind provided by British nannies or European *au pairs.* Nor would it occur to most American parents to seek such services from American girls or women. It just "isn't done." Because of our national history and traditions, we do not have at hand today—when we need it—a reservoir of trained (or even of untrained but willing) talent to accommodate the growing child-care requirements of this nation. Margaret Mead said:

Paid, well-trained nurses who are trustworthy, intelligent, and have the character appropriate for the continuous care of an infant are almost nonexistent today. And no State-supported child-care center can afford enough well-trained, nurturing persons.[4]

Despite much lip service to the "sacred role of motherhood" and repeated references to children as our "national treasure," American society has consistently derogated the task of caring for children. The U.S. Department of Labor, in its *Table of Employment by Occupations,* does not even list child-care workers as a category. Thus, child care today is not only a "nonprofession" in the United States; it is a low-status, miserable-paying, menial sort of make-do work usually relegated to the untrained and uneducated (who very often are foreigners with little or no knowledge of English).

There are exceptions, of course, and their numbers are growing. Some are college students who have taken early-childhood-development courses. But even those with training, who find employment in licensed child-care centers, frequently begin at the same wage paid to field laborers and others with minimal skills. The miserly wage scale ignores the fact that these child-care persons are charged with the heavy responsibility of helping to rear those who tomorrow will be the nation's teachers, industrial titans, governors, and presidents. The imbalance is obvious.

Will Substitute-Mother Child Care Hurt *Your* Child?

The most burning child-care issue in America today is whether a mother of preschool children can go to work with a clean conscience.[5]

All responsible parents who are deeply concerned about the physical, emotional, and intellectual development of their children tend to suffer—with varying degrees of intensity—certain predictable doubts and fears when they face the question of having others care for their children. Their concerns usually are related to one or more of three questions:

1. *Will my child's intellectual development be impaired?* Worded more bluntly: Will my child end up stupid if I turn his or her care over to others?

2. *Will my child become emotionally scarred if I do not assume all responsibility for him or her?* Will the child emerge from childhood unstable, antisocial, or otherwise maladjusted?

3. *Could my child become a juvenile delinquent if I do not raise him or her personally?* Parents of children in the eight-to-fifteen-year age range are especially susceptible to such fears, which have been fueled by the dramatic increase in juvenile delinquency linked to drug abuse, broken homes, and other social phenomena.

First, it is obviously logical to assume that the absence

of both parents from the home will have *some* effect on the children. To deny this would be silly. As has already been stressed, what one member of a family does inevitably affects all the others.

The crucial question, then, is not *whether* a child is affected by the mother's absence, but *how much* and in *what ways* her absence affects a child. Are the effects all negative, or a mixture of good and bad?

Even though there have been many studies of these questions by experts in family and human development in recent years, the results are as yet by no means conclusive. In 1975, Jerome Kagan, professor of human development at Harvard University, completed a survey of children between the ages of three and a half months and twenty-nine months who attended a Boston research day-care center, and compared them with a similar group of children raised at home by their mothers. Professor Kagan concluded that "there wasn't any difference in intellectual and social development" between the two groups.

But Professor Kagan pointed out that current testing methods may be too crude to detect such differences. "So logically," he said, "we can never say there are no harmful effects of day care. When the birth-control pill came out, it was supposed to be harmless, but we later found that it is harmful to some women."[6]

Two experts who had bitterly opposed the idea of day-care centers but later modified their position are B. M. Glickman and Nesha Bass Springer, the authors of *Who Cares for the Baby? Choices in Child Care.* In the preface to their book, they frankly admitted that they had "set out to write a book that would destroy day-care centers, and bring the babies back home" because they had "realized that the day-care center was rapidly supplanting the mother in the home . . ."[7] However, by the time they had finished their research and written their book, the authors had arrived at another viewpoint.

"We have come to believe," they said, in the epilogue to their book, "that these [the children's] needs may be met in many different day-care situations, and that with a great deal of selectivity and considerable expense children in full-time, other-than-mother care may be as competent, responsible, bright, and healthy as children raised at home."[8]

In a study funded by HEW, Ellen Rozelle Hock, assistant professor at the Ohio State University School of Home Economics, and five assistants interviewed 1432 mothers of new babies. They selected from this group 280 mothers of healthy newborns. Half of these mothers said they planned to continue working. When the babies were three months and eight months old, the women were interviewed again. Mrs. Hock reported that she and her colleagues found no differences in the development of the babies of working and nonworking mothers. The babies' adjustment and well-being appeared the same, she said, noting that "both groups of women exhibited the same type of loving, maternal attitude."[9]

As for the "juvenile delinquency" question, two authorities came up with this conclusion: "Despite the popular myths regarding maternal deprivation in families where mothers work, there is no solid evidence that the mother's employment status, in itself, leads to juvenile delinquency or other forms of social or psychological problems, at least for school-age children."[10]

It is worth noting, in passing, that a child's well-being and adjustment appear to be linked strongly to the attitude and state of mind of the mother.

"If a woman stays home only out of a sense of duty her dissatisfaction will show up in her maternal and family attitudes," observed Mrs. Hock.[11] An Iowa State University researcher's findings support the same view:

Research literature states repeatedly that mothers who like what they are doing, whether they are employed or not, have fewer problems in child-rearing. Mothers who like their work have been found to show greater affection to their children than mothers who dislike their work. Further, it seems clear that children of dissatisfied full-time homemaking mothers show more problem behaviors than do children of satisfied employed mothers.[12]

Other recent research into these questions has come up with the following findings:

1. Employed mothers tend to spend as much—or even more—time with their children, on a one-to-one basis, as nonemployed mothers do. And working mothers tend to enjoy child care just as much as nonworking mothers do.[13]

2. Sons and daughters of working mothers tend to have higher educational goals. In other words, their ambition to get ahead in the world, to improve themselves, is often awakened by the knowledge that their mothers have careers.[14]

3. The working mother is less susceptible to overinvolvement with her children than is the nonworking mother.[15]

4. Most mothers succeed in finding child-care substitutes who care for their children in much the same way as they themselves would.[16]

5. Although the children of working mothers tend to assume more household responsibilities than the children of nonworking mothers, there are few differences in the leisure activities of children in either category.

6. The daughters of working women have higher career aspirations than do daughters of nonworking women. And

the former more often choose careers in male-dominated fields than do the latter.[17]

7. Children of working mothers are less inclined to discriminate between masculine and feminine roles.[18]

The Other-than-Mother Options

What, then, in the face of the sobering realities, are the child-care choices actually available to two-career couples today?

Surprisingly, although there may not be many nannies or *au pair* girls available, there are a number of possibilities. You may choose to:

1. Work part time.

2. Employ a caretaker to live in your home.

3. Place your children in the home of a friend, relative, or a paid caretaker.

4. Place your child under the supervision of a competent person who operates a family day-care facility in his or her home.

5. Enroll your children in a good preschool or nursery school.

6. Seek out a first-rate day-care center (not the same as (3) or (4) above).

7. Take advantage of a company-sponsored child-care program. (These are rare, but may be increasing.)

8. Join a cooperative with other dual-career or conventional couples, and share with them—on a rotating schedule—the responsibilities of child care on a daily, continuing basis.

9. In the case of older children, enroll these children in afterschool activities, or help them to become involved in a number of nonschool programs during nonschool time.

The following sections will explore the pros and cons of

various options for, first, preschool children and, second, for children of school age through adolescence.

INFANCY: From Birth to Five Years of Age

MOTHER: What's the *best* kind of child care, doctor?

DOCTOR: Who really knows? So much depends on the child, the parents, the locale, the program, the people. Sorry, I can't give you a simple answer. But I *can* tell you how my wife and I select care for *our* kids. We ask ourselves one simple question: Does this child care *add* to their lives? If the answer is yes, we think it's child care worth at least a try. It should *add* something to the kids' lives, and not just fill time—like sitting in front of the tube.

OPTION 1: PARENTS WORK PART TIME

An obvious choice, but one well worth exploring. Many couples finally decide to work part time (either one or both members), spending the balance of their time caring for the children. We strongly support this option, which is also recommended by many authorities on child care. It is an especially strong choice for parents of children from infancy through five years of age. And it is a choice being made increasingly by young parents. Ellen Goodman has also said: "A survey indicates that the happiest working mothers are those in part-time jobs."[19]

Unfortunately, most American businesses, industries, and professions are geared primarily—and historically— to the full-time worker. What part-time openings are offered are available, in the main, to women. Men who seek part-time employment still tend to be viewed as oddballs.

Urie Bronfenbrenner struck a nerve when he urged that parents of young children do without some luxuries and work only part time. They could afford to do this "if [they] would be willing to consider kids as important as

[they] do color TVs and two cars . . . But that really requires the recognition and assumption that parenthood is at least as important as the rest of the things you do during the day."[20]

OPTION 2: CARE IN YOUR HOME

For a variety of reasons, most of them obvious, this option is regarded as the most attractive and satisfying by a large percentage of all two-career couples. Sara Wellington, a thirty-nine-year-old account executive, gives her reasons:

I've always chosen to bring in child-care persons to our home simply because my husband and I feel more secure in knowing that Jamie—our six-month-old—is in our home, in his own crib, with all his own things. There's an atmosphere of love there, and I want him to feel it even if we're not there. And if the babysitter changes, at least Jamie's environment remains the same.

The Carnegie Council on Children, in a recent policy statement, took the position that "the most satisfactory supplementary care arrangement to support the development of children in the first few years would probably be a *regular babysitter in the home,* since she could most easily provide the continuous, individualized attention needed by the young child. (Emphasis added.)[21]

We agree with the council except for its use of the term "babysitter." A babysitter is not enough. In present-day America, a babysitter is usually a person—generally female—who is paid between seventy-five cents and $2.00 an hour to "look after" a child or children for a short period during the day or evening. These usually are teenagers, with little or no training or experience in child care. As a rule, babysitters contribute little or nothing to a child's psychosocial needs. (See Chapter IV, Two-Career

Parenting, for definitive explanation of children's needs.)

More often than not, a babysitter winds up being a "baby-watcher" who has something else more important on her or his mind, such as a boy or girl friend, telephone calls, homework, a favorite TV show, food—you name it. Such persons are useful for stop-gap purposes; but even for fill-in functions, these workers should meet certain minimum standards. At the very least, you—and your children—should *like* the babysitter. And the babysitter should be intelligent and responsible enough to rise to an emergency and to carry out faithfully any instructions you may leave to cover contingencies.

But a babysitter is not, by definition, the answer for your child's needs for an entire day, much less for a weekend, or when you're away on a business trip or for any other extended period. That is a job for a real pro, not for an amateur.

We also support the idea that—with some exceptions—a child-care person should not double as a housekeeper, or vice versa. There are, of course, some outstanding people who are excellent housekeepers and who, at the same time, have all the qualifications of a skilled "other-than-mother." But these are such rarities that the average couple's chances of finding one are of the snowball-in-hell category. Should you by sheer luck stumble on one of these jewels, snap her up immediately, love her, pay her well, and feel blessed by good fortune.

Remember, "keeping house" and "keeping children" are contradictory terms; children and a clean house are naturally antithetical.

Later, in the section entitled "How To Choose One," we discuss some of the criteria for hiring a child-care person.

A child-care person can be hired either to live in or to live out. There are advantages and disadvantages in both systems, some of which are the following:

Live-In Child Care

Advantages:

1. The person is always available.

2. Arrivals and departures, and transportation, are not problems.

3. The arrangement is usually more economical than employing live-out help.

4. A live-in knows the family and its "rhythms," and can respond appropriately.

5. Under the best of circumstances, a live-in can become a true parent surrogate.

Disadvantages:

1. There is a lack of privacy. Someone is always in the house, "under foot."

2. The potential for "exploitation" of employee by employer is greater because of the former's constant availability.

3. Truly qualified live-in persons are rarities.

4. The live-in's needs and personality have greater impact on employer than do those of live-out help.

5. Special space in the home is required by a live-in.

6. Live-ins can suffer symptoms of "housewife's syndrome" as the result of extended isolation.

Live-Out Child Care

Advantages:

1. The reservoir of available live-out persons is greater than that of live-ins.

2. Live-outs are available part time as well as full time.

3. Employer becomes less involved with personality and personal needs of a live-out than with a live-in person.

4. Employment is not so isolating for the live-out worker as it is for the live-in.

Disadvantages:
   1. Transportation becomes important.
   2. The arrangement is usually more costly.
   3. Help is not available on a twenty-four-hour basis.

Who Are the Live-Outs?

There is a wide range of people available to you in this category. Not only are more live-outs than live-ins available, but—and more important—*the quality of the person in this category generally is higher.*

Here are some of the kinds of individuals you might find in the live-out category:

•people trained in early-childhood education (including college graduates unable to find the "right" job in a tight teaching market);

•part-time college students;

•other parents, including mothers whose children are away at school most of the day;

•senior citizens (there are *many* grandmother and grandfather types looking for rewarding, purposeful work to do);

•young people taking a transition year or two off from college or the job market;

•women who want to enter the labor force to do what they know how to do: mothering;

•young people wanting to experience parenting before actually raising children themselves.

Qualified people who have lives of their own often have familial or other ties that make a live-in experience unattractive or impractical. They also may avoid instinctively the live-in status because such a status—like that of housekeeper—has acquired (unfairly) low esteem in American society. These same qualified people also may shun live-in work because they fear exploitation by over-zealous or overly demanding employers.

Where do you look, then, for live-out child-care persons? Here are some resources:

1. Relatives.

Grandparents, aunts, older children of your own, may come immediately to mind as possibilities. Relatives can often provide precisely the kind of warm, caring attention you need and want for your children. But we urge you to be very professional about the nature of the work you expect them to perform. Make sure that the elements of child care specified earlier are provided.

I would really like my mother to care for the children while I work. But her way of doing things is just so different from Pat's and mine. We are really concerned about the kids not eating junk food, and my mother just doesn't seem to know how to choose healthy foods. She tries, but they end up having white bread, TV dinners, gobs of jelly and peanut butter, and canned fruits, instead of what we choose. Maybe they would be better off with someone we hired who would *have* to listen to us.

As you well know, family relationships are delicate and fragile enough without being subjected to employer-employee strains. Some relatives have their own—and very different—ideas about raising children, ideas that conflict with yours. Others may interpret "child care" to mean simply "baby-watching" or "babysitting." Some of them may feel embarrassed or unwilling to accept money from you for their services. If this is the case, be sure that recognition is given to them in some form; no one likes to be taken for granted.

If you decide to "hire" a relative, take special care to specify hours, needs, all the elements of the job at hand. And don't fail to have those weekly meetings to clear up problems or to discuss issues related to child care.

2. Friends or Neighbors.

Occasionally, friends or neighbors are available to provide professional-level child care. Just as with hiring relatives, however, this arrangement can entail both blessings and problems. Perhaps the most useful advice we can give in this situation, aside from urging you to maintain a good working relationship with the person employed, is not to compromise your children's needs by offering the job to a needy friend or neighbor while disregarding that person's qualifications for the job. Offer this important work only to the best person available.

3. College Students.

You may find a well-qualified child-care person through the student-employment office of the nearest community college, four-year college, or university. You can also consult the "situations wanted" listings in the student newspapers or on college bulletin boards. Many young people need to earn money to finance their education, and if your job is more than mere babysitting, in terms of responsibility and pay, this may be a good arrangement for both you and the student.

Students majoring in education, child development, nursing, or psychology sometimes seek firsthand experience with children as an adjunct to their class work. If they have had previous experience with the children of others, they may prove to be real finds. Though they usually are available only for part-time work, college students may give your children the energetic, experienced, intelligent care they need.

4. Senior Citizens.

Perhaps the least-tapped resource available for child care today is the senior citizen. There are thousands of healthy, intelligent, alert individuals in this category seeking purposeful work for themselves, and your child-care position may be the answer for a senior citizen's need as well as your own.

Again, it is very important that you let the prospective employee know that you hold both the job (child care) and the person ("old") in high regard. The double negative of being both "old" and at work in "child care"—two terms regarded as pejorative in some circles—can be a powerful force militating against your finding the right senior for your opening. State employment offices, senior citizens' groups and centers (many of which have bulletin boards), newspapers (some of them targeted at senior groups), churches, and synagogues are among the sources you might explore.

5. Others.

In times of high unemployment, many skilled people who otherwise would readily find work are looking for positions. The problem here, again, is to combat the negative image of the "babysitter" by wording your want ads imaginatively and by using good interviewing techniques. And certainly, after the person has been hired, by keeping your employer-employee relations on the highest possible plane.

Who Are the Live-Ins?

Many of the categories of people mentioned under "Who Are the Live-Outs?" are also available as live-in help. Traditionally, live-in help has tended to be that combined babysitter-housekeeper combination we warned about earlier. Some working couples have hired trained nannies from England. However, unless these individuals are legal immigrants with work permits, there can be problems with the immigration service. Work visas are rarely available to foreigners, and a foreigner is prohibited from working while in the United States on a visitor's visa (usually limited to from three to six months). Nonetheless, many of us have heard of cases in which someone's visiting English mother has somehow found her way into a home to take care of the children "temporarily."

The same visa restrictions and problems apply to *au*

pair girls. Add to the visa problems the difficulties associated with choosing someone, sight unseen, living thousands of miles away, and you can readily see that the hiring of foreigners is not the easiest of solutions.

For whatever reasons, there are still United States citizens who prefer to live with and work for a family. Some of these people have no family at all, at least nearby; so just as they function as a parent surrogate for the family, the employers provide them with a surrogate family.

With the cost of room and board constantly rising, the attraction of a job that provides these amenities is very great. Furthermore, some families in the more affluent brackets can provide a live-in person of a lower financial status with a standard of living that would, for him or her, normally be unattainable. This, for some people, is an impelling reason for working as a live-in child-care person.

OPTION 3: CARE IN SOMEONE ELSE'S HOME

As we began to look for child-care resources when Janet was pregnant, we found that most of our friends were choosing to take their babies to a sitter's home. We began asking around for the names of people doing this, and Mrs. Clay's was among them. From the moment we saw her clean, warm home, we knew this was where our baby should be when we were at work. This first visceral reaction proved to be right. Mrs. Clay has really added a dimension to Maryann's life . . . She seems to feel that Maryann is as terrific as we do.

Working parents can locate child-care people who will care for children in their own homes in much the same way live-in or live-out help is located.

Personal qualities to be sought in such child-care persons will be discussed in detail later, under "Choosing an Other-than-Mother Person." But there is another important consideration: the environment provided by the child-care person's home and neighborhood. Here are some of the environmental features you may wish to check:

•The neighborhood: Is it safe? Is it convenient to your home or work place? Is it attractive and clean? Are there parks and stores nearby? Are there sidewalks, or paths where walks may be taken?

•The caretaker's home: Is it safe, clean, attractive, well heated (or cooled)? Will your child have a place there that he or she can consider his or her own, such as a chest, a bed, part of a room? Is there a backyard, patio, or other outdoor play area? Is the area safe and attractive?

•Animals: If there are animals, are they kept inside or outside? Are there animal odors or droppings around? Are the animals well tempered and properly vaccinated? Are they licensed (if licenses are required)? Do you want your child to stay in a home where there are animals, and under what conditions? What about fleas?

•Other children: Does the caretaker have other children to care for, either her own or other people's? If so, how many? What does she say about how your child will be cared for if other children are present? If other children are present, observe them. Do they seem happy, well cared-for, and relatively healthy?

•Food: Observe any food being served or prepared for serving. Is there an abundance of junk food? What kind of meals can you expect your child to receive in that facility? Will the caretaker accept and faithfully follow any special instructions you may give her about food for your child? Are dishes and glasses clean?

OPTION 4: FAMILY DAY CARE

A family day-care setting is one in which a private home is adapted to accommodate children whose ages can range from infancy through school age. In some cases, the person or persons who run the home attempt to create a "little family" or "home" atmosphere for the children; hence the term "family day care." Some of these homes are oriented to younger children, infants to those five or six years of age. Others are geared for school-age children who come before and after school hours. Most states and some counties and cities license family day-care homes to impose and regulate standards of health, safety, and physical conditions. But we should stress that licensing requirements are almost as varied as the types of people and homes in which family day care is provided. Rarely do the licensing requirements take into account the all-important psychosocial needs of children.

The costs for such care vary widely, but the usual range is from $35 to $45 per week per child. For information on family day-care homes in your community (and we urge you to consider only licensed homes), contact one of the following:

(a) city or county Office of Human Resources or Services, or an office doing business under some comparable title;

(b) one of the many family-service agencies;

(c) a state or county public-welfare office.

OPTION 5: NURSERY AND PRESCHOOLS

Thousands of nursery schools already are in operation in towns and cities throughout America, and other thousands are being organized—some in rural areas. Although most of them offer only a half-day program, some offer full-day and extended day care. (Extended day care is, essentially, supervised play or child care before regular school convenes and/or after school ends.) These schools are open only to children between the ages of three and five (though some schools have a lower age limit of two years, nine months; and others have a maximum age limit of six years).

Nursery schools normally fall into one of the following categories: traditional, open structure, Montessori, or religion-related. Basically, what a child does during the time he or she is in nursery school will depend on the type of school. Some are cooperatives, with parents administering and helping to teach. Others are attached to regular private schools. Some are nonprofit; others are privately owned and operated as business enterprises. The cost of sending a child to one of these schools may be a few dollars a month, for parent-participation programs, or over $100 a month, for some private schools.

Two major challenges facing working parents in choosing a nursery school program for their child are: (1) taking the time necessary to investigate all the possibilities, and to choose the best available; and (2) finding a school that has a high-quality program that meshes with the parents' working schedule.

For information about nursery schools in your area, contact the National Association for the Education of Young Children, 1834 Connecticut Avenue, N.W., Washington, D.C. 20009.

OPTION 6: DAY-CARE CENTERS

You may have been misled, by frequent reports in the news media, into believing that we, as a society, have *the answer* to our child-care problems in day-care centers. But the statistics tell a different story.

In actual numbers, there are only about 2 percent of the children of working parents in day-care centers (as opposed to) 33 million of our 41 million children (who) are cared for by one of their parents when the children are not in school.[22]

What is day care? In reality, like family day-care homes,

day-care centers can be just about anything. They can be licensed or unlicensed (and we urge you to ignore completely the unlicensed ones); public (usually operated by public agencies for welfare or low-income families at minimal cost) or private (nonprofit or privately owned or cooperative); small (ten children) or large (100 children); and located in schools, churches, recreation centers, college campuses, or public facilities. Some centers are open from early morning (6:30 A.M.) to evening (9:00 P.M.); but many are open only from a few minutes before 8:00 A.M. until a few minutes after 5:00 P.M., with strict drop-off and pick-up schedules. Most day-care centers provide babysitting; a few provide high-quality care that includes attention to children's physical and psychosocial needs.* Costs range from $20 to $75 per week for full-time care, depending on the child's age.

For information on locating day care in your area, or on starting a center, write to Day Care and Child Development Council in America, 1401 K Street, N.W., Washington, D.C. 20005.

OPTION 7: INDUSTRY-SPONSORED CARE

Most places of work still do not provide day-care facilities for the children of employees. The February 1977 issue of *World of Work Report,* a publication of the Work in America Institute, Inc., states that only some 150 to 200 employer-supported day-care centers are operating in the United States, and that most of these are connected with hospitals, health-care facilities, and other nonprofit organizations. The report states further that a number of major corporations, including Control Data, American Telephone and Telegraph Company, and TRW, established day-care programs in the late 1960s and early 1970s,

*See section on children's needs in Chapter IV.

and that many of these have been closed owing to lack of participation by parents and the absence of real benefits to the sponsoring corporations. One notable exception to the rule is the Stride Rite Children's Center, operated in Boston, Massachusetts, by the Stride Rite Corporation. Functioning since May 1971, this center has been a success because of three factors (according to Stride Rite): (1) company sponsorship, (2) parent participation, and (3) outside sources of funding.

It would appear that unless work-place day-care facilities become the solution preferred by parents to meet their child-care needs, the prognosis for their increase is dim.

OPTION 8: SHARING CHILD CARE WITH OTHER WORKING OR TRADITIONAL COUPLES

This choice becomes more feasible after children reach school age, and the number of hours during which they require minute-by-minute care is reduced. Neighbors, friends, and relatives can provide care in the mornings, late afternoons, evenings, and weekends through such practical activities as car-pooling, taking turns attending school functions, and getting children to and from after-school lessons. They also ensure the kind of concerned, involved care described earlier.

Certainly, one advantage of this arrangement is that a sense of community begins to develop among the families, an element missing in the lives of many Americans today. Children are also exposed to a greater number of adults and children as role models, which aids them in their social adaptation.

As with families sharing housekeeping responsibilities, the disadvantage of this arrangement is that it demands a lot of coordination, communication, and organization if it is to work properly. But as long as the needs of both children and adults are being met, and the kids are not merely being dropped off at a neighbor's, this can be a workable child-care model.

The eight options just described constitute a sampling of the arrangements that parents are using today throughout the nation. Many couples rely on a combination in order to meet the different needs of their several children.

Some of the possibilities that were not discussed above are:

•communal living arrangements, where two or more families live together to share child-care and other responsibilities;

•private boarding schools in the United States or abroad;

•for summer child-care needs, summer schools, camps, or organized trips in this country or abroad.

Well-equipped libraries in cities throughout the United States have resource directories that can be consulted for more information. Local public-welfare offices usually can provide information about resources in their own communities. There are also child-care referral agencies in many communities.

(See also *Choosing Child Care: A Guide for Parents,* in the Suggestions for Further Reading portion of the book.)

School Age to Adolescence: When Children Are From Five to Twelve Years of Age

As children move out of preschool into elementary school years, working parents usually wonder what their kids should do after school, in their absence.

Nathan Talbot[23] tells us that more than a million children under the age of thirteen are being left alone in their homes, in what is called "latch-key status," to fend for themselves while their parents are away at work. He suggests that, although we do not really know what the result of this latch-key existence will be, many of these children feel unattached, unwanted, and unvalued, and end up as delinquents.

One aspect of the latch-key status is that children have "unlimited freedom to do as they wish." Children of elementary school age do have growing needs for independence. But they still require attention and a degree of supervision.

The kind of care you choose for your child in this age category will depend to a large degree on your own working schedule, and how it meshes with your child's (or children's) school hours. Because children of the ages of five to twelve are in school some of the day, the need for full-time care has—at last—finally ended! If your schedule permits, you may be available for child-care functions at this point.

If you must employ child-care help, here are some of the things to take into consideration in making your choice:

First, look for care appropriate to the child's age. Children grow up so quickly; a child at two may require an entirely different kind of caretaker from a child of four or seven. And children's needs differ. One may prefer to spend most of his or her time playing out of doors; another may enjoy more sedentary play (painting, drawing, and so on).

Second, if your situation demands it, you may have to find a child-care person who drives his or her own car. There is the trip to the doctor's office, music or dance lessons, parties or playtimes at the homes of friends—the list seems endless. With his or her own car, the caretaker can add to your child's life by taking him or her to museums, concerts, zoos, tide pools, farms—and even to shopping centers, which cannot be reached through public transportation means or on foot. Be sure to check on the caretaker's driving qualifications and safety record (no moving violations or citations), and on the car insurance (is the driver covered for liability, for medical aid to those riding in the car, and so forth?).

Third, keep in mind that, in a sense, a child-care person is an extension of the parent and should be able, on his or her own, to set limits ("yes, you may play outside, but you must come in at sunset"); to support the parents' wishes ("sure, you can have something to eat, but remember, only fruit or vegetables before dinner!"), and to uphold family rules and regulations.

Fourth, don't forget that caretakers are extensions of the parents in another important sense: by their presence, they often represent the parents at doctors' offices, schools, and at events involving the children. The caretaker may be the one to transmit information or instructions from the parents to others, and vice versa.

Fifth, if you are leaving more than one child for care, it is important to seek a caretaker who will provide equal treatment to each child and will not show favoritism to anyone. It is, of course, quite natural for a person to have favorites. But a caretaker's blatantly showing such favoritism cannot be tolerated.

Adolescence (Twelve to High School Graduation)

When Peter and Sally were babies, I looked forward to the day when we wouldn't have to worry about child care and the kids could manage on their own. Much to my chagrin, I'm finding now that—even though they're teen-agers—I still have to be concerned about their every waking moment.

Adolescence is a whole new ballgame. Some teen-agers need other-than-mother care when parents are working, and some don't. Some adolescents need to touch base with responsible adults throughout their trying teens. A surrogate parent can fill this need, sharing ideas with him or her, listening to an account of the day's happenings in school, and representing the parents' point of view and expectations regarding the child's responsibilities.

The kind of person you choose to perform this important task will depend, to a very large measure, on the needs of the child or children. One twelve-year-old may be so active and so responsible that he or she needs nothing more than a watch and a calendar to guide him. On the other hand, a seventeen-year-old may need a strong companion with the authority and ability to sanction him or her if necessary, to be immediately available in after-school hours for sharing, particularly if the parents are difficult to reach or reluctant to be disturbed.

Until children reach legal car-driving age, and often even after that milestone has been reached, a child-care person can chauffeur them to those important and necessary appointments with the dentist or doctor, athletic events, and so forth. Bicycles, mopeds, or public transportation may not be able to carry your teen-agers to all the places they may want or be required to go.

Such care for adolescents can be provided either in your own home or that of the caretaker, whichever is the better arrangement all around. Alternative arrangements are described below.

OPTION 1: AFTERSCHOOL PROGRAMS

If you, your spouse, or a child-care person is not available to provide such attention and supervision, you may wish to investigate the many community-sponsored after-school programs offered these days. City park and recreation departments, local YMCAs and YWCAs, public schools, churches and synagogues, and government-sponsored children's centers are some of the likely places that offer such programs. Usually these are provided as a community service, free of charge.

OPTION 2: LESSONS AND OTHER PLANNED ACTIVITIES

These include such time-honored activities as music lessons, Little League, sandlot ball and soccer, tennis, Cub Scouts, Girl Scouts, Boy Scouts, Campfire Girls, and many others. The most useful advice here is: Don't overdo it. There has to be some intelligent balance between what's out there beckoning the child, what the child *really* wants, and the time and resources you, as working parents, have to support such activities. Most parents err in the direction of wanting their children to do "everything." In the case of a two-career couple, this could be the result of some kind of guilt they may feel, an atonement, as it were, for their not being as available to the children as "normal" parents are.

Special Considerations

You know what drives me crazy? I just get our kids' school and afterschool schedules squared away . . . and one of them gets sick!

CHRONIC ILLNESS

If your child has a chronic illness, choosing child care will be even more difficult. All of the qualifications already discussed still apply, but there are others. For such specialized skills as nursing, teaching, physical therapy, and lifting, you must be prepared to pay more. Most schools are inadequately prepared to deal with chronic illness, so most parents with ill children elect, perforce, to bring someone into their home.

INTERMITTENT, ACUTE ILLNESS

Rare and exceptional is the child who escapes every childhood illness, whether it be flu, chicken pox, an ear infection, a broken arm, or any one of a score or more of afflictions to which the young body seems susceptible. Since one or more of these illnesses or accidents may occur in your family, it is useful to have a plan for such emergencies. Which parent will be available for home care on such occasions? Will you feel comfortable about leaving a child with a caretaker when illness strikes? How will your employer react if you ask for leave of absence to care for a sick child?

You may also want to line up a pediatrician who is near at hand, who will not make you wait interminably, and who will respond to phone inquiries. Also, you will want to locate a drug store that will take prescriptions by phone from your pediatrician and deliver them to your home.

SCHOOL VACATIONS

Don't let these creep up on you. Plan for them well in advance, much as a general would plan for a forthcoming skirmish.

For children enrolled in traditional, ten-month school programs, Christmas, spring, and summer vacations must be planned for. If you are planning ahead for summer, begin looking in January, because many camps and schools are filled up by March.

If your children are enrolled in year-round school systems, you will need to be especially vigilant. Your youngsters will need planned activities four times a year, and little may be available to them during those vacation times (although some schools now have intersession activities or planned classes).

Sit down with your children and confer with them on vacation plans. Arrive at a good mixture of planned activities and free time. Children usually clamor for far too much free time, which eventually takes the form of watching the Giant Eye.

CHANGES IN CHILD CARE

These are inevitable, so plan for them. Your child-care person may become ill, get married, or move out of town. Or you may decide to discharge him or her. Have a back-up plan formulated and ready to put into action at a moment's notice, because that may be all the lead time you'll have. And have a back-up for the back-up.

If you are uncomfortable with your present child-care arrangement, *change it immediately.* There is a kind of inertia that develops around child-care situations, usually born of the parents' not having a good alternative in the wings, or from their thinking there might not be anything better "out there" than they now have. We have found, in counseling two-career couples with child-care problems, that such problems rarely solve themselves, nor can they be solved by talking things over with the caretaker, setting new goals, or any similar expedient. If you really believe the situation at present is not very good, the odds are at least five to one that it will get worse.

So change. *Now!*

If a change in child care is imminent, there are a couple of things you can do to help your child adapt to a new arrangement. First, help the child say goodbye to the former caretaker (whether or not he or she is moving out voluntarily). Second, if you like your present caretaker, you may want to arrange an overlap of time so that the new person can learn from the old about the child's routine, habits, likes, and dislikes, and in general help both the child and caretaker adjust to the new arrangement. If it is not feasible or advisable to have the "old" caretaker on hand for this transition period, one of the spouses should assume that breaking-in role.

Choosing an Other-than-Mother Person: People and Programs

HUSBAND: Well, how much will a babysitter cost?

WIFE: Joe and Marian say they're paying about $400 a month, plus expenses.

HUSBAND: You're absolutely out of your mind! Never! My God, that's almost as much as you *make*.

WIFE: But, John . . . we're talking about getting the best care we can for the kids. I figured out that we spend about $400 a month on eating out, for movies, and clothes for ourselves. Why don't we just cut back on those things?

HUSBAND: Great! I get to sacrifice so we can pay a babysitter.

WIFE: What's more important to you?

Accept the cold reality: if you want more than a babysitter, or more than just a housekeeper, you are going to have to pay for what you get.

But what better investment can you make, especially if you are leaving very young children with a child-care person for substantial periods of time? Remember, this intensive, very special kind of service will be required for only a finite period.

We have found that most people strongly resist paying more for something for which others are paying much less. But what kind of money are we talking about, really?

At the very least, we are talking about the minimum wage (presently $2.90 an hour nationwide) for full- or part-time help. If your employee lives in, then an appropriate amount (negotiated with the person) can be deducted for room and board.

You should expect also to pay the employer's share of social security into the employee's social security account, along with the employee's share, which you will withhold. (This bookkeeping is your obligation under federal law.) You will need to include in the salary enough money for a paid vacation for the employee, as well as paid holidays and a certain amount of sick leave. In short, you will be expected to provide what any considerate employer would provide for any valued and trusted employee.

We have heard of couples who also buy or rent a car especially for the use of the caretaker for delivering and picking up the children at school, grocery-shopping expeditions, trips to the zoo and other attractions, plus some occasional use for the employee's own business.

Now, fasten your seat belt for a shocker: we know of some two-career couples who set aside one tenth of their combined salaries, and spend as much as $5000 to $10,000 for full-time child care. For couples who do not require full-time services, the amount can be modified downward accordingly.

Whatever the economics, we cannot emphasize too strongly our conviction that *child care should be your number one priority.*

What, for this kind of money, should a child-care person offer you as qualifications?

•Age? Unimportant, as long as the individual brings sound physical health, intelligence, and experience to the job.

•Disposition? Genuinely warm and loving with children; happy, outgoing, interactive with children. Smiling, patient. Dependable. Sensitive to the children's needs for sleep, activity, solitude, and affection. Capable of dealing with the kids during their fussy, limit-testing, and otherwise difficult times (of which there will be plenty). Able and willing to deal with sickness. And while with the children, making them her or his number one priority.

•Personal background? Ability to drive a car may be important. Smoking or not smoking, drinking or not drinking—these are matters whose importance you will have to determine for yourself. Naturally, such considerations as police records, drug addictions, and so forth should be cleared.

How do you find this paragon? In addition to the methods already mentioned, word-of-mouth advertising is still one of the best ways to find a good person. A friend knows a friend who has a friend.

Government employment agencies often maintain lists of applicants for such positions. Contact these agencies. As for private employment agencies, we must admit that reports we have heard to date on these from both employers and employees have not been too encouraging. Apparently, although there are exceptions, child-care persons with the high qualifications we have listed simply do not register with private agencies.

If you use the "Help Wanted" columns of your local newspapers, there are a few tips that may help you.

•Accentuate the positive. Tell the potential applicant something interesting or upbeat about yourself, your children, your job. After all, the purpose of the ad is to "sell" the position to the most qualified person among those reading the ad. One expert in the newspaper field told us that many people make a common mistake: they don't tell the reader enough. (He guessed they were afraid of spending too much money on an ad.)

•Give the reader the essential details: where, for how long, for how much, for whom. Number of children in the household, and their ages. Benefits. Responsibilities.

Here are a couple of examples of want ads that got excellent results:

Wanted: Mature, cheerful child-care person for professional working couple. Delightful one-year-old; drive another pre-schooler to school. Requirements: Experience with children, drive a car, no smoking, 5–5 1/2 days, live out. $500 a month, plus paid vacation, other benefits.

Wanted: Children's companion, teacher, interactor for two preteenagers of professional working couple. Requirements: Drive car, experience with children, no smoking, 20 hours a week, live out. Salary negotiable, paid vacation, travel with family, other benefits.

The same ad-writing principles apply whether your appeal is for a live-in, live-out, or a day-care–home person.

Hire Sensibly

Let's assume that you know what you want in a child-care person, for how long, and for what functions. You've placed your ads and called the appropriate agencies, and now the phone calls are beginning to come in. How do you begin to interview the candidates, and finally how do you select a winner?

Here are some guidelines:

1. If you've done your job well, you should receive a considerable number of phone calls. From a single two-to-five-day ad you may receive as many as twenty-five to seventy-five calls. The best way to deal with these responses is to screen them. If a person sounds good at the start, talk further with that one. If the applicant sounds really outstanding, set a time for an interview. If the caller sounds bad, in your judgment, or even not too good at the outset, politely end the conversation quickly and firmly.

It's not worth your time to talk at any length to people who obviously are not qualified.

On page 126 is an interview form that may help you in the process, not only to keep accurate records about the people who call, but also to be consistent in the questions you ask of them.

2. No matter how good a caller may sound on the phone, you must interview this person in your own home, with your spouse, and *with your children present.* The caller's initial impression on you and your children can be very telling. How are the "vibes"? Perhaps more than anything else, good gut reactions are vital. You will see what the candidate looks like, what kind of personality he or she has. Sense of humor? Smiles? Nervous, but pleasant at the same time? If your kids are very young, do they move away from or toward the candidate during the interview? After the interview, ask your children—if they are old enough to talk—for their impressions. Even after all this, you may not end up with a full picture of the prospect. But add what you have to your "inventory" on that candidate.

3. Be sure to ask for references and then call all of them, no matter how well he or she comes across in the interview. In fact, you may save yourself valuable time by checking references *before* the interview. In one instance, when we were interviewing for a child-care opening in our home, one of the candidates seemed absolutely fantastic on the telephone. All of her references were excellent . . . except one, the last one we called. This person, after a lengthy conversation, said that we sounded like such nice people with such nice children that she felt compelled to tell us that her friend, the candidate, did drink "quite a bit." We found later that her last employer had just fired her because of her drinking habits.

4. Last, but most important: never, *never* hire someone simply because you are desperate. Take the time neces-

Interview Form

Name_____Age_____Phone _____
Live in____Live out____Will work____5 days____5½ days
Drive?____Have car?____Where heard about job _____
Smoker?_____Health_____
Family Nearby?_____Where is home? _____
Experience with children _____
_____

How will you spend time with children? _____
_____

How do you think we should handle the first few days of
children's adapting? _____
_____

What are your interests? _____
_____

What won't you do or can't you do? _____
_____

What are your short-term and long-term plans? _____
_____

Last job: Employer_____Duties _____
Length of time worked____Why did you leave? _____
Applicant's questions:_____
_____

References: Name_____Phone_____
              _____   _____
              _____   _____
              _____   _____

Tone of applicant: _____

sary to do the hiring job correctly. It may take two days; it may take weeks. There's no way to predict. Take your time.

When you've finally settled on the winning candidate, develop a breaking-in plan for your children so that they can get used to the new person. Also, plan to be around during the first stages of a new child-care arrangement so that you'll have a chance to observe it in action.

If both employer and employee understand that each is on trial for a given period, it will be much easier to terminate the relationship if it doesn't work out to everyone's satisfaction.

You may not find exactly the kind of person you want for the length of time you want. Be persistent. Try to find the best possible person or combinations of persons. If your child-care person is willing to commit herself or himself for nine months, and seems to be really terrific, accept that nine months gratefully. It's probably unrealistic to plan on one individual or one arrangement for more than a year at a time. After all, your child's needs will vary, work schedules will change, and child-care people will come and go. The only certainties about child care are change and uncertainty.

Child Care Outside Your Home

There is no one best kind of out-of-home care for children. What's good for one child may not be a sound choice for another. The following are the various kinds of out-of-home care available to working parents. At the chapter's end are some guidelines to aid you in evaluating these options.

I can't tell you how many preschools I've looked at. The more I look, the more confusion I feel. They all seem rather alike

. . . the same toys, same schedules, and even the children look the same. How should I choose the best one for Timmy?

The most difficult task in choosing the right kind of child care is to learn what to look for in a care giver, in an environment, and in a program that will provide your child with care of the highest quality. Some of the factors you should search for, and assess, are:

1. The Care Giver.

Your child's welfare will be only as good as the individual responsible for his or her care, whether it be in a home, a center, or a school. The care giver is *the* thing.

(a) Educational experience. The care giver should have had at least two years of full-time experience with children. A preschool "teacher" should have, in addition, at least two years of high-quality training in the field.

(b) Adult-to-child ratio. No more than two infants per child-care giver; a ratio of one care-giver to four two-year-olds; one care giver to five three- and four-year-olds; one care giver to seven five- and six-year-olds; and one care giver to ten six- to fourteen-year-olds.

In addition, child-care staff members should be:

•sensitive to children's feelings;

•warm and responsive to each child;

•able to listen to and communicate with each child;

•able to preserve order in the facility without sacrificing spontaneity among the children or threatening them;

•physically relaxed with each child;

•able to look directly at the children when communicating with them and to *smile a lot;*

•eager to spend most of their time with children, not with other adults or with teaching materials;

•consistent and equitable in disciplining children and in dealing with children's skirmishes;

•encouraging and supportive of children's individual successes, imagination and humor;

•aware of each child's strengths, weaknesses, and potential, and able to act and react accordingly;

•aware of the teaching-learning process; and

•flexible, yet able to maintain a routine for each day.

When you visit a school, ask these questions of yourself as you observe:

Are the children held or hugged from time to time?

How does the child-care person handle an angry or a crying child?

How does the care giver respond to children's arguments?

What does the care giver do when a child says no to him or her?

Does the care giver praise the children?

Does the care giver seem to have control of the situation, or does he or she appear to be tense, harassed, frustrated?

2. Physical Environment.

The physical environment will probably have as much to do with your initial impression of a child-care program as any other factor. But don't be fooled! Sometimes the facilities that look the best—organized, neat, well outfitted, sparkling clean—are the ones that lack the real element you are seeking: a happy, warm, energetic atmosphere. Scan the facility for safety and health measures (no overflowing garbage cans near the children; no sharp edges on furniture; no overloaded lighting facilities; an out-of-doors play area far from traffic). Also check for the following kinds of equipment and space arrangements:

•adequate indoor and outdoor space to accommodate the number of children being cared for;

•kind and quality of toys, tricycles, outdoor equipment available suitable to the age of the children;

•availability of books, puzzles, art supplies, and other learning materials suitable for the children's ages;

•a place where a child can be alone for a few minutes;

•a place where a sick child can be cared for;

•areas for children to rest and sleep, if needed;

•safe storage places for medicines, household or facility cleaning agents, and other dangerous items;

•sufficient lighting;

•adequate and clean sanitary facilities; and

•a drawer, cubby, or cabinet for each child's belongings.

Such a facility also should serve nutritious food—fresh fruit, fruit juices, milk, whole-grain crackers, breads, and so on. It should not serve empty, high-caloric foods like candy, cookies, and sodas.

3. Other Children at the Facility.

Your initial impressions of the children enrolled at the facility also will be very important in helping you to assess the overall desirability of the facility. You can discern much about the teacher or care giver by observing the children in his or her care. Although we know that each school is different from the next, we sometimes forget that groups of children also may differ. One group may be happy, energetic, and sunny; another may be bullying, aggressive, and unkind. With which group do you want your child to mix? Remember, they will become your child's peer group and will help to form your child's view of the world. Among the children, you should look for:

•a spirit of concern for one another, caring;

•a feeling of togetherness;

•an ability to work out problems;

•a willingness to share, take turns, cooperate, work together;

•the taking on of responsibilities; and

•their willingness to "put away," to clean up after themselves.

Perhaps even more important is how the children seem to feel about the care giver. Do they seem to trust and like the person? Do they want to talk, show, demonstrate, ask questions of the care giver?

4. Program Considerations.

Whether the child is in a school, a home, or a center, he or she will be doing something each day. Whatever that "doing" consists of can be considered a program, whether or not it is a formal routine. For infants and very young children, a daily routine of fairly recognizable activities is important, whereas for older children more variety and greater peer-group interaction is more important. A good program should encourage the children to:

•live cooperatively with other children and adults;

•learn how to take care of themselves; and

•assume responsibilities for themselves and for others.

Such a program should also provide for:

•allowance for individual differences and likes;

•a balanced combination of individual freedom and guidance from the care giver;

•nonsexist expectations for both boys and girls;

•respect for various ethnic and cultural backgrounds; and

•means for the parents to act as observers, contributors, participants in some of the activities.

Behavior You Should Be Concerned About

Parents, even those of newborns, develop a sense about what is "normal" behavior for a child, and what is "abnormal." Behavior is a good indicator, especially in young children, of what is going on in their worlds. Here are some kinds of behavior you may want to watch for when your child is in the care of others.

Crying

It is, of course, normal for young children to be sad when their parents leave them, for any reason. The sadness can be acute if you are leaving a child for the first time or if you are leaving the child with someone new, either in a familiar or a strange place. It is normal for a preschooler to cry when left in a new school environment, though ordinarily the crying ends within minutes after the parent departs. But you should take note if the crying is chronic, long-term, or otherwise unusual.

Clinging

Again, there is almost always some clinging, with young children, on any new separation. If the clinging persists each time you take the child, or on your return to pick the child up, you will probably want to take a look at what happens to and around the child while you are absent.

Acting-Out

Jeffrey is an exceptionally happy, mellow child under normal circumstances. His everyday behavior includes singing, playing, much smiling, and a lot of climbing, jumping, and other physical activity.

When Jeffrey's parents picked him up, at the day's end, from new preschool, they noticed immediately that he was very quiet and morose, and that, very uncharacteristically, he "beat up on" the seats of the car and, later, a sofa at home. This acting-out was a clue that something was going on, something that was interfering with the child's normal behavior patterns.

As it turned out, Jeffrey had a teacher who did not like little boys. The teacher ignored Jeffrey as a new student and belittled his crying when the child was left by his parents in the morning. Jeffrey was changed to a new preschool, and his normal behavior returned almost at once.

Acting-out can mean very different things for different children. For quiet children, acting-out may involve suddenly becoming very noisy—or growing even quieter than they usually are. In noisy children, quiet behavior may be manifested. Whatever the norm is for your child, if you observe a change, take notice. Begin looking for the "why" behind this change.

At times, such changes may reflect a normal up-and-down period that many children pass through. The changes also may be part of a developmental period. It is generally known, for example, that two-year-olds go through something that has come to be called the "terrible twos," a movement toward negativism and independence.

But if the change in behavior is sudden and unexplained, one of the first places to look for an explanation (and possible trouble) is the child-care environment.

Dreams or Waking Up at Night

All normal children dream, have nightmares, and wake up at night. But again, if such behavior is persistent, unusual, or chronic, you may want to consult your pediatrician or a child psychologist or psychiatrist. You may wish also to check out the child-care setting for possible clues.

There are many other ways in which children's behavior can give you clues that trouble may be brewing. For children of school age, one obvious indicator is quiet withdrawal from normal activity. Often, the act of isolating oneself from the rest of the family can be a cry for help.

Chronic illness, as in adults, can be another clue to hidden troubles. Poor grades, when good grades have been the norm, may be another indication of difficulties. So may an increased need for sleep, a change in appetite (eating more *or* less than usual), crying, bedwetting, moodiness, or actively defiant behavior.

Margaret was hired to take care of our year-old daughter and our three-year-old son. She was a large, buxom woman who seemed to personify "mother earth." She became engaged with the kids almost immediately, and they with her. John and I felt that, at last, we had found *the* one! She did work out quite well, in fact, for several months.

Then, slowly, I began to feel uneasy about Margaret's behavior with our son, Alan. She would tear into him for leaving his toys out. She would get after him for spilling his food. She spent noticeably more time with Melissa than with Alan. When I came home from work, I would find Alan plopped down before the TV on one side of the house, and Margaret playing with Melissa on the other.

I worried more as the weeks went by. John and I began to see that Alan was making more out of our leaving every day than he used to. I found myself worrying about Alan at work, and leaving earlier each day.

The feelings described by this mother are indicative of something going awry. Inertia and the fear that there may be no better choice sometimes tempt parents to continue a child-care arrangement with which they are uncomfortable.

One word of caution: *don't.* If you are in any way uncomfortable about the way your children are being cared for, change it. Your feelings are probably being reinforced by the behavior of your children. If, in fact, they were happy and at ease with the caretaker, you probably wouldn't be reacting negatively.

Teachers, friends, neighbors, and the mothers of your

children's friends are all good sources of information regarding your caretaker and her relations with the children. Perhaps because they are outsiders, they may view the situation more objectively and perceptively than you do.

Be wary, however, about mothers who are not working and who take delight in making you uncomfortable about working by dropping snide remarks about your caretaker and the children. If you do receive negative feedback about your children's situation, examine the source. Crosscheck with other sources. And—best of all—arrange to spend time yourself in the environment and note your own reactions.

In choosing a child-care person and place for your child, keep in mind that there is a fine line between paranoia and vigilance. The choices available to most of us are less than optimal, so we need to take all the time we can, and invest all the money, patience, and work we can muster, to make sure that our choice is the best there is.

The key, in the end, may be the one we mentioned earlier: in choosing a situation, make sure that situation somehow *adds* to the child's life rather than detracts something from it. Once you have made a decision based on this criterion, you can go off to work, and enjoy your professional world, unhindered by worry, guilt, or frustration.

CHAPTER VI

Dealing with Dollars

The money: Whose it it? Who makes it? Who takes care of it, banks it, spends it, and accounts for it?

The questions are simple. The answers are not.

Two-career couples face the same dollar-dealing problems that trouble traditional marriages, in addition to an array of special problems that are peculiar to the dual-career relationship. In this chapter, the money problems most often encountered by working couples will be described, as will several approaches that working couples have developed to solve these problems. Also, some practical methods for keeping track of money will be suggested.

Money matters play a powerful role in all marriages, and a dominant role in some. Couples seeking help often identify conflicts over dollars as one major source of difficulty.

SHE: I feel as though I have to account for every penny. He is unrealistic about what things cost, but it's impossible to get him to go shopping with me. I don't like being treated like a slave on an allowance.

HE: No matter how much money I earn we seem to spend right to the limit. And when I ask her about it, all I get are tears. The checkbook is of no help because either the stubs are not filled in, or there are these fifty dollar checks for "cash."

Working couples should devote as much time and attention as necessary to mapping out guidelines for their financial affairs. The investment of hours and thought will yield precious dividends. Once a couple comes up with a model for handling their money, that model should serve them well for a long time. The payoff is the lessening or elimination of stress for a prolonged period.

Money Is Power

Most couples do not normally equate money with power. But make no mistake about it: money *is* power. Except in those rare cases where each marital partner has unlimited funds, issues of power are always present when money is involved.

Webster's defines power as "possession of control, authority, or influence over others."[1] Although it may be quite easy for a two-career couple to ignore the power issue in *other* areas of common concern, when dollars are involved it becomes apparent that the one with the authority over money matters enjoys special authority when it comes to making critical decisions. This partner, for example, probably has the final word on whether to hire a housekeeper or buy a new car, to move to a more expensive home or finance the start of a new career, to take a vacation or pay for a partner's tuition.

But you and your partner *can* devise a working, collaborative arrangement on money matters that will leave each of you comfortable both with the way the dollars are handled, and also—and this is perhaps more important— with the way in which the power these dollars represents is shared or delegated. We believe not only that you *can* work out a harmonious arrangement, but that you *must* if your dual-career relationship is to thrive and survive.

What Happens to the Dollars?

What really happens to the money that flows into your family? Who controls this wealth? Who decides when, and on what, it will be spent?

In most traditional marriages, one of several conventional models is followed in the handling of money. Among these are:

1. The Consultation Model.

The husband is the sole wage-earner. After depositing 10 percent of his take-home pay in the couple's joint savings account, he puts the rest of the money in their joint checking account. Though each partner has assumed the bill-payer role at various times over the ten years they have been married, the husband now performs the chore. When major purchases—of over $50—are contemplated, the partners consult, argue, or fight (depending on the item). In general, they have agreed not to make unilateral decisions about purchases.

2. The Budget Model.

The wife functions as "budget officer." She is in charge of a fixed amount of money set aside every month to run the house and to cover her personal expenses. The husband deals unilaterally with all funds over and above the budget.

3. The Allowance Model.

The wife assumes the primary responsibility for paying bills and financial planning. The husband has agreed to live within a specific allowance for his personal purchases, with his wife taking a like amount.

These models, with their obvious power discrepancies and other flaws, have long been traditional in America.

Can they be adapted to the exacting requirements of the dual-career relationship? Probably not, because they do not take into account the sensitive issues that arise when money is earned by both partners.

Nowadays, therefore, couples should draw up models that can be shaped to allow for greater collaboration in the use of income earned by both members. The need for such a model is highlighted, of course, when a partner either returns to or moves into the work force.

Know What to Expect

Once upon a time, young people headed for matrimony were told that "two can live as cheaply as one." Most of them discovered, to their sorrow, that the old maxim was fairy tale, not fact.

Today, in this new era of the dual-career marriage, the maxim might well be reworded: "Two working can live *better* than one." Attractive as it sounds, it ain't necessarily so.

One of the cold facts of life that many dual-career couples fail to comprehend is that *it costs money to earn money*. The costs are measured both in dollars and in energy expended. Unless they are aware of this hard reality, couples tend to hold unrealistic expectations about the amount of disposable income they will have when both are working, and the amount of strength they will have to enjoy this income.

This becomes especially true when both partners harbor the hope that the added income brought in by a partner's returning to work will allow them to accumulate enough disposable income to raise significantly their standard of living, or to accumulate substantial savings for investment or retirement.

One example involves the Greers. The Greers have two children, one of them a preschooler. Mrs. Greer decided to go to work, and found an ideal situation: a three-quarter-time job relatively close to home. She could report in at 9:00 A.M. and return home by 4:00 P.M. The company was very liberal about an occasional late arrival, and it tolerated absences now and then when child-care emergencies arose.

The Greers approached the change intelligently. They agreed to somewhat relaxed housekeeping standards. They concurred that high-quality child care was a top priority and a sound investment. And they planned to use *some* of Mrs. Greer's new income to pay for services she usually performed as homemaker.

Unfortunately, the Greers did not have in hand all the information they needed at the time they made their plans. As a consequence, after federal and state income taxes were deducted from her paycheck, plus social security and payments into the company's retirement fund, plus state unemployment taxes, there was *no* net increase in spendable income for the Greers. In fact, there was a slight *loss* in their net income in the initial months of her employment. Naturally, the Greers were disappointed and disillusioned.

Being prepared should obviously be an important component of every dual-career couple's planning. The costs involved in earning a second income are as follows.

Costs in Earning Second Income

(Note: The totals cited are what these goods and services actually cost at the time this book was written.)

1. Child Care / Housekeeping.

Depending on local costs of living and labor availability, these services can range from $400 to $1000 a month for a full-time, live-in housekeeper (if you are fortunate enough to find one), plus cost of food. You must also take into account these possibilities: the prorated cost of moving into a larger house or of adding a room to your present home to accommodate the live-in employee. Also bear in mind that child-care and housekeeping services, particularly when preschool children are involved, sometimes are regarded as separate functions performed by two people, and are paid for separately. (See Chapters III and V, on household management and child care.)

2. Nursery School/Extended Day Care.

Although these services may be considered optional in the traditional family, they are virtually obligatory for a working couple with small children. Cost: $100–$250 a month for a noncooperative preschool; less if one of the working parents can devote time to helping in a cooperative nursery school.

3. Food Budget Increase.

With less time on their hands, the partners are not free to go out of their way to shop for bargains. They also tend to use the most accessible food markets and to buy more convenience foods. Making dishes from scratch simply takes too much time. Added cost: 20 percent of the food budget.

4. Repairs and Household Maintenance.

Even though the house may be in good condition—perhaps even new—repairs can never be avoided. A working couple cannot afford the luxury of searching for the least expensive service technician, whose timetable may be erratic and whose working pace may be somewhat relaxed. If something needs fixing, the repair person must show up at a specified time and do the work as rapidly as possible. Extra margin for rapid and punctual service: 20 percent of the repair budget.

5. Transportation.

An unreliable car is out of the question. So the old clunker must be traded in or overhauled. Public transportation or a car pool may provide an answer of sorts. But if either or both partners must depend on a car, and if there is a lengthy commute involved, the expense can be significant. As of 1978, the cost of owning and maintaining an automobile was $3,310 a year, assuming you drive 10,-000 miles per year and keep your car three years.[2] Add at least 10–15 percent per year to keep pace with inflation and increasing costs of energy. Estimate: *high,* depending on commuting distances and type of transportation used.

6. Miscellaneous Additional Expenses.

Additional clothes, cleaning, lunches out, briefcases and other supplies, hairstyling, and so on. Estimate is variable.

The entry or re-entry of either partner into the work world should be seen in the same light as one would view the launching of a new business: there are always start-up costs, some of which one may not be able to anticipate. Another point to remember is that many new businesses do well just to break even at the start.

On the positive side, there are many payoffs. First, for most women the mere act of going to work for the first time, or of starting over again, nearly always has a deep personal meaning. Second, as the new worker's earnings increase, the family unit may well begin to show a "profit," with resultant increases in the family's sense of security and in creature comforts. Third, with some financial pressures lessened, couples are able to plan their lives more creatively.

A good point to remember is that most couples move through the financial challenges of start-up more easily *if their expectations are realistic.*

The worksheet on page 143 is designed to help those contemplating a return to the work world. To see where you stand, fill in the appropriate spaces and do the required arithmetic.

Profit-and-Loss Worksheet

I. Gross Salary per month $_____
    Less:

       Federal Taxes $_____
       State Taxes   _____
       Social Security   _____
       Retirement   _____
       Health/Life
         Insurance   _____
       Net Salary $_____

II. Expenses per month
    Child Care/Housecleaning $_____
    Nursery School/Extended
      Day Care   _____
    Food   _____
    Household Maintenance   _____
    Transportation
      (where applicable)
      Car payments   _____
      Gas, oil, repairs   _____
      Public Transportation   _____
    Miscellaneous Expenses   _____
    Total Expenses $_____

III. Net Income or Loss
                Net Salary $_____
                Less Net Expenses   _____
                Net Income $_____

Financial Issues

These are some of the questions every dual-career couple
must face, sooner or later, when dealing with dollars:
   1. Will there be "his" and "her" money categories?

2. Will one partner's paycheck be deposited to the other's account, even though he or she may not be able to write checks or make withdrawals?

3. Will "his" or "her" money be merged in a joint account, perhaps losing its identity as "his" or "hers" in the process?

4. Does earning part of the money increase the earner's potential influence over how the money is spent?

5. Is the second income to be used for basic expenses? Extras? Savings? Special purposes?

6. Does "her" income become part of "her" savings, "their" savings, or no savings?

7. Are the partners accountable to one another for what is spent, especially if one of them has operated independently for many years as the "number one" in financial matters?

Two-Career Solutions

Although the two-career relationship in America is still in its pioneer stages, couples have already devised an impressive variety of ways to cope with their finances. Here are some case histories of models we encountered in consultation with working couples, and some suggestions from which you may choose the ones best for you.

1. Proportional Contributions.

The Kelleys have been married for seven years, and during this period of time Wade Kelley has worked full time. Fran also works, but has left and returned to the work force repeatedly because of the birth of their three children. The last decision to return to work followed some careful re-evaluation by both partners. They are very independent people, have somewhat different interests, and sometimes take separate vacations. The relationship seems stable.

It costs the Kelleys approximately $1500 a month for basic living expenses, including money put aside for savings. At present the Kelleys are a fortunate couple, since their combined income exceeds their expenses. Mrs. Kelley brings home $500 a month, and Mr. Kelley approximately $1500. The Kelleys have decided that each of them will contribute to basic expenses *in proportion* to what each brings in, with any excess to be used as each individual pleases. In this instance, the contributions are as follows:

			Contribution to Household	Independent
Mr. Kelley's salary	$1500	× $1500	$1125	$375
Total salary (his and hers)	$2000			
Mrs. Kelley's salary	$ 500	× $1500	$375	$125
Total salary (his and hers)	$2000			
	Total		$1500 a month	

This means that Mr. Kelley has $375 a month which he currently banks (he is thinking about buying a power boat). Mrs. Kelley has purchased a piano, which she is paying for out of her independent funds.

The pluses: There is a relative degree of fairness here, in that both partners are contributing to the household upkeep while each retains some tangible reminder of his or her own earning power.

The minuses: The obvious disadvantage of the Kelleys' solution is that Mrs. Kelley has less independence in spending because she works only part time. She stopped working when she had her children, and she takes more time to care for the children. Since the Kelleys want children and jointly decided that Mrs. Kelley should work part time, the discrepancy in independent funds leads to some conflict.

2. Equal Contributions.

The Riordans are in their late twenties. Mr. Riordan is a department store manager. His wife is a research associate. Both have been working full time for more than five years.

Although they've been married for only a year, they lived together for eighteen months before their marriage, and at that time shared expenses but maintained separate checking and savings accounts. The Riordans have no children and have decided to defer the decision on children for at least two years. When they married they agreed to continue their separate bank accounts.

When the Riordans decided to purchase a house, each contributed approximately $6000, from savings, for the down payment. Having agreed to buy new furniture, they dipped into their savings again for the first installment, with the balance to be paid out of monthly expenses. However, Mrs. Riordan independently purchased a new car, using her old car as down payment and paying the monthly installments out of her own earnings.

Mrs. Riordan's job as a research associate yields a take-home salary of $14,000 a year, and Mr. Riordan nets $11,000 a year, for a joint take-home income of $25,000. For comparison's sake, assume that their monthly living expenses are $1500 a month. In this instance, unlike the Kelleys, each contributes the same amount of money, $750, and each keeps the balance of his or her funds in separate savings and checking accounts. Their model looks like this:

	Salary	House-hold	Independent
Mr. Riordan	$ 917 per month	$750	$167
Mrs. Riordan	$1167 per month	$750	$417

The pluses: The Riordans contribute equally and share equally in whatever benefits are derived from their relationship. A raise for either adds to that individual's independent funds. Even though they are now married, they maintain a sense of financial independence.

The minuses: What happens if the Riordans decide to have children? There would have to be a change in the model, since Mrs. Riordan would no longer be able to contribute, at least temporarily. Would this mean that Mrs. Riordan, who cannot contribute for a period of time, would not have any discretionary money?

This model works better when there is relative parity in the two partners' incomes. At a point at which one partner earns significantly more than the other, the difference in independent funds can cause resentment.

3. Pooling.

The Johnsons are a happy couple in their forties, married for sixteen years. Mrs. Johnson is a part-time bookkeeper, the part-time status dictated in part by the fact that one of the four Johnson children is only three years old. The couple agreed that Mrs. Johnson would give some of her time to child care during the early years of their youngest child's development. Her position allows her to move to full-time work whenever she elects, and she is contemplating such a move within the next two years. Mr. Johnson has a middle-management civil service job with the local planning commission.

Mrs. Johnson had not planned to work after the birth of her children, but because of the rise in their cost of living, she decided to capitalize on her salable skills by returning to the work force ten years ago. The couple is financially comfortable, with a combined income of $32,000 a year. Mrs. Johnson earns $10,000 for her two-thirds-time job; Mr. Johnson earns $12,000 more. This couple has opted for a simple pooling arrangement. Approximately $500 a month is earmarked for savings. The rest of the funds go into a joint checking account, to which both parties have access. Mr. Johnson is responsible for paying the major bills.

The pluses: One advantage of a pooling system is that the work of both partners is viewed as being of equal worth, regardless of the dollar amounts involved. Also, since Mrs. Johnson is working part time in order to assume greater household responsibility, she is not penalized by any decrease in influence over finances or by any decrease in independent funds available to her.

The minuses: Mrs. Johnson sometimes has difficulty in believing that her income is really important in this whole equation. In that sense, she sometimes holds back and exerts less influence in making decisions with respect to money. At times she also feels reluctant to make personal expenditures, particularly when they involve something that could be considered extravagant.

One major disadvantage is that neither partner has any privacy in money matters. It's difficult for either of the Johnsons to put aside money for a special purchase without the other being fully aware of it. For example, when one wants to buy a present, the money must come from the joint account, so there isn't any element of surprise or any way to do something special without the other being aware of it.

4. Pooled Funds plus Independent or Discretionary Income.

This model is similar to the pooled model described above, with one important distinction: each partner has a certain amount of money that, by agreement, is regarded as totally discretionary and is not subject to the influence or review of the other. The amount may be large or small, equal or unequal, and may carry with it certain prohibitions.

The Careys are in their mid-fifties. This is a second marriage for both, and they have been together for ten years. Their combined families number five children, ranging in age from twelve to twenty. Each partner has a full-time career. She is a management consultant; he is an accountant. From an income standpoint, they would be seen as well off, grossing in excess of $47,000 a year. However, with two children in college and with a large new home, they tend to be conservative about money.

Because they want to combine their incomes and still maintain some independence, the Careys have come up with the following solution: all of the money they earn is deposited to joint checking and savings accounts, except for $150 per partner, which goes into a separate checking account. This money is used by each to make special purchases. Mr. Carey was able to take his son to an out-of-town football game without checking with Mrs. Carey on the cost of the tickets. For her part, once a month Mrs. Carey spends a day at a spa at a cost of approximately $50. Each feels entirely free to make such expenditures without any review by the other.

In addition, Mr. Carey is buying a watch for his wife. Because she tends to return expensive items, he does not want her to know how much it will cost. So he is paying for the watch out of discretionary money, and will present it to her on their next anniversary.

The pluses: As in the pooled-funds models, work is considered worthwhile regardless of where it is done (inside or outside the home) and without reference to the amount of money earned. Another major advantage is that both Mr. and Mrs. Carey have a feeling of independence, a sense of privacy, and the freedom to do whatever he or she wishes with the $150, without review by the other. An extravagance cannot be challenged if it is bought with one's own money. Anything that cannot be negotiated with one's partner can be purchased on one's own.

There are some questions. How are the discretionary funds determined? Should the funds be equal for both partners? And are they subject to change? How does a partner who earns a major share of the money feel about having only a relatively small sum allocated for discretionary spending? Do frictions result from one partner's purchase of something the other considers unessential or frivolous?

Choosing the Model for You

Some couples have settled from the beginning on one of the methods outlined above; some have changed from one model to another to adapt to changing circumstances; still others have shifted to different models as their confidence in one another and in their relationship increased.

Dual-career couples tend to favor more formal accounting methods (such as proportional and equal contribution) at the beginning of a relationship or when they are entering second marriages. These are times when the need for independence is greatest. Couples who have been married for longer periods and who are accustomed to consulting with each other about issues tend to favor a pooled-income arrangement. *The need for independent funds is of special importance to a partner who has just entered or re-entered the work force; if all of the funds are pooled, that partner will have little or no sense of personal payoff for his or her labor.*

Discussing these models and adopting one, or perhaps creating one that will meet your special needs, will provide a base from which to discuss other kinds of money issues that are a part of any two-career relationship. How do you feel, for example, about giving equal spending power to your spouse? What's it like (and this is often an issue for men) to be in a situation where you must now *consult* with your partner rather than simply inform him or her, after the fact? To help couples to make a choice of a funding model, we have drawn up a worksheet (see pages below). There are two copies, so the man and woman may each fill in one, independently, to rate the models described. You may end up choosing the same model, and the issue then will be merely one of implementation. But you may wind up with some differences, in which case some degree of negotiation will be necessary. Whichever model you choose, adopt it on an experimental basis, that is, for a trial period of 60 to 120 days. At the end of that period, take stock to see if it serves your purposes well. If changes need to be made, make them.

Man's Worksheet

Instructions:

1. Rate each model independently on a scale of 1 to 7, where 1 means "like it very much," 7 means "I can't stand it," and 4 means "I can live with it, but . . ."
2. Then write down at least three reasons that support your rating.
3. Finally, exchange rating sheets with your spouse or partner and try to devise a model that will work for you.

A. Proportional Contributions
    1 2 3 4 5 6 7
B. Equal Contributions
    1 2 3 4 5 6 7

C. Pooling
    1 2 3 4 5 6 7
D. Pooled Funds plus Independent Discretionary Income
    1 2 3 4 5 6 7

Woman's Worksheet

Instructions:

1. Rate each model independently on a scale of 1 to 7, where 1 means "like it very much," 7 means "I can't stand it," and 4 means "I can live with it, but . . ."
2. Then write down at least three reasons that support your rating.
3. Finally, exchange rating sheets with your spouse or partner and try to devise a model that will work for you.

A. Proportional Contributions
    1 2 3 4 5 6 7
B. Equal Contributions
    1 2 3 4 5 6 7
C. Pooling
    1 2 3 4 5 6 7
D. Pooled Funds plus Independent Discretionary Income
    1 2 3 4 5 6 7

As stated at the beginning of this chapter, money is power. Many of the discussions (and arguments) that dual-career couples have about money really concern decision-making and influence. Often, therefore, what is really being discussed is not just a financial model, but a way of dealing with one another that may have implications in other areas of the couple's life together. What is most important is that both partners feel that there is a sense of fairness, and that they can maintain a reasonable balance between individual needs and what is needed for the family unit to prosper.

Banking, Bill-Paying, and Saving

The following information has been assembled to help two-career couples cope with several important money-management problems. Part 1 contains suggestions for choosing a bank, Part 2 describes various models for sharing or delegating the bill-paying responsibility, and Part 3 stresses the advisability, in dual-career relationships, of "savings for survival."

1. Choosing a Bank: Becoming a Customer.

Although banks, like car dealers and grocery stores, advertise aggressively for new customers, many bank users do not realize that banks consider their customers a valuable asset. Nor do most people know that they can, and should, develop a personal relationship with a bank, a relationship that opens to them a wide range of services and special help that most banks are ready and able to provide.

Wisdom dictates that couples should spend considerable time and care in selecting a bank. Here are the kinds of services a good bank should supply:

(a) Convenient hours. A bank that is open for business until 6:00 P.M. and on Saturday mornings is much more convenient for a working couple than one that maintains the traditional "banker's hours," that is, from 9:00 A.M. to 3:00 P.M. However, some banks that adhere to the conventional hours now supply twenty-four-hour service by means of automatic "teller" machines. These can prove surprisingly handy in emergencies. Look for them.

(b) Drive-in facilities. If you have only fifteen minutes between appointments, it's very nice to be able to cash a check or make a deposit or withdrawal without having to leave your car. This is especially true if you are in old clothes and don't want to change, or if you are taking care of the children and don't want to take them all into the bank with you. Caution: waiting lines at bank drive-up windows can sometimes be long, so be prepared for a delay at peak hours.

(c) A variety of account types and services. It's important to know about the various kinds of checking and savings accounts available, and the ability and willingness of a bank to create a package of accounts suitable to your needs. Does the bank offer banking-by-mail, and, if so, who pays the postage—you or the bank? Will the bank transfer your funds between your accounts by phone? What are its loan policies? Will it make automatic deductions from your accounts to transfer into savings or into other special-purpose accounts? Will it collect notes for you, and for how much? Is it equipped to handle Keogh, IRA, or other retirement-fund transactions?

(d) The personal touch. What kinds of amenities—trust services, notary services, cashier's checks, traveler's checks, letters of credit, and so on—is the bank able to provide, and how willing is it to meet such needs? Can you phone the bank to ask that a cashier's check be made out in the name of a certain person, and will it be ready when you come in to sign it at 3:00 P.M.? (You have only fifteen minutes of free time before you pick up your child at nursery school!) Some banks are very accommodating in such matters; others are not.

Take time to evaluate the services available, and base your choice on specific criteria. A checklist to aid you in your evaluation is provided on the next page.

2. Paying the Bills: Who Does What?

In addition to establishing a personal relationship with a bank, a dual-career couple must deal with other aspects of financial management. For example, no matter what

Checklist for Choosing a Bank

	Yes	No
Convenient location	____	____
Weekend hours	____	____
Drive-in facilities	____	____
Bank-by-mail	____	____
No-cost traveler's checks, notary service	____	____
Special services via phone request	____	____

account options have been agreed on, someone has to pay the bills.

We view the chore of paying the bills as something independent of the model agreed on for sharing expenses (that is, proportional or equal contributions, pooling, and so on). Somebody must review the bills, write the checks, decide which bills are to be paid, which deferred for a period of time, challenge an incorrect charge, make certain that medical forms are submitted to insurance companies, check to make sure that credits to charge accounts are being fully applied, and so forth.

The job is important. It is also boring, demanding, repetitious; and it yields few rewards except, perhaps, satisfaction for a job well done. As a rule, both partners want to wield the decision-making power, but neither really relishes the mundane task of keeping close track of the bills. But, somehow, the job must be done, and it must be done competently and systematically.

Many couples run into stormy financial weather not because they lack funds, but because they are disorganized and do not monitor their expenditures methodically. To help couples who are wrestling with financial problems, we offer four possible approaches:

(a) The person who likes to do it should do it. One partner or the other may actually find pleasure in organizing, or feel a need to be on top of what's going on financially, or may feel uncomfortable about giving responsibility to the other. If one partner feels strongly about doing this chore (for *any* reason), he or she should do it, as long as the task is not resented as an added load. In fairness, the other partner should accept other chores, to balance the workload.

(b) Do it together. The advantages of this system are that there are no unknowns for either partner, and the mistakes are shared. Twice a month, a couple can clear the decks, minimize the distractions, gird themselves for two hours of moderate discomfort, and get the damn thing over with. At the end of the work period, both partners are—or should be—clearly aware of where the money is going, and why.

(c) A rotation system. In your case, perhaps both partners dislike this kind of detailed work. And doing it together tends to invite disaster, because minor arguments can arise from the paying of bills. Furthermore, neither one is willing to spend his or her small amount of free time on such an unpleasant task. In this instance, the most effective and fair solution would be to rotate the responsibility every three to six months. One or the other thus handles the bills for a finite period of time, with an end in sight. This solution will work only if both partners are competent. (Incompetence is merely a way of avoiding the task, or never learning how to do it, so that finally the more competent partner must intervene to stave off impending bankruptcy.)

(d) Hire someone to do it. Finally, the couple may choose to pay someone to do the work. A qualified person, obviously someone you can trust, can be hired to go through the bills at month's end, list them on an appropriate display showing minimum and maximum amounts due, and present this listing to you. You can then indicate which bills are to be paid, and return the list to your part-time bookkeeper. That person can then write checks for your signature, Xerograph important papers (such as medical claim forms), and relieve you of all the busywork. In no way do you lose control, because the final decisions on disbursement of funds lie with you. The one thing you *do* lose is privacy, and you will have to decide whether the trade-off is worth it.

3. Savings for Survival.

We think that there are special reasons for dual career couples to put aside funds that are even more compelling than the reasons prevailing for families in general. If a couple is accustomed to using both incomes for survival, the loss of either can come as a severe blow. In addition, living up to the hilt of your combined incomes does not allow either partner the *right* or the *time* to be burned out. We strongly recommend that working couples arrange their finances so that either partner, because of illness or for personal motives, should be able to stop working for at least ninety days without the family's suffering any significant financial consequences. This may sound like a difficult goal to achieve, especially to those who are just starting on the path to solvency. But that kind of financial back-stopping will allow a couple an enormous measure of freedom to deal effectively with crises at work, illnesses, and the whole range of catastrophes that seem to afflict us all at one time or another.

One of the simplest and most sure-fire methods of accumulating funds is to instruct your bank or credit union to deduct a certain specified sum from your deposits on a monthly basis, and to put it into a savings account. People generally adapt quickly to having money deducted in this fashion. Automatic saving is a much more reliable way of accumulating cash reserves than a now-and-then, haphazard method of putting away a little after all the bills are paid.

Along with handling the day-to-day details of family financing, it is appropriate for each couple to do some long-term financial planning, preferably early in the game. What are your priorities? How will you achieve them? Early retirement, a very comfortable lifestyle, more education, an opportunity to retrain for a second (or third, or fourth) career—all of these will demand money, and the money will not be there unless you plan for it.

In dealing with these issues, couples often experience difficulty. Many women were raised in homes where their mothers were not knowledgeable about or necessarily involved in long-term financial planning. At the same time, most men's fathers did not necessarily engage their spouses in financial discussions; thus men have not had appropriate models, either. Even though intellectually committed to a more egalitarian type of relationship, they have difficulty in this area.

Although most financial planners talk in terms of retirement, we think it is difficult for couples in their twenties and thirties, and even in their forties, to grasp the implications of retirement. It is important, of course, to have long-term goals in mind and to put funds aside to realize them. But we think it is more realistic to plan how you want to spend your money during the next year, and where you would like to be five or ten years down the line.

Be very specific. Use pencil and paper as you do some anticipatory decision-making on funding and the use of your money. This strategy will increase the probability that the hard work both of you are putting in will ensure a comfortable and satisfactory life for you both in the years ahead.

CHAPTER VII

Some Special Challenges: Launching, Role-Changing, New Opportunities, Similar Careers, and Successful Women

It's February, and there are sixteen inches of snow on the ground. You have just been offered a promotion, a $10,000 raise, and a chance to move to exciting, snow-free San Francisco.

All the ingredients of a fantastic opportunity—right? And you should jump at the chance—right?

Wrong . . . if you are a partner in a dual-career marriage, and your spouse, to accompany you, must give up a newly acquired position as an advertising account executive, and it is known that San Francisco is at the moment glutted with Madison Avenue types fighting each other for every opening.

In this instance, by no means exceptional, you have reached the midway point between a rock and a hard place: Which of you comes first? Neither? Both? What do you do about it? Commute? Divorce? Or . . . ?

Until recently, many observers of the dual-career scene regarded *jealousy* as the prime troublemaker in two-career marriages. But jealousy is not, today, the major issue, and perhaps it never was. The real problem today is *coping with the realities* of a dual-career relationship, of confronting and solving such dilemmas as job relocations (mandatory or voluntary), promotions, new opportunities, rules concerning nepotism and conflicts of interest, and the complexities faced by and caused by couples working in the same field or profession or for the same firm. These special challenges are quite apart from problems arising from household management, child care, parenting, or finance, which have already been discussed.

The purpose of this chapter is to explore this host of special challenges, and to describe strategies for coping with them. We have grouped these special situations into the following four categories:

1. "Launching" Challenges.

Two-career couples who have already launched their separate-yet-joined careers may prefer to skip this discussion. For new dual-career partners, however, the strategies proposed below may be of help in meeting the problems arising from the simultaneous launching of two careers.

2. Role-Changing Challenges.

These challenges may occur at any point in a dual-career relationship, and they may occur more than once. One may arise very early in the relationship, when a partner decides to change his or her role (that is, job, career, or role within the marriage itself). Or one may not occur until midway or late in the marriage, perhaps after the "empty nest" stage has been reached. Whenever it is encountered, a role-changing challenge can be traumatic.

3. Challenges of New Opportunities (Transfers, Promotions, Offers).

These challenges are most likely to occur when both partners are well entrenched in their respective careers. New opportunities may appear for either or both, and difficult decisions must be made about these opportunities. Job relocations are offered—or mandated—and the partners must make some critical appraisals on which their separate and joint futures will depend.

4. Challenges of Similar Careers.

These challenges can occur at any point in the dual-career experience, from the launching period through the mature stages. They arise from the following:

(a) problems caused by antinepotism rules imposed by employers;

(b) conflicts of interest, either real or imagined, perceived by employers or others;

(c) the range of interpersonal issues that come to the fore when couples not only have similar areas of specialization but work together, as well.

5. The Challenges of Success for Women.

An increasing number of women are finding themselves in a situation where they have surpassed their partners in status, earning power, or achievement. How does *she* handle it; how does *he* handle it; how do *they* handle her success?

"Launching" Challenges

We recently conducted a workshop at Stanford University on two-career marriages. Many of our earlier workshops had drawn participants from urban, middle-class sectors, most of them in the thirty-to-forty age bracket. So we were well prepared for questions about household management, child care, finances, and other more or less typical problem areas. We were, therefore, taken by surprise by the large number of couples whose primary concern was *how to launch two careers at the same time,* and to do so in an enlightened manner, with fairness to both partners. Our experience echoed that of Patricia K. Light, chief psychologist in the Office of Career Development at the Harvard Business School. Ms. Light, on assuming her job, had expected to encounter the usual run of student difficulties. But she was astonished to find that one of the most common pleas for help came from young couples who posed the same question: How can we handle two separate careers?[1]

Here are some of the many vexing problems that can manifest themselves at the launching stage:

•Both partners receive job offers, but the two opportunities are separated by thousands of miles. Which one should they accept? Neither, and continue to search for two offers in the same community? Both? Can they live together while living apart?

•One partner is invited to fill a superb position in a community in which there are no prospects for the other. What does the second partner do? Vegetate? Rebel? Resist?

•The job offers are coming in, and the partners find it hard to talk with one another. How do they reduce the tension, decrease the conflict, call a truce?

Several strategies can be used to meet these various challenges. These are described below, along with a decision-making formula and some case histories that illustrate how these techniques were successfully employed by two-career couples.

Problem-Solving Strategy 1: Identifying the "Better" Opportunity

The decision-making model that follows was derived from our work in group sessions with couples who were attempting to deal with the launching problem in an anticipatory fashion. Those who have applied the formula outlined here have, in the main, found it a satisfactory strategy for reaching a fair and reasonable solution.

The assumptions here are that (a) the partners are entering the job market simultaneously, (b) both are receiving attractive job offers, and (c) the jobs are located so far apart that they cannot accept both and still live under the same roof.

The strategy calls for the partners to examine and "grade" both job opportunities in the light of criteria that are meaningful to them. Some of these may be:

•location (urban or rural; north, south, east, or west; United States, foreign, coastal, mountainous; and so on);

•quality of each position;

•opportunities for advancement in each;

•beginning salaries and known (or estimated) rates of increase;

•the emotional "fit" of each job, in light of the partners' personalities.

A grading system (for example, poor to excellent, on a scale of 1 to 5) and the list and definitions of criteria can be set up in any way acceptable to the partners. (See the Position Rating Scale, page 164.)

The partners will agree on the following:

•Whichever of the two openings is adjudged the "better" of the two opportunities will be the "winner," and that job will be accepted by the partner to whom it was offered.

•The partner whose career will thus be launched first agrees that, after a specified period (we suggest two to four years) the couple will relocate, if necessary, to give the other partner a chance to start his or her career.

•The partner whose career is launched first will devote a reasonable amount of time, energy, and resources helping the other partner to find suitable employment. This effort would include, but not be limited to (a) soliciting help through contacts in his or her place of employment, (b) moving to the community one month early to begin the search, and (c) staying actively involved in the search process until the other partner finds a position.

Position Rating Scale

	Partner 1	Partner 2
Geographic Location	_____	_____
Quality of Firm	_____	_____
Quality of Position	_____	_____
Opportunities for Advancement	_____	_____
Salary Level	_____	_____
Quality of Schools (if the couple has children)	_____	_____
Other (specify)	_____	_____
Other (specify)	_____	_____
Other (specify)	_____	_____
Total	_____	_____

To use this form successfully, the couple must specify the criteria to be used and the number of points to be allowed for each criterion *before* the offers arrive.

Problem-Solving Strategy 2: Searching for Less Obvious Opportunities

Martin and Abbie Frick faced a familiar problem: a good job for him in a new location, but apparently no job openings for her.

ABBIE: I'm tickled pink that Marty has gotten this offer in Cleveland. But we've checked around, and there simply are no college-level teaching jobs in sociology open to me. I've located several other possibilities in smaller communities on the East Coast, but there's just nothing in Cleveland. So it looks as if my years of graduate studies for the doctorate will just go down the tube . . . and that makes me feel both sad and furious.

MARTIN: I'm really sorry there's nothing open to Abbie in Cleveland—and the place is loaded with colleges and universities. Maybe later, but not now. And I just don't see how I can pass up this chance to put my new master's in business administration to work. I *need* a big city like Cleveland to make an M.B.A. pay off, and all the smaller communities where Abbie has found openings are just not the right setting for me.

The Fricks were in their mid-thirties, with two school-age children, when they made the Big Move by quitting their jobs and returning to school for advanced degrees. During those years, they lived on savings. Both graduated at the same time, and Martin immediately received a very attractive offer in Cleveland.

But Abbie's dilemma threw the Fricks into a marital crisis. Abbie, it became clear, was identifying with her professors. They had encouraged her—and her colleagues in the Ph.D. program—to seek academic careers (that is, to be "like them"), in spite of the cold reality that there were few openings for teachers in her field at any of the important colleges or universities in the East.

The professors' influence on Abbie had been so strong that she had never considered using her training for anything but teaching. Perhaps, we pointed out, she should widen her horizons, think imaginatively. We asked if she had ever thought about working in student affairs, where an applied sociologist might be of great help in organizing training programs for dormitory staffs or in planning social activities for students and faculty. We also asked Martin whether his firm was involved in any form of social-science research, and discovered that the firm was, indeed, so involved.

Our purpose in discussing these and other possibilities with the Fricks was to motivate Abbie to explore some of the less obvious outlets for her background and talent, and not to limit herself to one narrow field. The result was very salutary. Abbie began to channel much of the energy that had earlier taken form as anger against her husband into more creative problem-solving. By the time our group consultations were finished, the Fricks were energetically engaged in examining a whole new range of options. At last report, both were employed in the same city, living together, and moving ahead in their respective careers.

Problem-Solving Strategy 3: Commuting

Strategies 1 and 2 are designed, of course, to permit two-career couples to carry on their separate careers while living under the same roof. Strategy 3 is for couples who prefer not to restrict their career choices in any way, and who are willing to abandon the conventional living-together mode—at least temporarily—to achieve their objectives.

Radical as it seems, commuting is the arrangement being chosen by increasing numbers of dual-career couples. Many of these are highly successful executives in the top salary echelons, some of whom commute regularly from coast to coast, or for hundreds of miles so that they can carry on the career of their choice. Although we believe that commuting is a very difficult way to solve the problem, we include it here so that it can be considered along with other strategies.

Ms. Light, of the Harvard Business School, wrote:

Over the long term, there are very few couples who can pull off a commuting arrangement and manage to have anything left in the usual context called marriage. A crucial ingredient in marriage is shared experience, and if these experiences are decreased beyond some lower limit, the relationship is fragmented."[2]

For some, experiments with commuting have turned into nightmares. A Washington, D.C., businessman tried commuting between the capital and St. Louis to direct a corporation in Missouri, while his wife, an attorney, maintained her practice in Washington. After a year of shuttling, the businessman resigned from the St. Louis post because he had found the burden of commuting "outrageous."[3]

For many others, however, career "yo-yo-ing" has worked out very well. In one instance, the wife worked in New York City while her husband operated his own business in Boston. The wife admitted that keeping a ten-room town house in Boston and a New York apartment, flying to Boston on weekends, and hiring household help and part-time child care "costs all you can make." The arrangement worked, she said, only because they both invested "an incredible amount of organization and planning, energy and stamina."[4]

For some, commuting has proved to be a boon. In one instance, the wife, vice president of a prominent restaurant chain, lived and worked in Boston. Her husband owned an air-freight business in Newark, New Jersey, and lived in a small community across the Hudson in New York State. The wife flew or drove every weekend to the New York residence to be with her husband, and he flew twice weekly to Boston to spend the night with his wife. This way, they were apart only two nights a week. Their children were in their twenties when this regimen began. The couple charged off this rather exhausting and costly commuting schedule as part of the price of maintaining separate careers. The husband was enthusiastic about the plan, because, he said, it gave them each "a whole new vista." He enjoyed his trips to Boston, maintaining that it took him less time to fly there from New York than to drive from his suburban residence to his Newark office. But the wife admitted she would not have considered commuting had her children been below high school age. She also pointed out that she would not have embarked on a separate career without her husband's backing and cooperation.[5]

We firmly believe that all arrangements involving commuting should include the following provisos:

First, that working arrangements permit some flexibility regarding time away and travel time.

Second, that vacations will be taken together.

Third, that there will be frequent use of the telephone to maintain contact.

Fourth, that the couple will plan to come together for at least one weekend every month, and more often if possible.

Finally, that there will be some agreement on general ground rules in regard to social activities. Can she accept dates with other men, and he with other women? Should these be restricted to group affairs? What about sexual contacts? Will the rules of monogamous marriage be respected, or are extramarital relations condoned?

We urge couples who are considering a commuting arrangement to spend as much time as necessary to define their ground rules in advance, and to agree not to alter them without prior consultation.

Although commuting is widely practiced in dual-career marriages today, we think this strategy has many inherent difficulties, difficulties that are compounded when there are small children in the household. However, as the whole two-career concept is moving rapidly into new areas, we feel it is appropriate for couples seriously to consider this choice, and to decide for themselves whether it may work in their case. We do advise, however, that if commuting is contemplated, the couple should agree to view this strategy as experimental before abandoning all the old, conventional routes.

We are convinced that the outcome will be sheer disaster if the commuting option is chosen because of anger or despair born of a couple's inability to work out rational, harmonious solutions to their problems.

It is obvious that commuting is not limited to couples who are launching careers simultaneously. Couples at any stage in their lives together, from beginning to end, may be faced with the dilemma of accepting attractive job openings in widely separated locations. Or one partner, with roots deeply set in the community where the couple has lived for some time, may prefer not to leave that community, and his or her current job, to accompany the other partner to a new job location. In this event, commuting may provide an answer, albeit an imperfect one.

Some Final Thoughts on Launching

First, about children. If you, as a dual-career couple, are planning to have children, it is helpful for the *wife* to establish her career before the first child is born. It will then prove much easier for her either to maintain her position after a relatively brief maternity leave, or to return to work in her chosen field if she has chosen to devote more time to child-rearing.

Second, both partners must do some soul-searching before answering the following question: How comfortable will *both* of you be if the more attractive and advantageous opportunity is offered to and accepted by the woman?

. . . When the interviews started, it was devastating. She's now sitting on four good offers starting at over $21,000, and he's had only two nibbles—both at about $19,500. They're both having a very hard time, and frankly I don't know whether the marriage will make it . . . The thing that is most surprising is that *she* seems more upset than *he* does.[6]

We will be discussing the issues relating to successful women in a later portion of this chapter. It is an issue to be faced at the launching stage.

Finally, we want to stress—very forcefully—that decision-making for a two-career couple will, at times, be loaded with emotion. We have tried to present models that will make the process more manageable and lessen the strains. If you are lucky, you may receive similar offers in the same city or area, offers that require no agonizing decisions. But don't depend on it.

PETER: While we were getting ready, it seemed easy. I would finish my traineeship, and then the company would give me a choice of five different locations. Barbara would finish her computer-programming course at the same time. But when we got down to the finish line, the fur began to fly. She didn't want to leave the West Coast, even though she could get a good job in any of the three cities I'd listed as my top choices. It was really heavy for a while.

BARBARA: I never knew how much being close to my family really meant to me, until the time came to leave. I don't think we've ever fought so much or so hard. Finally, Peter agreed to stay in Oregon for the first three years, and I agreed to leave if his first offer after that is a really good one. But I hope this doesn't happen, especially since I've been promised the department-head spot. Maybe we won't have to face it.

Tension, passion, and—at rare times—logic will be present, in some degree, in the decision-making process. Expect it to be difficult, and feel relieved if it isn't.

Role-Changing Challenges

FRANCES: With both of the kids in school, I was forced to deal with the fact that I had been bored for the past three years. At first, particularly when Jeannie was born, the idea of doing the homemaker scene was fine. I had done everything "right" until then—getting married before graduation, working as a teacher while Jack was in sales, then getting pregnant and quitting work. So it seems reasonable to me, now, to think about going back to work, and I'm ready. But any time I bring up the subject, Jack gets this pained look, asks if I'm unhappy, and begins talking about "latch-key" children.

Role Change: What Is It?

Partners in a dual-career marriage may decide to change roles at any time, and for any one of a variety of reasons. But whatever the reasons, role change means that the person involved is deciding to do something else, something different, either more or less than he or she has been doing. There are many variations on the theme: the homemaker to student; the surgeon to writer; the executive to sculptor; the four-hour-a-week volunteer to full-time director of training.

Why this radical turnabout in barely a decade? The reasons are many. First, and perhaps most compelling, is the economic pressure that is squeezing middle-income families. It is becoming more apparent that soaring costs of housing, education, and energy are forcing many families to conclude that two wage-earners are needed to maintain the lifestyle they both want. Also very compelling is the social pressure born of the women's movement, supporting women to seek a way of life they regard as more rewarding.

What has been sad for many women of my generation is that they weren't supposed to work if they had families. There they were, with the highest education, and what were they to do when the children were grown—watch the raindrops coming down on the windowpane? . . . Of course women should work if they want to. You have to be doing something you enjoy.
—Jacqueline Kennedy Onassis[7]

But tradition also is being shattered on the male side. Many men are no longer content to continue working in jobs or professions they find unfulfilling, and are consciously—even aggressively—searching for ways to change roles. Other men, having achieved what they consider success in their fields, are abandoning them to search for new adventures. These are behavior patterns that a generation ago would have been looked on, by society at large, as odd if not antisocial.

HE: When I was in school, being an engineer was both exciting and secure. Doing research for NASA and then in the aerospace industry was fairly satisfying. But now I'm thirty-five and a section chief, and I am bored out of my skull. Call it a midlife crisis if you like; it doesn't make the feelings go away. I wanted to study law, and had begun at night about three years ago, but the pressure of work *and* study was too much. Now it seems like the right time, and we've decided to sell the house, buy a condominium, cut back our lifestyle for at least two years, and I'm going to become a full-time student. Beth is willing to go back to work, but she seems rather resentful.

SHE: He just dropped it on me one night, and things have been kind of crazy since then. He's very excited, but I'm not sure that we've thought it through carefully. Every time I begin to ask questions, he gets angry and says I'm being negative. I'm not negative. I'm scared!

Role Change: The Emerging Patterns

Though the phenomenon is still relatively new, certain identifiable patterns are emerging.

First are the women like Frances, quoted above, who originally planned to devote themselves to homemaking as a career, then find themselves unsatisfied with their full-time "apron-string" routines. Once the children are in school and nothing is left but those bouts with the vacuum cleaner and the kitchen stove, women like Frances grow restive. In the past, some turned to books, bridge, gourmet cooking . . . or the bottle. Now, more and more, they are scanning the world of work-for-pay or volunteerism for a better mode of living.

Second, there are older women whose children have finished the home cycle, ended their schooldays—or at least their live-at-home schooldays. These women find the empty nest intolerable, and they search for useful, rewarding activity outside the home.

Unfortunately, this often occurs at about the time that men begin to tire of the breakneck pace and think of devoting more time to home, their wives, and the education and adult development of their children.

I sell more Cuisinarts and copper pans to middle-aged men who are ready to do the "more-time-at-home bit" than to women. I have a feeling that if their wives are like me, they'd rather have a book on going back to school, or a new briefcase. I wonder how they work it all out.

Third, there are men who are unwilling to continue working at the self-destructive pace that is so common in commerce, industry, and the professions. Men today are well informed about the end effects of continued stress. They are concerned about heart attacks and strokes brought on by unrelieved tension. And they recognize that they probably will die seven to eight years before their wives. So, more and more men are crying "enough" before it is too late.

Fourth, working men and women alike often grow dissatisfied with their current work and decide to shift to entirely different activities. Thus, an aerospace engineer drops his calling to study law. The dermatologist cited in Chapter I begins to wonder if he wants to spend the rest of his life studying abnormalities of other people's skin.

Role Change: Why Does It Cause Problems, and What Are They?

First, all change is difficult, whatever its nature and whatever its degree. Any time you change any part of a system, all the other parts must adjust. If a partner in a two-career marriage breaks with his or her earlier pattern and takes up a new direction, it is not only the spouse who is affected. The partner's friends, children, and relatives— among others—are also part of his or her "system," and they, too, must accommodate to the change.

Tom was just fine about it. What I really wasn't ready for was the way my mother would react. When I told her I was going back to work I might as well have said I'd entered a bawdy house. Now that I've been working half time for almost a year, Tom still hasn't left me, and neither of the kids seems any stranger than before. Mother has settled down somewhat, but she still mutters and shakes her head in that way she knows gets to me.

Second, most role-changers do not know how difficult a role change is, nor do they anticipate adequately the resistance they may encounter. Sometimes a partner will fall into an accusatory mode, viewing (as the case may be) a husband as chauvinistic or a wife as selfish, and perhaps seeing the marriage as faced with irreconcilable differences. We continually warn two-career couples not to interpret this normal, universal problem as one that is unique to their relationship.[8]

When I came home and told him that I had not only passed my real estate exam, but had a job with a realtor, Fred exploded.

I was bewildered and resentful. After coming down hard on Fred as a chauvinist, I called the manager to ask about the first staff meeting. She asked me how Fred had reacted, and I told her. She laughed, and said the same thing had happened to her.

Another woman said:

No one told us how to deal with our husbands, or even that we would get negative feedback from them. But my husband said that his taxes went to pay teachers and I shouldn't have to spend time doing their work. I was furious with him for being so selfish. Why weren't we warned about this problem, as part of the orientation program for new volunteers?

Finally, the partner who is changing may be viewed by the other as the one who is getting the best of it. For example, if the woman is returning to work or school, the tasks to be redistributed are, in the main, the dull, repetitious, and odious household-management chores she has done alone. A husband who has never taken care of the children may suddenly be faced with nurse-maiding a sick preschooler, chauffeuring a car pool, sitting in on a P.T.A. meeting, or advising a sobbing youngster how to cope with his or her frustrations, big or small. Even though he may be a very caring father, doing it is different from helping out.

If it is the man who is cutting back, going on for further training, or changing careers, the family's finances and lifestyle may be considerably altered. What initially seemed to the wife to be a reasonable plan may, on sober reconsideration, be interpreted as a threat.

When Bob talked about just doing real estate and cutting out the tax work, it seemed ideal. It did make it easier for me to be working. Suddenly, though, there is much less money coming in, and I feel under the gun. He appears to have lots more time —and I really do like that—but I don't like the financial pressure. I thought I would *enjoy* working. But now—enjoy it or not —I *have* to!

Role Change: Making It a Success

The experiences of couples who have successfully changed roles would indicate that the chances for success are greatly heightened if the move is taken in three steps: gearing up, implementing, and rechecking.

GEARING UP

This is the planning phase. There is ample opportunity for all hands to anticipate what is coming, to discuss it fully, and to unburden themselves of any objections. During this lead-time period, initial resistances can be explored and resolved.

We continue to be amazed by the number of couples who think nothing of spending six months to plan a vacation, a year searching for the right house, or even weeks shopping for clothes or a household appliance, but who will decide almost overnight on a change that will affect their lives.

If a role change is contemplated for either partner, it is absolutely vital that both partners allow reasonable time for discussion and for the anticipation of the many problems that can arise from role changes. Specific planning is necessary to minimize disruptions before any change is made. We generally advise a six-month "accommodation period."

If children are involved, they should be included in the planning. Children should not be informed after the fact of changes that will dramatically affect them. Through participation in the planning, children will be given an opportunity to reveal their feelings about the changes in the offing. And be forewarned: in many cases, their feelings will not be positive.

If it is the woman who is changing roles, at least the following three topics must be dealt with:

1. The Household.

If the wife is leaving the home, the home will still need managing. Are some tasks formerly performed by her now to be performed by others? By whom, and which tasks? Will outside help be hired? To do what, and for how much? Who will hire and supervise this help?

It is usually very difficult for couples to shift from the traditional relationship in regard to household management. Our experience has been that unless household-management problems are handled with great care, either of two things will happen: the wife will give up her career aspirations, or there will be a marital crisis.

The worst possible arrangement—which, unfortunately, is still the rule rather than the exception—is for the woman to continue with total responsibility for all household and child-care functions while shouldering the added burdens of part- or full-time work, or of a heavy study schedule at school.[9] This will inevitably lead to resentment, fatigue, and an eventual confrontation between the partners.

Things will be equally bad if the role-changing woman makes no provisions for any of her conventional home functions and, in an act of rebellion, simply lets home and family fall into disarray. She *thinks* she is saying, in effect, "Now you will appreciate me." But what she is really saying is *"I'll* show you! To hell with it."

2. Children.

If a mother is to move successfully into the work world, there must be adequate provision for the well-being of the children. Parenting functions that before were her sole responsibility are now to be shared by others. Thus, the husband whose wife will be working may need to invest much more time and energy in his parenting role.

3. Lifestyle.

New two-career couples rarely anticipate the radical changes their leisure time will undergo. There is likely to be a significant cutback in their social activities for the following reasons:

(a) The woman's traditional role as social-activities coordinator will be sharply curtailed because she will have less time for planning and executing social affairs.

(b) Women often develop new interests that they may find are not shared by their earlier circle of friends.

(c) New dual-career couples find that, as their free time diminishes and their fatigue increases, they allow traditional social activities to fall by the wayside and choose only those activities that seem worth the effort.

Dual-career couples appear to restrict their friendship patterns almost automatically to other couples with similar lifestyles.[10] We are not suggesting that two-career couples should end up as recluses. It is simply that they usually experience a shift in the kinds of social activities they participate in, and some decrease in the range of their social intercourse.

Unless this change in social patterns is anticipated, it may be interpreted as a negative experience rather than the norm in two-career marriages. The norm, for dual-career couples, called for them to choose all social events and activities with greater care and, as a consequence, to find those activities richer and more satisfying than do their counterparts in the conventional-marriage framework. There is, in sum, a shift from quantity to quality in terms of time invested.

If it is the man who is either cutting back or dropping out even for a short period of time, there are different factors to consider.

1. Economic.

In most instances, the decision of the man to cut back will be accompanied by some decrease in income. Even though this has been anticipated, the reality often causes trauma.

2. Others' Reactions.

Many times there is difficulty in dealing with the reactions of others—family, relatives, friends—to role change.

When John told me how the mothers had reacted to his arriving at the pool with Elaine for the "parents-and-tots" swimming program, I laughed. But when two of my friends phoned to ask if John was still working, and made some thinly veiled cracks about his masculinity, it made me very uncomfortable. I thought about taking leave during July so *I* could be with the kids. For *their* sake, I told myself. Baloney! I was just uncomfortable. Fortunately, John saw what was going on, and we were able to work things out. But we were both relieved when other fathers began showing up with their kids.

3. The Role-Changer's Own Reactions.

Even though a man may have initiated and anticipated the change as an opportunity to have more time, to vary his activities, or to feel less harried, the "doing" often proves less exhilarating and satisfying than the "anticipating." His reactions may stem from feelings of guilt or other sources, but more frequently he simply feels depressed rather than, as he had hoped, excited.

The most important thing that I had to learn was that it was okay not to be busy all the time. It wasn't until my second semester in graduate school that I began to appreciate that I was feeling lousy and that Sandy was getting irritated with me. Here I was, the one who had initiated this whole thing, and I was moping around. It's tough not to be the breadwinner. I *thought* it wouldn't bother me, but it does.

Armed with the knowledge that certain reactions and problems are normal in role changes, a man will find the process much easier.

IMPLEMENTING

First, try to choose the most comfortable time for the change. This may not always be possible, as the time may be dictated by the job or by the employer's needs.

I thought we had considered everything, and that summer would be the easiest time. But I was mistaken. First, I was tired when I got home from work, and really not up to evening picnics on the beach. Second, I'd forgotten how much more dependent Jody would be on me for transportation, with no school buses or car pools. Finally, I resented having no free time to spend outdoors, what with all the indoor chores to do. Please tell all returning-to-work women to try to time their return to coincide with the months when the kids are in school. It's just easier that way.

Second, realize that no matter how good the planning was, there will be hitches. Expect them. Regard the initial months as experimental, a time for restructuring, re-evaluating, negotiating. Remember to set aside a meeting time, once a week, to review progress and problems with all members of the family, as well as a time to talk with any hired helpers. Fine-tuning may be required, or perhaps even major restructuring. What seemed simple in theory during the planning may prove much more complicated in practice.

If there is consultation and negotiation at this stage, the chances of resentment, disappointment, misunderstanding, and failure will be greatly reduced.

RECHECKING

After the change has been in effect for a trial period—perhaps three months, or six months if that seems more fair—re-evaluate the whole experience. Ask yourselves:

(a) Does it still seem a good idea? Is your first-blush enthusiasm for the role change vindicated by the realities?

(b) Are the plans you made to accommodate change really working? Should some tasks and responsibilities be reassigned, altered, or dropped? How do all members of the family answer these questions?

(c) What else, if anything, needs to be done to ensure the success of the change?

Finally, it is imperative that all hands fully realize that there is more to supporting a role change than mere intellectual commitment. The husband who tells everyone that his wife is "fantastic" for having gone to work, but who still expects gourmet meals, a spotless house, and hand-ironed shirts, is being verbally supportive but behaviorally resistant. The wife who says she encourages her spouse to reduce his workload, but also voices concern about the economic consequences, is just as inconsistent.

It's not a question of deception or duplicity. The reactions described above are not at all unusual. Until the change is really made and is in effect, it is difficult to *know* what will happen. Anxiety, or even panic, may be normal under such circumstances. As we cautioned at the outset, change is hard under the best of circumstances. It is even more difficult if expectations are unrealistic.

Challenges of New Opportunities

The San Francisco job offer described at the opening of this chapter came to a couple whom we shall call Sharon and John. Here's how they reacted initially:

JOHN: I know that Sharon's position is important to her, but we have to be reasonable. This is a fantastic opportunity to get out of middle management and to head a profit center of my own. If things work out, we're on our way. What the hell—

I'm thirty-four, and the next few years are critical. How *can* I say no? I don't want to turn it down. Sharon knows that I support the idea of her working, but I would be stupid not to say yes. If she really refuses, I just may go myself.

SHARON: John is absolutely insane. This is his third "promotion" in five years, and I've had it. It took me six years and three universities to get my B.A. in communications, and my jobs until now have all been part time, underpaid, and disgusting. I've finally gotten a *real* job, and now he wants me to give it up! If we could be here for another year, I'd have the experience and contacts to make a move feasible. But right now it would be professional suicide. Sure, he's all for my working, but it damn well better not interfere with his plans or . . . No, that's unfair. John does care, but he's also scared to say no.

A generation ago, John and Sharon would have been anomalies—oddball exceptions to the general rule. Today, Johns and Sharons are all around us. We see their counterparts in our seminars and our family-counseling and mental-health practice. What we have to say on this subject is drawn both from our extensive contacts with two-career couples involved in such dilemmas and from our continuing interchanges with personnel managers, corporate executives, and government officers whose daily work brings them into contact with dual-career couples.

First and foremost, bear in mind that moving, even when it involves a single-worker family, is an extraordinarily difficult process. One management consultant has suggested that "relocation is known to be a major source of stress in that multiple changes occur at once and affect the entire family."[11]

Second, for two-career families this anticipated trauma is further complicated by the question "shall we" as well as "how to."

Third, in most instances the contemplated move has, at least on a short-term basis, clear benefits for one of the partners.

Finally, two-career couples are just beginning to realize that the cost-benefit ratio involves career, partner, and family.

To help couples cope with this challenge, we will begin by emphasizing that job relocations can be of several kinds. Here are some of them, with suggestions in each case for dealing with the problems each raises.

Short-Term Changes

The key element in the short-term change is the assumption that the employee will return to his or her post after a brief period away. Under this heading are opportunities for specialized training (at a technical center or home office, for example); further education in one's field; or, perhaps, a trouble-shooting assignment. Any one of these could last from one to six months.

Short-term changes are nothing new. They have been routine for years in industry and business. And until recently they posed no special problems. Employees, believing (rightly) that these short-term assignments would bring added recognition, almost always accepted without a question.

Today, a "yes" response is no longer automatic, for two basic reasons. First, the key employee now being selected for a short-term assignment is just as likely to be female as male. Earlier, when a man was offered a temporary change, generally he was the sole breadwinner, and it was assumed that his wife and children would accompany him. But in the growing number of instances today when the opportunity is extended to a woman, do the same ground rules hold? Is her working husband expected to resign from his job to follow her? Is she to take the children with her, or leave them with her husband, or . . . ?

Second, what about those cases in which a husband who is offered a short-term change is married to a wife who has a job she likes very much and for which she is paid hand-somely? Is she expected to resign, to follow him? And if the man, out of respect for his wife's career, chooses to reject the offer, can he use his wife's career as an excuse to his employer for doing so? What happens if the man accepts?

Because of this welter of conflict and confusions, the divorced male or the confirmed bachelor is now consid-ered by some employers as the ideal employee![12]

A number of imaginative solutions have been worked out by couples faced with these dilemmas. Here are a few:

1. Commuting.

The pros and cons of this system were discussed at some length earlier in this chapter. But this solution is certainly worthy of consideration if the opportunity is of such mag-nitude that turning it down would seriously jeopardize one's career; and if moving the family en masse for such a short period would be too disruptive to the other part-ner's career or educational plans, to the children's school and social life, or both.

If the opportunity is a *time-limited* option—that is, for a few months—the discomforts of a commuting solution can be more readily tolerated, because the partners know that the assignment will soon be over.

2. Request for Temporary Reassignment by the Other Spouse.

It may be possible for the other partner to negotiate a temporary assignment that will allow the family to capi-talize on the short-term opportunity without commuting. This will depend on the breadth of the individual's skills and the enlightenment level of the organization for which he or she works.

In discussing this particular dilemma with many dual-career couples, we found that it had not occurred to them to approach their superiors with their problems. In many cases, companies are willing to be helpful, and may show surprising inventiveness in arranging temporary assignments.

3. Leave of Absence for the Other Partner.

If a temporary assignment cannot be arranged, the employer may be willing to grant a leave of absence, with *guaranteed right to return.* Important: ask for, and obtain, that guarantee in writing, specifying that the same or an equivalent position will be available on your return. The guarantee should not be qualified with any condition like "if there is a position available." Though management may at first resist a categorical promise, they may eventually agree in the face of firm and persuasive arguments.

4. New Opportunity for the Other Partner.

Another option is for the other partner to find a new opening. In one instance, a woman professional was offered an opportunity to go to Washington, D.C., for special training. Her husband, an accountant, stepped out of his practice and lined up a temporary teaching assignment at a university in the capital. They moved to Washington together and had a thoroughly enjoyable and fruitful half-year. When they returned to their home base, the husband did not resume his practice; he turned to full-time teaching and research.

5. Saying No.

More and more two-career couples whom we counsel tell us they are choosing to say no to what might have been a tempting opportunity for one partner because acceptance would have damaged the other's career and, in all probability, their relationship.

Increasingly, men and women are weighing their career needs and desires against their need for a stable and productive marital relationship and family life. They are beginning, in greater numbers every day, to question whether any new opportunity offered them is worth the upheaval, disorientation, and disruption of long-established ties. Men are becoming ever more sensitive to the impact their career decisions may have on other family members. For their part, women are becoming more and more aware that an "opportunity" may, in the end, not be worth the bother.

Going to Venezuela for four months to set up the new branch office was viewed as a real plum—the kind of assignment that usually precedes promotion to overall responsibility for a department. I was also the first woman who had been given this kind of chance. There was tremendous pressure on me to say yes. Tom was just finishing up his master's project and had spent the last six months setting up the lab. There was no way he could go with me, and it just didn't seem fair to take on all the responsibility for Tim and Wendy. We had just gotten the children settled with school and sitters.

As we talked about it, the Venezuela opening changed from an opportunity to a problem. I finally decided to turn it down. The people at the home office weren't too thrilled, although Charlie was quite understanding and said that personnel was becoming more aware of how complex it was to deal with working couples. He also said that he would still support a promotion.

6. Temporary Separation.

Obviously, a couple may decide that the benefit to be achieved through a short-term change is worth whatever strain a temporary separation will create. If the distances involved or the nature of the assignment make commuting out of the question, certain issues must be dealt with.

Temporary housing and loneliness are two of the problems that will face the partner who goes. We advocate that, if at all possible, the dingy motel room be avoided. Find a comfortable, attractive place, a place that makes you feel good, even if it costs a bit more. The difference between a $200-a-month dreary efficiency and a $300-a-month one-bedroom apartment with pleasant furnishings may be worth much more than $100. Sixty days—or six months—in a shabby cell can become damn depressing.

The problem of loneliness needs to be anticipated and discussed. What are the ground rules about social contacts, parties, dating? Avoiding the issue is likely to lead to trouble.

For the partner who's staying, the question becomes: Who will fill in for the partner on the road? Once again, the major concerns are the household and the children. Dishwashers break down, cars overheat, children catch the measles whether or not Father or Mother is at home. The staying partner should line up standby help for just such emergencies. He or she should also let supervisory personnel know what's happening so that allowances can be made if he or she is less than efficient or is occasionally late to work.

How often will you write one another? Telephone? Will there be one or more visits? With what frequency? Talk about these matters in advance to minimize misunderstandings and hurt feelings.

Long-Term Changes.

If we were asked to identify the single most difficult problem facing dual-career couples today, we would cite the problem of dealing with permanent relocation (whatever "permanent" means in today's mobile society).

Merrill Lynch Relocation Management, Inc., estimates that U.S. companies relocated some 300,000 employees in 1978. Of these, only a small fraction—8 percent—were women. Even so, the 1978 total for women was twenty times greater than the number of women transferred only five years earlier.[13]

One middle-management employee of International Business Machines Corporation was relocated nine times in his twenty-year career; the moves took him and his family from Hyattsville, Maryland, to Tujunga, California, back to Maryland, and then to New Jersey, then to the Marshall Islands, back to Maryland, and (at last reports) to Texas.

"There's a loss. I can't measure it," said the IBM executive.[14]

And a writer in the *Wall Street Journal* wrote: "The nomadic existence of America's managers sometimes exacts a heavy price, and most of it is paid by the wives and children of the men who are transferred."[15]

Several forces are at work in causing relocations. Among them are:

1. Ambition.

Often the best chance for advancement comes from leaving one company to join another—but this usually entails moving.

2. Competition.

Outstanding workers often are wooed by competing firms, which may be located in other cities or states.

3. Company policy.

Many large industries and businesses consider relocation the best form of management training, so they move their key personnel every two to four years. These companies also are likely to link promotions to these moves.

Relocation may also be a form of sheer survival: a contract is lost and an aerospace industry shuts down; tax reforms force universities to release tenured faculty members in an area where no other openings are available; a worker is fired for the right or wrong reasons. Those affected have no choice but to move. However, the three major forces affecting two-career couples are those cited in the previous paragraphs. But what additional factors make relocation so difficult?

1. Corporate Insensitivity.

During a panel discussion in which four female personnel managers representing large corporations sat as panelists, the attention centered on promotions for women.[16] The following panel-audience interchange took place:

MEMBER OF AUDIENCE: How do we handle the question of a promotion which requires a move when you're married and have a family? It's really difficult just to pick everyone up and go. My husband's job doesn't allow much mobility.

PANEL MEMBER: That's not our problem. You just have to work it out on your own. If you can't, then perhaps you should get some marriage counseling.

Unfortunately, many major employers still operate as if there were only one breadwinner in every family, and still interpret an employee's reluctance to leap at an advancement opportunity as evidence of disloyalty. They are also inclined at times to interpret such reluctance on the part of a man as evidence that he is not "in charge" of his own home, or in a woman, as a sign of insufficient commitment to her career.

Until recent years, relocation overtures *were* traditionally made to men who were the sole breadwinners in their families. Even when only one wage-earner was (or is) involved, moves were (and still are) traumatic. But the problems raised by relocation in families where there are two wage-earners are infinitely more complex than those for the one-breadwinner family.

Too many personnel administrators are still insensitive to this established fact. They are inclined to shrug it off with "that's *your* problem," even though the Merrill Lynch report indicates that "about 22% of all firms interviewed said they have experienced transfer difficulties with employees who have working spouses . . ."[17]

2. The Fantasy Move.

Dual-career couples sometimes precipitate their own crises by shopping for new opportunities before discussing frankly their willingness (or unwillingness) to move, and before resolving the critical question of timing.

Then, when fantasy shifts to reality, the problems begin.

When the recruiters came around and gave me the pitch, I figured what the hell, why not? Patty at that time didn't even bat an eye. Within a month, I had an offer to go to Wichita which means a raise of nearly $5000. But now we don't know *what* to do. Patty is dragging her feet, because she finally landed that teaching job in the school and grade she always wanted. So what the hell *do* we do?

3. "I Didn't Know What I Was Getting Into."

In Chapter VIII we point out that a company's transfer policy is one of the things to assess in choosing a potential employer.

If you know, in advance, that your firm's stated policy is to move its people around every three years or so, and if you accept the job knowing this, you will then be able to plan your own lives more intelligently. You will, for example, know then how to plan an education program that may require you to complete it at three universities. You can make plans regarding when to have children (or not to). And your partner can look for job opportunities with an employer who has branches in other communities so that, at relocation time, both of you can move your careers together.

Possible Solutions
Make It for Both

If one partner is offered what really looks like a fantastic opportunity, perhaps what both partners should do is work on *extending* the opportunity to *both.* Relocation need not be all negative, especially if it appears to be a move ahead for both partners.

Although you may be on your own when doing most of the looking for the other partner's opening, don't hesitate to ask for help. The partner whose position is assured should ask his or her employer for any aid possible in lining up a spot for the other partner.

People knowledgeable in personnel matters know that there is an informal agreement among personnel directors to try to find jobs for the spouses of transferring or newly hired employees, when such spouses are known to be seeking employment. This fact is not generally known to outsiders. But the practice is growing . . . so make use of all possible resources.

Find Better Opportunities for Both Partners

If one partner's move requires the other partner to abandon a promising career (at least temporarily), it may prove wiser to give up the move until new opportunities can be found that are acceptable to both. One couple's experience provides a good example, and suggests a problem-solving model. Dr. Kendall, a research biologist, was unhappy with his employment and was job-shopping. He finally received an offer requiring a move to another city. But Mrs. Kendall had just completed her one-year probationary period as a city planning analyst and was expecting a promotion. The Kendalls investigated and found that there would be little or no opportunity for Mrs. Kendall in the city to which they would have to move if Dr. Kendall accepted the offer.

The company recruiting Dr. Kendall showed little interest in Mrs. Kendall's problem. Although they gave vague promises of help, they spent the bulk of their time and energy in trying to woo Dr. Kendall. The proferred position attracted Dr. Kendall, but Mrs. Kendall was adamant in her stand that she would not move unless she received a firm offer comparable to the one she expected on her promotion.

How did the Kendalls resolve their dilemma? First, they listed all the factors that both *favored* and *weighed against* the move. Candor was the key word; every pro and con felt by both partners was included. The list they drew up appears below.

The major items *against* the move were those related to Mrs. Kendall's career and the absence of any clear commitment by Dr. Kendall's prospective employer to help her find a new position.

As the negotiations advanced, Dr. Kendall tried several times to stress the importance of his wife's career. He had little success. Result: the Kendalls turned down the offer.

Dr. Kendall reopened his job search and eventually

Factors Influencing Decision to Move

For	*Against*
Husband very excited about new position:	No current opportunity for job for wife:
Much more pay	No income from wife
Greater research independence	Husband's new company unwilling to help in wife's job search
More opportunities for advancement	Wife unwilling to defer career plans
Very attractive city	Potential husband-wife conflict about career potential for wife
Good climate	
Good schools	
Near other family members	Children don't want to move

found another opportunity. Although it did not offer some of the attractions of the first offer, the new prospect proved more favorable to both partners. (See below)

So the Kendalls opted for the second offer, *even though it was not as good an opportunity for Dr. Kendall.*

This was an agonizing decision, but a wise one in the long run. It is never easy to reject an attractive offer, especially if one is near the bottom of the career ladder. There is the haunting feeling that one is turning down a final chance.

However, creative and responsible people are always in demand. As long as they continue to produce at a high level, they will be sought after and will advance.

Negotiating a Delay

In some instances a couple may wisely decide to *defer* a move until it can be made without undue hardship for one or the other partner. For example, if one partner is involved in an educational program that will require an-

Factors Influencing Decision to Move

For	Against
Husband relatively pleased about new position:	Unfavorable climate
	Extended family not close
Some greater pay	Children don't want to move
More opportunity for advancement	
Good position for wife:	
Salary earned by wife	
Good schools	

other year or two to complete, a temporary delay could be negotiated to permit the partner to complete the program. We know of a number of women who have studied at as many as *six* colleges, but have never been in one place long enough to obtain a degree because of the grasshopper-like career moves of their husbands.

Take a Stand

Refuse to go. More and more two-career couples today are refusing to accept transfers or promotions that demand relocation if it will adversely affect their partner's career development. Many others are leaving companies whose policies conflict with a dual-career pattern. It is becoming commonplace for employees—often the best ones—to confront their supervisors and personnel officers and to argue their positions. Numerous instances are on record of companies backing down or modifying policy for fear of losing a valued employee.

At a recent conference attended by the personnel directors of more than 200 major companies, much of the discussion centered on moves and transfers. The following are three of the conclusions reached:

Companies must be more open in involving spouses in the relocation decision-making process. They must lay out all the opportunities to the couple and give them a chance to make a decision—the company should not try to make the decision for the couple.

> —Deborah D. Conner
> Manager, Employment and Development
> Cummins Engine Company, Inc.

Corporations can no longer assume wives must follow their husbands if the husbands are transferred.

Firms will have to make transfers more palatable.

> —Marvin Trammel
> Corporate Employment Manager
> General Mills, Inc.[18]

The Challenges of Similar Careers

Time was when the males of society left the cave in bands and, through craft and cunning, killed an elk, buffalo or musk ox for their women and children at home. The women were gainfully employed in caring for the children, preparing skins for clothes and cooking the food. Everyone was fairly content in his or her job role, because those roles were challenging and necessary . . . No woman in her right mind wanted to change roles . . . Today, of course, it's a bit different.[19]

Things are, indeed, a bit different today.

Among the revolutionary transformations that have taken place in the past decade or two are those that affect men and women in the world of work. Today, women are employed in tasks that a generation ago would have been unthinkable for "the gentler sex." Women installers shinny up phone poles; women plumbers install piping and bathtubs and toilets; women teamsters drive giant trucks; women fire-fighters jump aboard the engine when the alarm sounds; and women carpenters drive home nails alongside the men.

In academe, women Ph.D.s teach college-level courses in fields that, until barely a few years ago, were dominated by men: nuclear physics, astrophysics, oceanography, medicine, engineering, and many others. Women compete with their male counterparts for presidencies, deanships, and department chairs in universities throughout the nation.

In the rough-and-tumble world of commerce and industry, women slug it out with the men for supervisory jobs at all levels.

This frontal assault by American women on the world of work has created a number of special problems in the relations between employer and employee, and between men and women. The segment of the work force to feel the impact of these problems most strongly is the segment made up of two-career couples.

Changes in the career patterns followed by women today, as contrasted with a decade ago, have heightened the likelihood of competition between the sexes in the working world. Arline Bronzaft, in a 1974 study of women graduating from a New York university, discovered that nearly eight in ten of them expected to have careers, marry, bear children, and resume their careers after building a family. She disclosed, further, that between their freshman and senior years (1970–1974) the number of the women in this sample group who chose the career option increased from 48 to 79 percent.

Perhaps even more significant than the sheer increase in numbers was the finding, in this study, that 68 percent of the women sampled expected to follow careers that required postgraduate study. In other words, they intended to seek more specialized careers, including many that historically have been male preserves.[20]

Ms. Bronzaft's sample group contrasts sharply with the model of the early 1960s, when women who opted for careers tended to choose the more traditional occupations —teaching, social work, nursing—and elected to stop working altogether with the arrival of children. In the intervening years there have been marked increases in the number of women enrolled in schools of medicine, law, and engineering, and in other graduate programs.

What does all this mean? Among other things, it means that men and women at the graduate school level are being thrown together in growing numbers. In turn, this means that friendships and marriages are being formed between men and women with similar or identical career aspirations.

The marriage of people with careers in similar fields poses a set of special problems—and, of course, some special opportunities. Around twenty-five years ago it was widely believed that marriages between professionals would ultimately destroy the marriage and the professional advancement of both.[21]

More recently, however, this belief has been subjected to a closer look. There are now good reasons for believing that not only may it not be *harmful;* it may even be *helpful* for couples to be in the same or similar fields. The most extensive research has been conducted on couples who were highly advanced in their training (Ph.D.s in sociology, Ph.D.s in psychology, lawyers). Little is yet known about working couples at less specialized levels of training, so our conclusions are somewhat cautious.

The questions most frequently raised by two-career couples in similar careers are:

1. Productivity and Advancement.

Is the productivity of either partner likely to be affected adversely by similarities in careers? Will your advancement be inhibited by antinepotism rules? Will your career paths run parallel to each other, or follow a collision course?

How will employers react to having on the payroll an employee whose spouse, working in the same specialty, is on the payroll of a competitor? Will the employer fear that company secrets will be shared over the breakfast table or in bed; that a conflict of interest is involved? Will one or both partners be listed as "poor security risks" for this reason, and their advancement, as a consequence, be prejudiced?

2. Satisfaction.

Will the similarity of your careers lead to boredom because neither of you can ever "escape" from work, even at home?

One student of the subject has commented that "couples who share professions or employers often find that they have too narrow a range of interests and acquaintances." She also points out that, for couples who run a business together, there is no outlet, after work, for discussion of the problems of the day. Each is a part of the problem, and cannot therefore serve as an impartial, neutral sounding-board.[22]

3. Settings.

What is it like to share not only a home and a career, but also the same office? Issues of conflict of interest and nepotism aside, what are the pros and cons of two-career couples spending the better part of their waking, sleeping, and working lives in each other's presence?

Fortunately, there are answers (though some of them are tentative) to all these questions. Those which we give below are based on data developed thus far by research, as well as on our own discussions of these subjects with two-career couples.

1. Productivity and Advancement.

At one time it was generally believed that a husband and wife in the academic world had to choose different disciplines if they were to have successful individual careers. This belief was based on two factors. First, many institutions had antinepotism rules that prevented the husband and wife from working in the same department or in an area where the other was the primary supervisor. Second, it was believed that being in the same field would inevitably lead a couple to compete and thus destroy the career of either or both, or their marriage.

But there is recent evidence that casts doubt on the

notion that a wife's academic career is inhibited by the presence of her husband in the same discipline. Thomas Martin, Kenneth Berry, and R. Brooke Jacobsen, of Colorado State University, compared sociologist husbands, wives, and other female sociologists on the basis of their degree level, academic rank, promotions, kind of employment, and career longevity.[23] The primary aim was to determine whether a woman's career was supported or inhibited by her partnership in a dual-career marriage. (There was no examination of the husband's career pattern; this is indicative of a common bias in current research.) The results were fairly clear.

"In brief, it was found that compared to other females in the profession, sociologist wives were proportionately much more successful at obtaining the Ph.D., achieving higher academic ranks, gaining more promotions, avoiding demotions and practicing longer professional careers."[24]

The study noted, however, that "wives tended to be employed on a half-time basis more than other females and husbands, and it was hypothesized that department or university rules concerning nepotism might account for this irregularity in the data."[25]

Another study, which concentrated on married psychologists, found a mixed picture. "Wives in a professional pair tended to be more productive than other females [psychologists] but less productive than their husbands."[26]

This study also noted, in its subjects, the traditional distribution of labor. "Among professional pairs, there are five activities for which wives have the major responsibility: cooking, marketing, school age child care, preschool age child care, and laundry."[27]

Finally, some lawyer couples who work together were studied. Here again, the issues are very complex, but "this study seems to indicate that working partnerships between husbands and wives in a career-level profession offer structural opportunities for successful combination of work and family life."[28]

So, at least for some professional and academic couples, similar careers are not a burden.

When we look to the worlds of commerce and industry, we find again the questions of antinepotism and conflict of interest.

Typically, conflicts between working husbands and wives tend to arise only when they both work as professionals or executives in key areas, such as sales, research and development, finance, planning, or personnel . . .

Formerly confined to blood relatives, clashes of working and personal relationships are occurring more these days between spouses—the result of more women working, especially as professionals and executives. Such conflicts arise when the man's employer has business or political dealings with his wife's organization or when she works for a competitor or vice versa . . .

Real or potential, the conflicts affect couples in banking, law, computers, accounting, advertising, management consulting and the media, as well as in politics . . .[29]

The above quotations from a front-page story in the *Wall Street Journal* reflect the uneasiness about conflicts of interest that currently pervades business and professional sectors.

Understandably, an employer may be highly sensitive about information that is potentially useful to competitors, such as promotional plans, new marketing ideas, inventions, salaries paid to some senior executives, and so forth. They are also aware that "industrial intelligence," that is, the obtaining of secret information from one employer for the benefit of another, is now big business. They are, therefore, acutely aware of the potential perils of having one partner of a two-career marriage on their payroll while another partner is working for a competitor.

The partners in such cases can, of course, privately agree to observe certain ground rules. For example, it's okay to complain about the boss, but not to tell your partner that the boss is about to be fired *if* that information could be used to an advantage by the partner's employer, a rival company. Sometimes partners agree to avoid *all* discussion about work, but this kind of an accord probably is impossible to rely on or enforce.

Some organizations are responding to this problem by becoming *openly* restrictive, and by developing very specific rules against the hiring of dual-career couples.

Civil rights experts say that companies can develop specific policies for couples without fear of successful litigation as long as they enforce the regulations equitably . . . But most concerns just muddle along. Personnel officers complain that they cannot avoid the conflicts issue in advance because federal antibias rules prevent them from inquiring about a job applicant's marital status . . . Other companies simply ignore the situation, saying they respect their staffer's loyalty.[30]

In our research on employment practices among major United States corporations, we found that half of the corporations responding to our questionnaire said they have restrictions on the hiring of husbands and wives. Most of these restrictions deal with partners working in the same department or with the supervision of one partner by the other.

But there are signs of change.

Many corporations, law firms and banks have discarded rules that prohibited employment of both a husband and a wife. Some companies even believe that employing married couples is good for business. Debbie Foster, a representative of H. J. Heinz Co. in Pittsburgh, says her company has found that competent people usually marry competent people.[31]

Ironically, there is a Catch-22 aspect to all this. If, for example, the husband and wife have both been trained in advertising or banking, but are barred from working in the same department by antinepotism rules, do they go to work for competing employers? Which is worse?

There are certain potential difficulties for working spouses in the conflict of interest and nepotism problem areas, but we think they can be dealt with. In the first place, prospective employers may not ask specific sex-related or marital-status-related questions of job applicants.[32] Therefore, in a situation where the spouse is already employed by a firm, the nepotism issue may not even arise until after his or her spouse is hired. Then, if the newly hired spouse becomes a valued employee, the employer may be very reluctant to dismiss this employee solely in order to abide by company nepotism rules. This is particularly true if the rules are unwritten.

In general, however, we would counsel any dual-career couple to anticipate these issues, and not to be surprised if they arise. Frank discussion with a potential employer about how you would deal with any possible conflicts of interest will demonstrate your alertness to the dangers involved. Couples also should be prepared to challenge what they may regard as inappropriate or capricious rules. Such a challenge may prove to be risky, but it is a necessary step.

Finally, if it becomes readily apparent that the specializations of the two partners are directly competitive, they may be well advised to concentrate, at the planning stage, on fields that are complementary rather competitive. Doing so may stave off conflicts of interest that could thwart or stunt the career development of either or both.

We understand full well the concerns about jealousy and competition. But to a large extent, research data and our own considerable interaction with two-career couples convince us that these concerns—however acute and, at times, painful—are largely groundless. One of the most moving statements we have heard on this subject comes from two male psychiatrists who wrote regarding their physician wives:

We share one final perspective: we write in celebration of wives as well as marriages we consider highly successful—which is not to say without problems to be resolved and tensions to be managed. And yet for our investment in marriage we have in return experienced interpersonal adventures of higher intensity than we had been able to imagine in the romantic dreams of our adolescence.[33]

We believe, then, that opportunities to work in similar careers or areas will more than likely tend to *increase* productivity in both partners, and to heighten their satisfaction in their work. Certainly, employment in similar or identical areas should not be avoided or feared. Although there may be significant differences in productivity between men and women in a given profession, or even in their comparative levels of satisfaction in their work, these appear to be attributable more to the difficulties of managing a two-career family than to the fact that the partners are employed in similar occupations.

2. Satisfaction.

Research evidence and our own observations indicate that (a) women whose careers are similar to those of their partners may produce *more* in their work, and (b) there is no marked negative effect on the productivity of men whose partners are employed in similar or identical fields. But there remains, nonetheless, the question of job satisfaction, of a sense of fulfillment.

It has been evident for many years that the choice of a career by any given individual is based not only on that individual's particular skills and abilities, but also—and perhaps to an equal degree—on the individual's personal interests and lifestyle. A large part of career counseling is based upon this observation.[34] A person skilled in mathematics may elect to capitalize on this skill by becoming a certified public accountant, an engineer, a high school math teacher, a comptroller, or a banker. Satisfaction in one's career derives from more than one's aptitude for a given kind of work; it is a well-established fact that certain kinds of people tend to be more comfortable in, and better adapted to, certain types of work environment.

It has been observed that, in general, people in the same professions tend to share, to some degree, likes, dislikes, and interests. A couple working in the same field is likely to share a variety of interests. Therefore, a prediction could be made that—in theory, at least—similar careers will tend to enhance a dual-career marriage.

This obviously conflicts directly with the old adage that holds that opposites attract. But we have found, in our work with two-career couples who come from a diversity of settings, that there is a considerable degree of satisfaction derived by such couples from personal and professional involvement in the same fields or disciplines. In some cases, there is the special empathy that comes from an understanding, by both partners, of the kinds of pressures generated by their work. Many people who work in the entertainment world, for example, have stated flatly that it would be virtually impossible for them to be married to anyone who is not in entertainment, and to maintain a career. As one well-known woman television personality said to us, "Only a person working in TV is willing to accept the time pressures and the scheduling demands which broadcasting exerts on his or her partner."

Partners in other fields also appreciate this shared understanding. Each is likely to sympathize, for example, with the emotional demands of dealing with a classroom of children for six hours, the bureaucratic stresses that are part and parcel of university life, the pain of dealing every day with sick and dying people in the medical world, or the trauma of negotiating with difficult and demanding clients in commerce and industry.

So what's the bottom line? Here again, we'll give you our conclusions. We believe that working in the same field can enhance career development for both partners (assuming that barriers in the work environment can be dealt with). Our reasons for so thinking are admittedly somewhat speculative, because there has not yet been time for serious study of the matter. First, partners profit from being parts of a social-professional network in which intelligence about opportunities, new developments, and other matters of common interest are interchanged. Second, partners with similar careers can profit from the exchange of ideas, and from testing out each other's premises and conclusions. Finally, couples with common careers often can share professional events and thus have more opportunities to be together.

If the marriage is a good one, the sharing of career interests can contribute to the personal and professional growth of both partners.

3. Settings.

But what about working together? Having a fight at home and then storming away to the office is fine, but what if you then must face your partner anew—planning a contract, jointly laying out a sales campaign, or editing a book you are co-authoring?

When couples share an office *and* similar responsibilities, as Robert Anthony and Bernadette Evangelist do in their graphic-design firm, knowing where personal life begins and professional life ends can be a problem. Although they try to maintain a 9:00-to-6:00 business day, frequently it stretches until 10:00 P.M. The tightness of a partnership can pinch when there is reason to disagree. When arguments are unresolved, Evangelist said, "Neither of us sulks or stops working; we get very formal with each other."[35]

There's no cooling-off time, then, to put things in perspective; no relief from physical togetherness.

But there is the added bonus of shared triumphs, as well as the convenience of propinquity if an emergency should arise at home. Writer Sally Koslow has said:

Perhaps the most glowing positive of all in working together is what brings most couples to the decision in the first place—they enjoy each other's company . . . For a lucky few, working with the one you love works.[36]

In sum, the decision to work together is highly personal, and the arrangement should be undertaken experimentally. If your relationship already is rocky, this move will not stabilize it.

There is one caveat: if there is a marked difference between the pecking-order level of husband and wife in their work, it may be advisable for them to work in different settings. Examples: one partner is a lawyer, the other a paralegal; one is a school principal, the other a teacher; one is a dentist, the other a dental hygienist; and so on. In instances where the differential is very great, strain could develop. In such cases, we suggest that the partners not work in the same setting, simply because it is difficult to forget the hierarchical relationship that prevails in the work world when the couple returns to the home.

Putting It Together

In the main, we have found that conflicts occurring between partners working in the same field tend to be less related to their career similarities than to other factors involved in the dual-career relationship.

For example, when there are noticeable differences in the partners' advancement patterns, these frequently are traceable to the fact that one has assumed (or has been pressed to assume) more home responsibilities than the other. The usual pattern, still, is for the woman to take on the major share of house-care and child-care duties, often to the detriment of her career advancement. The issue here, therefore, is not related to similar careers, but to the who-goes-first predicament.

Many men who feel threatened by their wives' success will suffer this reaction even if their wives are not working in the same field.

The Challenge of the Near Future: Successful Women

It was the most exciting thing that had ever happened to me. The editor said I'd be getting my own column, and that my writing had been nominated for a national award. That meant a trip to New York with the other finalists. I'd receive at least $5000, but if I won the top spot . . . ! So, I called Don to tell him what had happened. Know what he said? "Oh. That's nice." Then a long silence. That made me very uncomfortable about the award, the column, the trip to New York—everything! I thought Don was really pleased about how well my writing was going. But now I don't really know.

Little dramas like this are being acted out regularly, these days, as more and more women enter fields of work that, until very recently, were dominated by men.

Success Has Been a Male Thing

In American society, "success" has historically been associated almost entirely with men in their work. Men have been viewed as "successful" when they earned better-than-average salaries, when they attained advanced degrees (education), when they rose to executive levels in the business world (status), when they became persons of influence in the public or private sectors (power),[37] or when they demonstrated superior intelligence. Success has rarely been attributed to men in their roles as husbands or fathers. Cynthia Fuchs Epstein, a sociologist, has noted: "Men . . . must succeed or fail primarily on the basis of occupational achievement. They get few extra credits for being good husbands and fathers."[38]

Conversely, a "successful" woman in the working world has been, until now, an oddity. "Success" for women traditionally has been measured by how they have performed as wives and mothers, and whether or not they have married "successful" men. In short, men have been *expected* to outrank their wives in income, education, status, power, and intellect.

But things are changing. Women, penetrating the world of work, are in numerous instances beginning to equal—if not surpass—their male counterparts in success, as defined in masculine terms. And because the inequality in status sometimes now favors the female, problems without precedent are beginning to emerge. These problems affect the women themselves, their partners, and their marriages.

The balance of this chapter will discuss two important facets of woman's success in the world of work: his feelings, and hers. We will also point out the circumstances under which problems are most likely to occur, and what to do about them.

Her Feelings about Her Success

HE: Do you enjoy success?

SHE: Yes . . . and no.

Although on occasion we have, in our work, met a woman who does *not* like her own success, we have found most women ambivalent in their reaction to success. Usually such mixed reactions are traceable to values that were instilled in *all* American women as they grew up. In generations past, girls and young women were led to believe, by custom and tradition, that only certain goals were appropriate for women, and that success in the work world was not one of them. Matina Horner observed:

> ... Women still tend to view competition, independence, intellectual achievement, and leadership as basically in conflict with femininity. They respond with anxiety to cues about successful women. Thus, despite the fact that our educational system purports to prepare both men and women identically for meaningful work, the data indicate the existence of internal psychological barriers for women, particularly for those who seek upper-echelon positions and training.[39]

The successful women with whom we have worked have expressed their ambivalence in such ways as the following:

I like being successful, but the notoriety scares me.

It's really great to be successful, but sometimes I wonder if it's going to change me.

Being successful also means I have to give much more to my work, and consequently less to my family.

Women also admit to mixed feelings about their success as it affects their relationships with their partners—and probably for good reason. Furthermore, they sometimes admit to changes in their own feelings about their partners *because* of their own success. Take a look at these typical expressions of concern:

I love being successful, but I worry about how much of it my husband will tolerate before ... well, before something drastic happens.

I would really feel much more comfortable with John if he were at *least* as successful as I am.

The dilemma I feel is this: Do I hold back on how successful I could be, and keep our marriage together? Or do I risk the marriage, plunge ahead full steam, and face the possibility of later years alone because my husband couldn't take it?

His Feelings about Her Success

Men's feelings about successful partners range from fierce pride to outright terror. But here again, as with the women, the men's feelings are generally ambivalent.

A university colleague, knowing of our interest in the dual-career phenomenon, shared his personal experiences with us. It seems that, after twenty years of traditional and happy marriage, his wife decided to return to work. Because her earlier education was inadequate for the positions she sought, she signed up for a master's degree program.

She was doing very well with her studies and had a full-time job awaiting her when she finished her course. Her husband was confiding to us his feelings about his wife's accomplishments:

She's probably the top student in the program. I'm really proud of her. One of the things I do wonder about, though, is what happens if we go to a party with all her friends and colleagues, and somehow *I* don't come across as bright enough? Imagine somebody saying about me, "He seems nice enough, and probably he's a very interesting fellow. But obviously *she's* much brighter than *he* is." I wonder if I could take that. [Pause.] On the other hand, I'd feel terrible if she weren't doing *really* well, because I'd feel that was a reflection on *me,* too!

So the men, though expressing approval of their partners' successes in one breath, may, in the next, admit that they "feel jealous," or "feel diminished" (as males), or "feel afraid that her success will somehow change how she feels about me," or "feel uncomfortable about being 'Mr. Jane Doe' [or whatever name] at social events."

The feelings of both men and women, and the depth and dimensions of the problem, are just now beginning to surface. More than anything, what we are dealing with is a phenomenal change that has taken place under our very eyes. There are few role models, because the change is so recent. It is *new* for women to be as successful as their partners, and in some instances even more so. Women lack role models on how to feel and act successful. But men are even more handicapped, because there are few if any male role models known to them who are comfortable with and supportive of their successful partners.

As an ambitious woman, you must find an enlightened man [who] is willing to share in the family responsibilities [and has] an ego strong enough to withstand the assaults that you will make on it. He must possess a tremendous sense of self-esteem. Because such men are rare, I have reached the conclusion that those executive women who have successful marriages are very lucky indeed.[40]

When To Expect Problems

Obviously, not every woman has difficulty with her own success, nor does every man respond negatively or ambivalently to a successful partner. But negative or mixed responses are common. Rhona and Robert Rapoport note:

For example, one of the tension points in the dual-career families we studied centers on how far the wife could go in developing high career aspirations without arousing competitive anxieties in her husband. The norm that is involved is the cultural assumption that the male is the principal provider and as such his occupational role must take precedence. Where some of the wives outstrip their husbands, or are at the point of doing so, there is often discomfort unless it is seen as a temporary expedient or something that the husband wants for his own purposes.[41]

We believe that difficulties are more likely to arise at certain times than at others. These are:

•when the man in the relationship reaches a low point, or feels confused, or suffers defeat in his own work just at the moment his partner achieves success;

•when the woman becomes significantly more powerful than her partner in earning capacity, visibility, or prestige;

•when the man is directly affected by a woman's success, as, for example, when the woman's success requires him to move, with her, to another community; the man must assume more responsibility for the home or children or both; his partner becomes less available to him because of her travel schedules or her added work responsibilities;

•when the woman's behavior changes markedly because of her success; or

•when her success is sudden and unanticipated.

Knowing that the woman is about to achieve success, you, as a two-career couple, can:

(a) anticipate that her success *will* have an impact, and discuss the possible implications of success before it "arrives";

(b) keep cool until the first blush of success passes, and you have had a chance to evaluate what's happened;

(c) try to enjoy the heady feeling while it lasts (after all, success is usually only a part of a total experience; few people are successful all the time);

(d) search among your friends for couples who have already shared the same experience, and ask their guidance;

(e) keep talking with one another about your real feelings; and, finally,

(f) if the problem is too big for you, seek the help of a professional counselor.

Of all the challenges we have discussed, this one is potentially the most dangerous for a marital relationship. It is also the one about which researchers, writers, and mental-health professionals know the least. For the working couple, the challenge of the successful woman may well become the major new challenge of the 1980s.

CHAPTER VIII

Choosing the "Right" Employer

The way we work in America is the major source of strain on family life.[1]

The quality of life is becoming as important a concern to people as their career progress or their financial standing.[2]

When it comes to *technological* change, American enterprise grasps its significance immediately and reacts rapidly.

But when it comes to *social* changes (like the two-career phenomenon), America's business and industrial communities tend to respond very slowly, if at all.

Perhaps this is because technological change manifests itself in the profit-and-loss statement, whereas the correlations between social change and the bottom line are difficult to determine.

Also, most senior decision-makers in today's corporate world are older men who were raised in traditional family environments, and whose own immediate families, in the main, were formed in the same mold. They naturally tend to view the world in the light of their own experience.

As a result, personnel policies in today's corporate world still mirror the times when the traditional family was the only acceptable model. Policies governing personnel matters assumed that the one-breadwinner family dominated American life. This kind of thinking, is, of course, archaic, as all the statistics on the nation's current work force will testify.

However, resistance to social change is still strongly evident in the personnel policies of businesses and industries, major and minor, throughout America today. Evidence of this fact surfaced in a survey we conducted of 100 randomly selected companies from the *Fortune* 500 list. From the information obtained in this poll, we learned that:

•only 35 percent of the corporations responding permit paternity leaves under personal leave or other special arrangement. None has formal paternity-leave policies;

•only 30 percent allow sick-leave time to be taken by employees while they care for sick children. An additional 9 percent permit use of other leave time for this purpose;

•only 17 percent offer "flextime," or flexible work schedules. None of our respondents offer shared positions.

Though the present odds are somewhat less than optimal, they do indicate that, even now, dual-career couples may, and should, "shop" for the employer who will offer them the most advantages. *In searching for positions, therefore, working couples should attempt to single out firms that offer some or all of the following attractions:*

1. Flexible Hours, or Flextime.

"Flextime" has won [great] popularity. Under flextime, all employees of an office or factory are obliged to be at work during a core period that might run from 10 A.M. to 2 P.M., but each employee can decide which other four hours to work. About 6,000 European companies are on flextime. In the U.S. about 90,000 federal employees and a few hundred private companies are on flextime.[3]

Research by two investigators, Allan R. Cohen and Herman Gadon, disclosed that more than 2500 United States companies had some form of flexible working hours at the time of the survey. Among these were such prestigious firms as Hewlett-Packard, Control Data, Exxon, Nestlé's, John Hancock, Pacific Gas & Electric, and the First National Bank of Boston.

Most of this shift to flextime, said the investigators, had taken place since 1973, and the concept is spreading very rapidly. The major reason for the change does not seem to be the two-career phenomenon, but of course it all works out to the advantage of dual-career workers. Companies appear to be adopting flexible working hours to make it easier for mothers who are the sole earners in their families to adjust their working hours to demands in the home, or to allow employees to attend to personal business, or even "to reduce commuting time," the survey revealed.

The investigators were told by the U.S. Geological Survey, after that agency had experimented with flextime for one year, that its 3000 employees had been permitted to set their starting and stopping times flexibly. Three fourths of these employees reported they were able to spend more time with their families. More than 50 percent said they had increased their recreational activities, and 43 percent reported that they had taken greater advantage of educational opportunities because of flextime.

The investigators also found that flextime reduced short-term absenteeism resulting from causes other than employee illness (such as child-care complications), tardiness was cut, turnover was decreased, and morale was improved.[4]

There are several variations on the flexible-hour concept. One, called the "punch-in" system, allows employees to work any combination of hours that adds up to

forty per week between certain broadly defined beginning and ending points. Another is the ten-hour-day system, with a four-day week. Many companies and public
agencies are on the ten-hour-day regimen now, and it
appears to be working with varying degrees of success. In
some cases, the arrangement has not worked (as at *Forbes*
magazine and at a Chrysler plant in New York State), and
has been dropped. The ten-hour day apparently exhausts
some workers and cuts them off from social life. Also,
some businesses trying the system have found it difficult
to conduct their affairs in a five-day world with a four-day
production schedule.

Flextime offers a decided advantage to dual-career couples who want to undertake their own child care, because
flextime will usually free both parents to share this responsibility. The system is also useful for couples who want to
spend more time together (such as long weekends), or to
attend continuing-education classes.

Flextime is seen by many observers of the American
labor scene as a sure thing in the near future. In *Money*
magazine, Jeremy Main wrote:

One way or another, an American's work schedule is going to
become more and more a matter of personal choice. And why
not? The eight-hour day and the 40-hour week have only become the norm in the last generation. Earlier this century people worked more hours a day and often six days a week. The
whole idea of a rigid work day was imposed by the factory clock
and the factory whistle in the 19th century. Before that most
people worked like farmers, by the sun and the season.[5]

2. Leave Options and Opportunities.

For working couples, the primary leave requirements
are maternity leave, paternity leave, sick leave for themselves, and leave to attend to a sick child.

Most organizations today have maternity-leave policies allowing authorized absences ranging from thirty to ninety days. These are usually regarded as sick leaves or leaves without pay. In most cases, such leaves are granted only for the woman to give birth; she is expected to return to work as soon afterward as possible. Few companies appear to regard it as appropriate for a new mother to spend six months to a year with her newborn to watch over the child's early development.

Any organization that demonstrates an enlightened position on these points should certainly rate a "plus" when you are conducting a job search.

Paternity leave is rarely granted. In fact, it is likely that few personnel officers have ever heard of paternity leave. This is one more instance of the long-term bias that sees child-rearing as essentially a woman's responsibility. As more and more men involve themselves in child-rearing tasks, a change in this attitude will be inevitable.

A firm that makes allowances for paternity leave should certainly be given a preferential rating during your job search.

Sick leave for employees normally is granted by most firms. But leave to attend the needs of sick children is still not granted by most large businesses and industries. Employees in the higher echelons tend to have more latitude in this matter, but women still are given greater freedom than men in responding to child-care emergencies.

In seeking employment, it would be advisable for you to discuss this matter with the interviewing officer. You might ask if employees may charge some of their own sick-leave or annual-leave time against any period of time needed to care for a sick child.

3. Permanent, Responsible Part-Time Employment Opportunities.

One worker in five today is a part-time worker (that is, he or she works fewer than thirty-five hours per week), and the part-time work force is growing at double the rate of the full-time force.

Full-time Equitable Life Assurance Society employees now may switch to part-time employment after five years of service, and continue to enjoy the full range of fringe benefits. But they must agree to work at least half of a full-time schedule. "Most of Equitable's part-timers so far have been women, mostly in child-rearing years."[6]

Many companies, and many workers themselves, report that part-time employment is more productive and more satisfying than full-time.

Working part time "has been great," she says. "I feel I'm much more productive. I don't put things off until tomorrow and I don't find time-filling chores. I get things done."[7]

Some types of part-time work are better suited than others to the needs of two-career couples. These are:

(a) The straight part-time position, or "compressed day." In this instance, one or more people work part time during a five-day week to perform a function that otherwise would be performed by one or more full-time people.

Students of the work scene have long agreed that there is tremendous waste of manpower in the eight-hour-day routine. Though most workers do not consciously attempt to cheat their employers, the tasks in some assignments are less than challenging, and often are simply boring. Workers therefore tend, at times, to fill up hours without accomplishing the work for which they have been hired.

Taking advantage of this fact of life, some enterprising applicants for openings have offered to do the same work in fewer hours as normally has been assigned to an eight-hour employee. They argue that they can increase productivity and lower costs at the same time. This is an approach worth considering.

(b) The "split-location" job. This is a job that may be done partly in an office, partly at home. Research work, telephone sales, secretarial functions, editing and work of a creative nature (design, architecture, and the like) are examples.

(c) Consulting. Consultants offer to work on a part-time basis for organizations that need special expertise but do not want to hire such talent on a full-time basis. For example, a specialist on personnel matters may work part time, giving counsel on special projects, research programs, and so on. The consultant works on his or her own schedule, is paid by the hour or assignment, and may work simultaneously for several firms on this basis.

(d) The "paired-shared" position. In this instance, two persons divide one full-time job, with equal responsibility for doing the whole job. Each works half time, and together they provide full-time coverage. Although this arrangement is most common in professional circles, it is also found in the academic world and in secretarial work.

A variant of this formula calls for job-sharing on an unequal-time basis, with one worker giving the minor fraction (one-third, one-fourth), and the other making up the difference.

(e) The "split-level" position. This arrangement calls for a "heavy," or professional person, to team up with a clerical-level worker to fill one job. Many jobs call for people with highly developed skills working with those who do routine clerical chores. The teamwork arrangement allows such jobs to be fully covered without the full-time presence of highly paid heavies.

4. Realistic travel expectations.

A job that requires the employee to do a large amount of traveling, often on short notice, can really disrupt a dual-career relationship (and, of course, a conventional one). If your type of work is likely to involve travel, look for an employer who will understand that you have home as well as office responsibilities, and will use discretion both in the amount of travel assigned and in the lead time you are given to make arrangements.

5. Considerate Transfer Policies.

Stress research suggests that relocation may be among the *most* stressful of voluntary events which families undertake.[8]

It is important to determine beforehand the general expectations and policies of any employer in regard to relocation and transfer of personnel. Our survey of major corporations, cited earlier, indicates that most corporations are unaware, or only slightly aware, of the overall implications of job transfers. Their policies appear to be based on the outmoded belief that most workers today come from one-breadwinner families.

Two-career partners should look for organizations that offer opportunities for transfer, but allow the employee ample preplanning and consultation time so that the transfer can be made in an orderly fashion. Employees should be given options with respect to the most appropriate time for a move. And the careers of both spouses should be considered whenever transfers are contemplated.

When the Aluminum Co. of America decided it wanted compensation-analyst Larry Wyatt to move to Knoxville from Pittsburgh, it also arranged a job interview in Knoxville for another Alcoa employee—Mr. Wyatt's wife, Katrina.

"We had pretty much decided we wouldn't go if I couldn't get a job, too," Mrs. Wyatt recalls. Her husband explains, "It would have been quite a strain on us to lose Katrina's income."

. . . [Only] 16% of 686 major corporations surveyed last year by Merrill Lynch Relocation Management Inc. said they had programs to help career-minded spouses find new jobs when their husbands or wives are transferred.[9]

6. Enlightened Sex-Role Policies.

It may prove very difficult to assess a company's real attitudes toward sex roles. However, it may be useful to inquire about its affirmative-action policies, and to ask such questions as:

•Are there attitudes at the management level that could make it difficult for women to progress?

•Are there expectations—spoken or unspoken—that all men will be tough, aggressive, competitive people who will demonstrate single-minded and total devotion to their jobs?

•Is there evidence that management believes it may be difficult for a woman to be a manager because she might have to travel with men (sexual fears)?

•Does management seem to feel that a woman's devotion to her career will be only fleeting, and therefore she will not be as productive as a man?

•Is there a feeling—expressed or tacit—that women are incapable of functioning for several days of the year because of menstrual periods?

•Do management-level personnel appear to feel that women are overly emotional and illogical, or tend to be less devoted to their jobs than men?

A recent investigation of these and allied questions revealed evidence of two patterns of sex discrimination, at the management level, that could negatively influence the career progress of women. First, men's careers were viewed with more concern by the organizations surveyed. Second, doubts were expressed by those polled as to the ability of women to balance their work and family demands.[10]

Obviously, these matters are of greater concern to women than to men. However, for the male employee it may be just as vital to determine a given firm's attitudes toward women workers, since, in some sense, this attitude will reveal the firm's expectations in regard to its male workers.

7. Child-Care Facilities.

Some business firms and industries already provide child-care facilities, and some have done so for years. These have historically been viewed as aids to working mothers, but, whether they were planned for this reason or not, they also answer the needs of dual-career couples.

The number of organizations providing such facilities is relatively small. Problems involved in such on-site care are still being ironed out. In a few instances, firms that have supplied such service have canceled it after a trial period, alleging, in some cases, lack of interest and support by working parents.

Whether you opt to use a company's child-care facilities —if they are available—it is important to determine if such facilities are offered. The very fact that a company has installed such a facility is evidence that the firm is concerned about meeting the needs of employees who are parents as well as producers.

8. Antinepotism and Conflict-of-Interest Rules.

In the late 1940s, Katharine Hepburn and Spencer Tracy starred in an amusing movie entitled *Adam's Rib*. There were married, and both were attorneys. They ended up in court representing opposing clients, with entertaining results.

In the 1940s, this was pure fantasy. But this kind of conflict-of-interest problem is no longer fantasy, and it is no longer atypical. With more women meeting men in professional or graduate schools, and marrying them, two-career couples are more frequently faced with finding jobs not only in the same fields but often in the same specialized sectors of a field. These couples may run afoul of antinepotism or conflict-of-interest rules.

Developed initially during the Depression of the 1930s

as a means of spreading jobs around, antinepotism rules forbade an employer from hiring both partners in a marriage at the same time, or from employing the spouse of a current employee. The rules are now interpreted by different organizations in different ways, including the following:

•not employing both spouses under any circumstances;

•not employing both spouses in the same department;

•not allowing one spouse to be the supervisor of the other; and

•not employing both spouses, yet allowing two unmarried people who live together to be employees simultaneously.

Antinepotism rules, at this time, are regarded as legal by the federal government. The Equal Employment Opportunity Commission has held that such rules are legal as long as they are enforced without regard to sex.

Conflict-of-interest rules prevent an employer from hiring anyone whose spouse is working for a competitor or for an organization that has any interest in the employer's business. Examples: a politician's wife seeking employment with a newspaper or broadcasting station, or an advertising executive's husband applying for work with the executive's major account.

Either or both of these categories of rules can adversely affect the working lives—and therefore the personal lives —of dual-career couples. It is advisable, for this reason, to check into a prospective employer's policies on these rules. Further suggestions on handling these issues may be found in Chapter VII.

9. Perquisites, or "Perks."

Finally, what is the overall work climate of the prospective business or industry? Is the employer overdemanding, inflexible, intolerant or ignorant of the needs of a two-career couple in or outside the work place?

The most successful corporations are sometimes viewed, by the unknowing, as the most tough-minded and the most demanding. Yet it has been our experience, through contact with various business sources and through our survey of the *Fortune* 500 list mentioned earlier, that the very opposite is generally true. The giant, prestigious firms often are the ones that provide employees with the most "perks."

What are these? Any one organization is not likely to have them all, but the following are the perks one may encounter in a random sampling of progressive, employee-oriented enterprises:

•regular, well-executed in-service training programs dealing with both technological and human-relations subject matter;

•human services, including mental-health counseling, physical-fitness facilities, job- and career-counseling programs, preretirement counseling;

•company newsletters and bulletin boards that are up to date, interesting, and employee-oriented;

•clearly written personnel policies available to all for review;

•profit-sharing plans;

•employee-satisfaction studies; and

•worker health and safety programs.

Since you will probably spend most of your week in your work setting, it simply makes good sense to choose the setting in which your chances for finding satisfaction and comfort in your job are the strongest. So perks are important.

The checklist on page 226 may help you to determine which of various employers that you are considering will offer you the greatest attractions. Circle those factors which you regard as the most important. Then rate the prospective employers on a scale from 1 (poor) to 5 (excel-

Factors to Consider in Choosing the Right Employer

	Organizations		
	A	B	C
	1 2 3 4 5	1 2 3 4 5	1 2 3 4 5
TRADITIONAL CONCERNS			
Salary			
Advancement possibilities			
Immediate supervisor			
Working conditions			
TWO-CAREER CONCERNS			
Flexible hours			
Leave opportunities			
Part-time work opportunities			
Travel policy			
Sex-role stereotypes			
Child-care facilities			
Antinepotism/ Conflict-of-interest rules			
Employee-oriented company attitude (perks)			
Other concerns you may have:			

lent). Discussing your findings with your spouse will aid you in making a sound decision.

A Final Word

If you have been reading the popular publications serving the business community (*Business Week,* the *Wall Street Journal, Fortune, U.S. News & World Report, Forbes,* and so forth), you have noted the steadily increasing concern about, and coverage of, the dual-career phenomenon. Though at times the reporting still centers on "working women," the terms "two-career couples" and "working couples" are appearing with greater frequency.

In the fall of 1978, the *Wall Street Journal* printed a series of front-page features on the concerns of working women and two-career couples.[11] *Fortune* and *Business Week* offer continual coverage of these subjects, as do the business sections of such leading newspapers as the Los Angeles *Times* and the *New York Times.*

Forward-looking organizations, like the Association of MBA Executives, have begun to give discussions of dual-career couples top billing at their national meetings.

The result of all this publicity is that more business leaders are becoming aware of the phenomenon. At the 1978 national meeting of AMBA, the following statements were made by three distinguished panelists, touching on dilemmas facing two-career workers:

Corporations might consider instituting policies that require them to honor transfer agreements. For example: a company might tell an employee that if relocation from the home office doesn't work out after eighteen months, the executive can return to the home office. When the eighteen-month period is over, the company should honor the commitment. Oral agreements are sometimes ignored, but a formal policy could prevent that from happening.

> —Deborah D. Conner,
> Manager Employment and Development
> Cummins Engine Company, Inc.

In conflicts between corporate and individual goals, corporations must be very realistic with their employees when they discuss the ramifications of an employee's decision. If, for example, an executive is offered a transfer that he or she doesn't want, corporations should be careful not to discuss the issue in socially acceptable terms when they really mean they'll fire the employee if he or she refuses to move.

When an employee is brought into a company, the firm should be aware of the spouse and his or her career needs.

Corporations shouldn't try to make decisions for their executives; a corporation could run into trouble by forecasting problems that may not exist. In some cases, the decision may be easier than it seems.

Corporations, particularly in large cities, may be confronted with dual-career issues that involve single people living together as well as homosexual couples.

> —Richard A. Collister, Vice-President
> Recruiting and Staffing
> Chase Manhattan Bank

Corporations should review policies on nepotism, conflict of interest, and employee transfers to better accommodate dual-career couples.

Corporations might form agreements and working relationships with companies and institutions in locations where they have offices. Under these arrangements, cooperating organizations might be able to provide jobs for spouses of transferred employees.

As businesses hire more women, the dual-career issue will be accentuated.

> —Marvin Trammel
> Corporate Employment Manager
> General Mills, Inc.[12]

These are encouraging signs. As a wise man once noted, nothing is so inevitable as change. Evidence of change, although sometimes subtle, is all around us. And one day that unique lifestyle we call the two-career phenomenon will no longer be regarded as a phenomenon.

CHAPTER IX

"Help!": Coping with Overload

HE: This is it! I'm going crazy. The bills haven't been paid for two months . . . I've got three writing assignments I haven't touched . . . the kids are off the wall. And Jean isn't helping out one damn bit.

SHE: "Helping out?" Good Lord, what am I supposed to do! I've got finals coming up . . . the house is so filthy I don't want to go home . . . and Dick has become the bastard of the century. I wish I could find a nice warm hole, and crawl in.

The partners in this two-career marriage are rapidly approaching the point of overload.* When this point is reached, a fuse will blow and the partners will be in deep trouble.

Many—if not most—working couples approach, or actually reach, the overload point at least once, and perhaps several times, in their married careers.

---

*The concept of overload dilemmas was introduced by Rhona and Robert Rapoport, in *Dual-Career Families Re-Examined,* p. 301 (see Suggestions for Further Reading).

What Is Overload?

Many of the friction points common to two-career marriages already have been discussed: conflicts on household management, money, child care, relocation, and so on. Overload is something apart from these separate and distinct problem areas and it may be defined as: *the sense of distress and helplessness that a couple suffers when, through their individual and joint efforts and capabilities, they are no longer able to deal effectively with personal or professional problems.*

In this chapter, the symptoms of overload will be identified, and means for coping with it will be described.

How Do You Know When You've Got Overload?

Ordinarily, most couples are not aware of the onset of this malady. They realize, rather, that they are tired, that they feel distressed, that anger comes quickly and unexpectedly; and they are vaguely aware that something big is wrong.

Overload comes to different couples in different guises, at different times, and under differing circumstances. In one instance, there may be a sudden deluge of things to deal with. In another case, the buildup may be slow and insidious, one more task or responsibility being loaded upon those already in place until, in the end, physical collapse becomes inevitable.

In these instances, and an infinite variety of others, life becomes just too much, and the whole mechanism registers "tilt."

The Danger Signs

The following are the more common overt symptoms of overload:

1. Communication Failure.

You and your spouse are no longer on the same wavelength. Such an innocuous question as "What do you want to do this weekend?" may arouse an inflammatory response, like "Get off my back!" Discussions about even the most insignificant details tend to end in argument. Hours, days, sometimes weeks, pass, during which verbal interacton between the partners dramatically degenerates and diminishes.

2. Fatigue.

If the level of your tiredness begins to increase more than it really should with the addition of a new time or work demand, and neither of you is able to share the other's burden, the overload point may be at hand, or may even have passed.

If the wife is very tired because of an increased work schedule, and the husband recognizes this and eases the pressure by taking the children on a Saturday morning outing, the couple is dealing with a spot fatigue problem that is not necessarily overload. If, however, the wife's fatigue makes her husband angry and resentful, and he is unwilling to come to her aid because of pressures from his own set of chores and priorities, then the couple may be approaching—or at—the overload point.

3. A Sense of Helplessness and Hopelessness.

Overload may be at hand if, in trying to deal with your day-to-day regimen, you, as a couple, feel overwhelmingly ineffectual. Nothing works. Everything goes wrong. Your ineffectiveness seems endless. As a facet of this particular syndrome, couples often feel (needlessly and incorrectly) that they do not have the resources, the time, the money, or the energy, to work out the problem.

Those are the most common symptoms of overload. Following are seven of the most common mistakes made by couples in their efforts to deal with it.

Seven Common Mistakes

1. Denial.

One or both partners refuse to admit the reality of overload, and deny its existence or impending threat.

HUSBAND: You seem awfully irritable and short-tempered. Is something wrong?

WIFE: Nothing's wrong. I'm just a little tired, that's all. Please, I really don't want to talk about it. Not now.

Obviously, the wife is doing the denying. Usually, the partner who is most overloaded is the most prone to deny. Her denial in this example is likely to have two immediate results.

First, the husband will feel confused if he takes his wife at her word. He may even begin to feel, incorrectly, that something is wrong with him, rather than with her. Or that he is doing something to make her tired, irritable, or short-tempered. Second, her denial is actually paralyzing the couple's ability to correct the situation. As long as she denies that anything is wrong, the couple will not be able to diagnose the difficulty and deal with it effectively. They —especially the wife—have swept the thing under the rug.

2. Blaming and Scapegoating.

Blaming, obviously, means seeing another as the cause of your distress, or turning your anger outward. Scapegoating means transferring your anger from a menacing target to one that is less threatening. Both of these responses occur with some frequency in dual-career relationships threatened with or experiencing overload.

Example: Mr. Benson has been working at what he considers maximum capacity in his very demanding factory job. In addition, he has been preparing dinner and tending to all the child-care chores two evenings every week so that Mrs. Benson can attend night classes.

During the busy Christmas season, Mr. Benson is informed by his supervisor that, in addition to his regular duties, he will be responsible for a post-holiday inventory. Mr. Benson is upset. But he fears a confrontation with his supervisor and rationalizes the extra load as "legitimate." Feeling overwhelmed, he grows angry with Mrs. Benson, and she becomes the scapegoat for anger that should rightly have been vented on the supervisor.

MR. BENSON: Damn it, ever since you went back to school, I've had more and more to do around here. What's more, I don't like the way you've been ignoring the kids and me. Nothing and nobody around here gets any attention except those damned books.

MRS. BENSON: What on earth are you talking about?

As in the case of denial, the danger of blaming or scapegoating is that the *true* source of pressure is being ignored by both parties. Effective problem-solving is, therefore, impossible. The usual response of the blamed or scapegoated partner is—understandably—anger, resentment, and a tendency to fight back. These are hardly responses that will alleviate the overload.

3. Depression.

A depressed person feels profoundly sad, hopeless, and overwhelmed. In addition, he or she is unable to associate these feelings with any particular situation or event. Almost the opposite of scapegoating, depression is a kind of self-blame, or anger turned *inward*.

This syndrome, another common response to overload, should be carefully distinguished from the occasional—and transitory—sadness or "down" we all feel at one time or another.

Other characteristics of depression are inactivity and the substitution of sleep for activity. Example: Mr. Johnson, usually an active early-riser, begins to stay in bed longer and longer. Called by his wife for breakfast, he may respond, "I'm bushed. Leave me alone." When he finally does get up, he complains bitterly about his fatigue. Jogging has been an important and regular exercise for Mr. Johnson, but now he seldom jogs. Mrs. Johnson is worried about her husband and tries to be understanding, but is annoyed by his constant lying around.

If depression is not recognized for what it is, the sufferer will tend to do less and less, sleep more and more, and may even be supported by his or her worried spouse in this kind of behavior. However, support for such behavior is really not very helpful.

As with other faulty coping mechanisms, depression veils the real causative factors, making relief difficult or impossible.

4. Psychosomatic Reactions.

Overload at times manifests itself physiologically, as a psychosomatic illness or pain. Some of the more common forms of psychosomatic illness are headaches, backaches, hypertension, stomach upset, asthma, and a variety of skin eruptions. It is important to understand that psychosomatic illness is *real,* and not imagined, as some people think. Psychosomatic illnesses, however, have causes that are both psychological (mind-related) and physiological (body or organism-related), with the distinctions sometimes very blurred.

Clearly, recurrent physical symptoms that do not seem to have a physiological basis are one expression of overload. This is not to suggest that every physical symptom you or your partner may suffer can be traced to a psychological base. But it is wise to recognize that if, after some consultations with a physician, nothing is found, it is time to begin considering that something else may be going on.

5. Withdrawal.

Withdrawal is a retreat from normal interaction with other humans. It can range from the simple form of communication breakdown described earlier to an all-out withdrawal of the person from everything and everybody. Feelings accompanying withdrawal may include a sense of being totally overwhelmed, of not wanting to make one more decision, or be faced with one more person or one more of anything. In short, virtual retirement from the human race.

The wife, returning from work, is asked by her husband, "What would you like to do for dinner?" Her response, typical in withdrawals, may be "I don't know. And I don't care. I don't want to make any more decisions. You decide. I'll eat whatever you put down in front of me."

Withdrawal often is accompanied by denial. If asked what was wrong, the wife in this case would probably answer, "Nothing's wrong." Withdrawal may also mimic depression, but usually it is not accompanied by the depressed person's fatigue and sense of hopelessness.

Withdrawal sometimes is a way for a person to gather energy for dealing with an overload, but more often it is a way of avoiding recognition of it. Clearly, withdrawing makes it difficult for the partner to help or to intervene, and is not a very useful approach to solving problems.

6. Rigidity.

Rigidity, another response to overload, is characterized by a person's unwillingness to consider possible solutions. In fact, what often occurs is that the person develops an even greater resolve to leave things as they are. Example: the wife is feeling particularly harassed by her work and her home responsibilities. Seeing that his wife is "beside herself," the husband suggests they go away for the day to "get a handle on things and do some planning." She not only rejects his suggestion, but decides to clean the closets, the drawers, and the garage—chores she has postponed for months. He leaves the house, feeling rejected and angry.

As is true of all the other faulty coping mechanisms described above, rigidly adhering to the status quo is a nonproductive approach to decreasing stress levels. The wife's rejection of her husband's efforts to improve the situation, in the above instance, is destructive to both of them. Neither gets his or her needs met. Incidentally, his reaction in angrily walking away is also a very typical and natural response to rigidity.

7. Going Crazy.

Virtually every human being, at one time or another, feels under such pressure by people or circumstances that he or she goes momentarily "crazy." What does "crazy" mean? The manifestations are yelling, crying, trying to run away, throwing things, physically or psychologically abusing one's spouse or children, and a whole range of other inappropriate actions. A person unable to cope with a given situation usually seeks relief by behaving in irrational ways.

The term "going crazy" is used here in both its colloquial and its diagnostic senses. Colloquially, such behavior represents an intensifying of actions that a person normally has under control. People who are normally a little sad will cry incessantly when they are going crazy. People who normally shout when they get angry will start throwing things when they turn a little crazy. People who normally withdraw under stress may, when going crazy, take off for a few days.

Diagnostically, "going crazy" means that an individual is temporarily unable to function or know what's going on. Psychologists and psychiatrists sometimes refer to this inability to function as a psychotic reaction. Obviously, not every instance of abnormal behavior is a sign of incipient psychosis. But "going crazy" is one way in which people may respond to unresolved and chronic overload.

Dealing with Overload: Positive Measures

You know what, Babe? I think we are really overloaded. Right now!

There are several steps that can be taken to deal with overload. Among them are:

1. "Calling" an Overload.

The first and most difficult step is to admit that overload exists. Either partner can "call" an overload. The call can result from recognition, by one or both partners, of any of the symptoms described above, or any combination of them.

Important: the partner not calling the overload must agree to cooperate in the diagnostic phase to follow (even though that partner may not agree that there really is an overload).

2. Diagnosis of Overload.

Once overload has been acknowledged, the next step is to determine the sources of stress. Some of the questions that may be posed in this phase are:

(a) Which partner is feeling stress the most?

(b) What kinds of (mistaken) coping mechanisms were observed?

(c) What are the sources of the pressures, on each and on both?

(d) Is the center of these pressures at home, at work, or elsewhere?

(e) When did stress begin?

(f) Have there been any significant changes at home, at work, or anywhere else, that may have contributed to the stresses?

(g) Is either partner trying to avoid a problem, a decision, or some other event or act?

At the practical level, try to determine whether added responsibilities have crept into your lives, at home or at work. Have the children been sick, or up at night? Have you, as a couple, been experiencing a diminishing of sexual activity? Are holidays in the offing, with the inevitable parties, gifts, cards, family gatherings? Are the children home from school for holidays or vacation? Has the boss of either partner laid on any added assignments?

Diagnosis may be resisted by one or both partners simply because the sheer act of diagnosis involves added work and decision-making for an already overloaded couple. Sometimes, considerable effort is required to encourage the one experiencing the most stress to cooperate, especially if that partner is already resorting to one of the mechanisms described above. Individuals who are depressed, withdrawn, or angry often are loathe to involve themselves in the diagnosis, even if it is in their best interests.

The objective of diagnosis is to identify the factor or factors that have caused stress in one or both partners.

Having (1) acknowledged and "called" the overload and (2) diagnosed its causes, you are ready for Step 3: Reducing or Ending the Overload.

3. Reducing or Ending the Overload.

HE: It sounds to me like what we need to do, first off, is to get a housekeeper, or at least someone temporarily—maybe a few times a week—until we get the chaos under control.

Lessening or, even better, eliminating an overload may require your asking others for help. This can prove difficult for some individuals. Working couples often see themselves as "superpeople," able to do anything, take care of any situation. Asking for help, they sometimes feel, is a threat to their self-image as competent, effective people.

To preserve this superperson self-image, some couples turn to ineffective problem-solving models, such as "working harder" rather than working more effectively. But asking for help can be a sign of strength and maturity, not an indication of weakness.

Relieving or ending an overload can be accomplished by one or a combination of the following approaches:

(a) Turning to one another for help. Although this may appear an obvious option, it is really the first line of offense against the enemy, overload. Who knows—or at least *should* know—your dilemma better than your partner? A partner can devote time and energy, and provide support, care, and relief, in a measure no one else can. If, however, the partner is part—perhaps the major part—of the overload problem, you will probably have to seek help elsewhere.

(b) Seeking help from an employer, supervisor, or instructor. You may need the special kind of help that can be given only by an employer. For example, you may request time off, as for sick leave or vacation, or a reduced workload, or flexible hours for a specified time period (if flextime is not already an option at your place of work).

There may be other, more creative, ways of asking your employer, supervisor, or instructor for help. At worst, the response can only be no. Here again, your superperson self-image may try to intervene to prevent your requesting such help. Interventions of this kind can defeat your purpose.

(c) Calling a temporary halt to everything.

HE: As of right this moment, let's not do one more thing. Cancel our dinner party for Saturday. I'll tell Mom we won't be able to visit her this week. What else?

If there is one single item that most two-career couples lack, it is time. Time to think, time to plan, time to reflect, to catch up on sleep, to regenerate.

We have found, in our practice, that the most effective way a person can deal with an overload is to agree to do nothing, and to agree further not to accept one more commitment from *anybody* to do *anything*. This allows the affected parties to regain control over their lives, to install some priorities, and to do some planning.

(d) Lining up emergency help, hired or otherwise. Relief sometimes comes from hiring someone to take care of some chore, or chores, or to tend for someone. In short, to perform tasks you simply don't have either the time or energy to take care of yourself. Most short-term emergency help is expensive, often more expensive than hiring the same service on a long-term basis, but it's worth it.

What kinds of help? Employing a temporary clerical person to catch up on paper work or correspondence, or to reconcile bills and bank statements for the month(s) you are behind. Hiring a bright, energetic college student to help with the children while they are home for holidays or vacations. Renting a car while the second car is in the garage for an overhaul. (This prevents your hassling with the inconvenience of a car pool or using slow, crowded buses or streetcars.)

(e) Getting away from it all.

HE: Now that we've canceled out of that dinner party Saturday, why don't you and I go up to the mountains for the weekend . . . just the two of us. It's been a long time since we've done that.

Often the best panacea for what ails a two-career couple is a little time alone, unburdened by pressures of any kind. "Getting away" can be as simple as a night at a local inn, five minutes away from home. Of course, if time and resources are available, getting away can also mean backpacking into the hills or forests, or—if money is no object —letting the staff of the Mauna Kea Beach Hotel in Hawaii take care of you for a few days.

What you, as a couple, really need is to turn off the world and all its demands, and concentrate on taking care of yourselves. Even a mere twenty-four hours of such unadulterated aloneness can perform miracles in recharging your batteries. Revitalized by such a rest, you can face your problems with new vigor.

Long-Term Strategies for Coping with Overload

The five strategies just discussed are essentially short-term solutions. They will provide a two-career couple, it is hoped, some relief from immediate pressures.

But overload is often caused by forces too large for short-term remedies. For example, if both partners are working full time and are trying to maintain a busy household (with perhaps three children) without much outside help, the mere act of getting away for a few hours—or even for a week—will not solve the problem in the long run.

One possible long-term strategy is to re-examine carefully the distribution of responsibilities in your individual and collective lives, including those already discussed at length (household management, child care, finances, and so forth). It may prove to be the case that one of the partners is overburdened with some or all of these responsibilities, and that you need to renegotiate, redistribute, reallocate the chores.

If you, as a couple, find that your overload cannot be relieved by your own voluntary acts, and that it tends to be chronic or repetitive, it may be time to seek the help of a licensed mental-health professional. The specific kind of mental-health professional, whether it be a psychologist, social worker, psychiatrist, or marriage and family counselor, may be less important than that the individual or a therapist team has the following characteristics:

(a) experience in working with couples;

(b) knowledge of two-career couple issues; and

(c) a willingness to work on dual-career issues (communicating, managing, decision-making, and so on) in addition to therapy relating to individual personal problems.

How can you find a person or therapist team with whom to consult? There are a number of ways. First, you may talk with other two-career couples to see if they have worked successfully with someone. Second, look over college adult-education programs or in local newspapers to see if any local professionals are offering seminars on the subject. Third, ask other professionals, like your family physician or attorney or school official, if they know of people who are competent to deal with dual-career problems. A final suggestion is for you to call one of the local mental-health information and referral services (usually listed in the Yellow Pages of the telephone directory) for names of professionals who work with two-career couples.

Ultimately, the choice of whom you work with is up to you. As you get the names of potential therapists, call them to find out about what kinds of experience they have, what their particular therapy orientations are, and what they charge. Most therapists work either as private practitioners or as members of clinics, and the costs of their services will vary accordingly. Private-practice charges, depending on the educational background and experience of the individual, usually are in the range of $25 to more than $100 per session. Some therapists charge clients on a sliding scale, according to their ability to pay. Others have a standard fee, like $50 per session for individuals or couples. Still others may charge more for sessions with couples. Clinic fees often are based on one's ability to pay and vary from no charge to the upper limits of private-practice fees.

Overload is one of the major stumbling blocks confronting two-career couples, so if you even *suspect* that you are suffering from this malady, take action. Action, to summarize, includes the following steps:

•Recognize the symptoms, don't avoid them.

•"Call" the overload.

•Investigate its causes, and begin plans to eliminate them.

•Make sure your plans include not only short-term but also long-term strategies, and thus ensure that the overload—once eliminated—will not recur.

When you have acquired the skills and strategies to deal with overload, you will have advanced along the path to "making it together."

CHAPTER X

The Couple Relationship: Some Final Touches

This final chapter is devoted to you—the partners in a two-career relationship—as individuals and as a couple.

Until now, the discussion has centered on problem-solving. But most of us who have formed two-career partnerships have done so not because we want to solve problems, but because we hope to spend many rich years together.

The difference between *doing* and *hoping* lies in the observance of certain ground rules. The recommendations that follow are based on those ground rules. Our own experiences as a two-career couple, together with those of hundreds of couples with whom we have worked and taught, convince us that the living-out of these recommendations will make the difference between merely existing and really enjoying.

Some of the points that follow are restatements of points made earlier. This is purposeful; the redundancy is for emphasis. Other points will be new; they were not presented earlier because, in the context, they were not relevant. As we have said before, accept that which is useful and applicable, and reject that which is not.

The Art of Including

"Including" your partner is one way to strengthen your relationship. We mean this, here, in the career sense rather than in the merely social and conventional sense.

How does this work? Include your partner, if you can, in any professional invitations you may receive. If you both work in the same field (as we do, for example), the opportunities for this kind of "including" are numerous. For instance, one of you is invited to speak at a conference, a seminar, or some other occasion. Why not suggest that your partner be invited as a joint speaker? We have found that most organizations are delighted to hear from both of us, each giving a somewhat different (or even a totally opposing) version of the joint message. Being invited as co-speakers not only gives each of you a chance to share the rewards; it provides you an opportunity to work together and to enjoy one another.

If you work in different fields, why not—*when it is appropriate*— suggest that your partner also be invited? Some organizations will even pick up the travel tab for a spouse.

Most two-career couples have little enough time together as it is. Including your partner whenever possible in professional activities is a thoughtful gesture on your part and is also a way to see that recognition is shared. In sum, it is sound methodology.

The Art of Supporting

What if your partner enjoys skiing, but you get chilblains whenever the thermometer dips below 52° Fahrenheit? What if you enjoy art auctions, but your partner begins to doze off by the time the third lithograph comes up for bid? What if you enjoy watching prizefights, but your partner finds them offensive and boring?

It is important to "include." But it is also important to know when to "exclude," that is, when each of you should develop his or her own personal interests and activities, to the exclusion of the other.

In the personal life of each of you, there will be things, activities, people that are important to you but not at all important to your partner. Each partner should recognize this and should encourage the other to "do his (or her) thing." One may truly enjoy trout fishing; the other may delight in macramé. Neither should attempt to force a favorite hobby on the other unless it "comes naturally" to both.

It is all too easy to throw one's partner for a loop by dropping a few words like these:

•"I really hate to be alone" (expression of personal distress);

•"Do you think this is a good way to be spending our money?" (blocking); or

•"I can't understand why anyone would want to spend such a beautiful day watching football on TV" (subtle put-down).

Every individual has his or her own need for self-expression and fulfillment. Such needs usually were engrained in the individual long before marriage, and they do not abruptly terminate with the marriage ceremony.

A really rich, successful two-career relationship allows for individuality and strikes a perfect balance between joint and solo performances.

The payoff will come when each partner, with tolerance and understanding, can enjoy the good feeling that results from seeing the other "do his (or her) thing," without suffering any resentment whatsoever.

The Art of Accepting

People come together for all sorts of reasons. Some are realistic; others are not. During what once was quaintly called "courting," each partner puts his or her best foot forward, behaving and appearing in ways designed to please the courted. Eventually, however, it becomes plain that the "fantasy" partner and the "real" partner are somewhat different. It also becomes clear that the older the relationship gets, the more set and "characteristic" each partner becomes in terms of behavior and personality.

The art of accepting lies in accepting your partner as he or she really is. This does not negate, in any way, the importance of communicating, to your partner, the things that bother you about his or her behavior. Changes are possible, of course—particularly specific changes in behavior—but any effort to reorganize completely your partner's personality is bound to end in disappointment, if not catastrophe.

There is a part of living with a partner that most people are unaware of: more often than not, the very aspects of your partner's personality that you most admire and cherish are the ones that annoy you. There is an explanation of this paradox. People who are always responsible and upon whom you can depend (traits that please a partner) also tend to be compulsive (which drives their partners crazy!). People who are creative and spontaneous (admirable traits) tend to be impulsive and disorganized (characteristics seldom admired by a partner). Usually, under stress, people tend to be *more* of what they are: the organized become compulsive, the spontaneous turn chaotic, and so on. It would be lovely if this were not true, but usually a behavior characteristic is present in any given individual in both its mild and its extreme manifestations.

Thus, accepting will help you and your partner toward a better, more solid relationship. If one (or both) of you thinks of your partner in terms of how you want him or her to be, that's dangerous. We offer this observation because those experienced in human-relations counseling tell us that a major characteristic of deteriorating marriages is the effort by either or both partners to change the other to conform to a desired image. It doesn't work. Instead, such an effort produces stress, which can lead to very serious problems.

The Art of Applauding

If your partner wins applause for some distinct accomplishment, what do you do? Unfortunately, men or women too often take the accomplishments of their partners somewhat for granted. More attention may be given to the problem, the issue, the difficulty, than to some meritorious act. This is the norm. Think about it: If your partner comes home with a problem involving a colleague at the office, perhaps a supervisor, how do you react? If you are "normal," you spend considerable time listening to the problem and helping the partner arrive at a solution. But if your partner announces that he or she has just received an award, how do you react? The usual response is a smile, a "Gee, that's nice," a hug—then a quick return to whatever you were doing before.

On the next occasion, take special time and pains to applaud your partner's accomplishment at some length. Your partner will be feeling *good* about this triumph. Let him or her know that you, too, feel good about the recognition and are proud that it was granted.

The Art of Pleasing

Another way of "making a difference" in your relationship is to make genuine efforts to *please* your partner. We don't mean to be cute about this. But we have found that a simple act that pleases often goes a long way toward bringing partners closer together.

"Pleasing" can take many forms: choosing a particular gift that will have special meaning, instead of merely buying "the usual"; fixing a favorite meal without waiting for some special occasion that demands it; getting up early the morning after a dinner party to clean up the kitchen before your partner awakens. It could take the form of supporting a partner's occasional extravagances. For example, if your husband likes relaxing through physical activity, encourage him to spend a Saturday at an athletic club for racquet ball, sauna, shave and a haircut—and you pay for it. If your wife is a horsewoman, buy her that long-wanted saddle she thought she couldn't afford—and pay for it yourself.

The art of pleasing, like the art of including, is more *attitude* than *act*. Whatever form it takes, the art primarily involves taking the time to know what your partner likes and needs, and acting on those likes and needs.

Practicing these arts can give those added touches which will make the difference between merely *living* together and *making it* together.

The Art of Being Close

As each of you becomes more productive, it becomes easier to drift into different orbits. Schedules, deadlines, children, obligations, all can contribute to a sense of distance, alienation, or isolation. Although each couple will develop their own ways of maintaining contact, two things that we want to focus on are touching and sexuality.

Touching

Even for couples who have been together for a long time, touching is difficult. Our culture does not emphasize touching except when it is sexual or when it involves small children. Men who hug one another are viewed with suspicion; women can touch, but only just so often and in special circumstances. This taboo reaches into the confines of a couple relationship to the point where many children rarely see their parents hug one another or hold hands. Think about how children react when they see their parents hugging: "Wow, did you see Daddy hug Mom? I wonder what's happening!"

In our professional world we have been impressed by the number of people who have difficulty in reaching out spontaneously. We think that couples can measurably enhance the quality of their relationship by being willing to touch, to take a hand, to hug, to hold one another, to reach out to one another physically as well as verbally. A physical act—that of making contact—is one way of being close.

Sexuality

Why do we include sexuality as a separate topic? Although sexuality is part of any couple relationship, two-career or not, there are some specific issues for the two-career couple. First, there is the fear on the part of some men that their wives, particularly when leaving the traditional role for a career, will be more available to other men and perhaps more interested in them. In general, we have no evidence that two-career couples are any more or less faithful than their traditional counterparts.

Second, it has been observed that the frequency of sexual contact for two-career couples decreases. What's this all about? What two-career couples are dealing with most of the time are the issues of availability and fatigue.

If you're on different schedules, then the actual time that you have with one another may be lessened. Similarly, when both of you are wiped out, the likelihood of having sexual contact that is mutually satisfying is very much reduced. Not knowing that this is common in two-career relationships, a partner may interpret decreased sexual contact as rejection by the other, or possibly conjecture that his or her partner is involved in an outside relationship. Sure, there are times when availability and fatigue may be used as an avoidance of sexual contact, but usually they are real issues.

So what do you do? First, we think it's crucial for two-career couples to talk openly about their sexual needs and preferences, including frequency of contact or lack of it. Second, we think that *spontaneity* as the critical ingredient of a satisfying sexual relationship is much overplayed. Two-career couples in particular need to anticipate, yes, even to schedule sexual time. Saying at the beginning of an evening "Let's go to bed early tonight so we can make love" is far more effective than hoping your partner remembers that it's been almost a week and will spontaneously make himself or herself available and desirable.

If you have children, it may even be necessary to deal with their schedules, too, if you're going to be able to create the time, setting, and attitude that both of you want. Many two-career couples plan an occasional midweek overnight just to make sure they can have some uninterrupted time together.

Becoming a two-career couple certainly will not help to alleviate any sexual problems that you may have; if anything, problems can be exacerbated by the additional stress. If, in fact, you find you're dealing with an issue of sexual dysfunction, then we urge you to seek helpful professionals in this area. If the issue is not one of sexual adequacy or function, then probably you're dealing with issues of availability and energy, and these we think can be solved by open dialogue and anticipation.

The art of being close is a skill that every couple needs, but we think it's particularly critical for the two-career couple.

The Art of Planning

Talk with one another about your hopes and dreams. Plan together to reach long-range goals. You will find that the mere act of planning together, of sharing your dreams and aspirations, will have a cementing effect on your relationship. And joint planning for the future also will give you more control over your own lives.

By long-range goals we mean those which you may realistically achieve in, say, five or ten years. Such objectives may include additional education for one or both of you, a work sabbatical, travel, living abroad (or even elsewhere in the United States) for a year or so, or changing careers. You may or may not actually carry through with your plans, but we think that you will find the very act of planning a positive experience in itself.

The Richer, Fuller Life

Certainly, two-career living is not the easiest of choices. But then, "ease" is not the reason couples choose this route. A two-career relationship offers women the chance to be everything a woman can be: a career person, a wife or partner, and a mother. It offers men the chance to share the family financial burden, the potential for having more time for personal pursuits, and the opportunity to be more involved in family life. In short, the two-career relationship offers us the chance to "have it all" while "making it together."

Reference Notes

Suggestions for Further
Reading

Index

Reference Notes

Chapter I   The End—and the Beginning
(pages 1–9)

1. Shirley Streshinsky, "How Working Couples Work It Out," *Redbook*, June 1977, p. 232.
2. Delores Fryling, Janis Porter, and Lynda Taylor, "A Behavior and Attitudinal Study of Dual Career Marriages." Unpublished master's thesis, School of Social Work, San Diego State University, 1974.
3. "America's New Elite," *Time*, August 21, 1978, pp. 56–57.
4. Kathryn E. Walker, "Who Shares in the Family Work?" *American Vocational Journal*, February 1975, pp. 52–54, 56.
5. "$61,100 Nationally for a New Home," San Diego *Daily Transcript*, February 12, 1979.
6. U.S. Department of Commerce, Bureau of the Census, *Current Population Reports:* Series P60, No. 116, July 1978, Money Income and Poverty Status of Families and Persons in the United States: 1977 (Advance Report), p. 12.
7. U.S. Bureau of Labor Statistics, *Monthly Labor Review*, November 1978, Family Budgets, pp. 33–36.
8. Leslie Bennetts, "Mid-Life Crises Called Order Amid Chaos," San Diego *Union*, March 13, 1978.
9. Sharon L. Connelly, "Geographical Relocation of Dual Ca-

reer Couples." Dissertation proposal, September 8, 1978, p. 4.

10. Ibid, p. 4.

11. Harold H. Frank, *Women in the Organization* (Philadelphia: University of Pennsylvania Press, 1977), p. 305.

Chapter II Two Careers: The New Game in Town
(pages 10–31)

1. Shephard G. Aronson, "Marriage with a Successful Woman: A Personal Viewpoint," in *Women and Success: The Anatomy of Achievement,* ed. Ruth B. Kundsin (New York: William Morrow & Co., Inc., 1974), p. 232.

2. Ann Blackman, "Problems of the Two-Paycheck Family," Los Angeles *Times,* March 10, 1978, p. 4.

3. Alvin Toffler, *Future Shock* (New York: Random House, 1970), p. 99.

4. Jessie Bernard, *Women, Wives, Mothers: Values and Options* (Chicago: Aldine Publishing Co.), 1975.

5. "An Overview of Women in the Workforce," National Commission on Working Women, Center for Women and Work, Washington, D.C.

6. Fritz Perls, *Gestalt Theory Verbatim* (New York: Bantam Books, 1969).

7. Shephard G. Aronson, "Marriage with a Successful Woman: A Personal Viewpoint," in *Women and Success: The Anatomy of Achievement,* ed. Ruth B. Kundsin (New York: William Morrow & Co., Inc., 1974), p. 236.

8. Kathleen Neumeyer, "Conflict-of-Interest Marriages: How Los Angeles Couples Are Coping," *Los Angeles* magazine, November 1978, pp. 164–169, 355–357.

9. A. C. Bebbington, "The Function of Stress in the Establishment of the Dual-Career Family," *Journal of Marriage and the Family,* August 1973, p. 530.

10. "An Overview of Women in the Workforce," National Commission on Working Women, Center for Women and Work, Washington, D.C.

11. Shirley Streshinsky, "How Working Couples Work It Out," *Redbook,* June 1977, p. 230.

12. Rhona and Robert N. Rapoport, *Dual-Career Families Re-examined: New Integrations of Work and Family* (London: Martin Robertson & Co., Ltd., 1976), p. 310.
13. Jessie Bernard, *Women, Wives, Mothers: Values and Options* (Chicago: Aldine Publishing Co., 1975).
14. Jessie Bernard, *The Future of Marriage* (New York: Bantam Books, 1973).
15. Ibid.

Chapter III Who Takes Out the Garbage?: Managing the Household
(pages 32–65)

1. Mary-Ellen Banashek, "Two-Career Couples: How They Make It Work," *Mademoiselle,* September 1977, p. 168.
2. Rhona and Robert N. Rapoport, *Dual Career Families Re-examined: New Integrations of Work and Family* (London: Martin Robertson & Co. Ltd., 1976), p. 301.
3. Lyn Tornabene, in Donna Goldfein, *Everywoman's Guide to Time Management* (Millbrae: Les Femmes Publishing, 1977), p. 40.
4. Michael Grant, "Working Parents Share Chores," San Diego *Union,* March 20, 1977.
5. Shirley Streshinsky, "How Working Couples Work It Out," *Redbook,* June 1977, p. 103.
6. Theodore Nadelson and Leon Eisenberg, "The Successful Professional Woman: On Being Married to One," *American Journal of Psychiatry,* October 1977, p. 1073.
7. "How the Man in the House Shares the Work," *Vista Press,* February 8, 1974.
8. Shirley Streshinsky, "How Working Couples Work It Out," *Redbook,* June 1977, pp. 103, 224, 226, 228, 230, 232.
9. Rhona and Robert N. Rapoport, *Dual Career Families Re-examined: New Integrations of Work and Family* (London: Martin Robertson & Co. Ltd., 1976).
10. Linda J. Beckman and Betsy B. Houser, "The More You Have, the More You Do: The Relationship Between Wife's Employment, Sex Role Attitudes and Household Behavior," *Psychology of Women Quarterly,* in press.

11. Ibid.
12. Mary Bralove, "For Married Couples, Two Careers Can Be Exercise in Frustration," *Wall Street Journal,* May 13, 1975.
13. Theodore Nadelson and Leon Eisenberg, "The Successful Professional Woman: On Being Married to One," *American Journal of Psychiatry,* October 1977, p. 1074.
14. "When Mothers Are Also Managers," *Business Week,* April 18, 1977, p. 156.
15. Alan Lakein, *How to Get Control of Your Time and Your Life* (New York: Signet Books, 1973).
16. Donna Goldfein, *Everywoman's Guide to Time Management* (Millbrae: Les Femmes Publishing, 1977).

Chapter IV   Two-Career Parenting
(pages 66–91)

1. Constance Rosenblum, "Should We? Here's How They Decide," New York *Daily News,* September 25, 1977.
2. Ibid.
3. Mel Roman, "How Do the Children Feel?" *Parents* magazine, April 1977, p. 37.
4. Linda J. Beckman, "Relative Costs and Benefits of Work and Children to Professional and Non-Professional Women." Paper presented at the American Psychological Association meetings, New Orleans, August 1974.
5. Margaret Mead, in Alice Lake, "Three for the Seesaw: How a First Baby Changes a Marriage," *Redbook,* April 1974, p. 99.
6. Ursula Vils, "Testing Aptitude for Parenthood," Los Angeles *Times,* May 1, 1978.
7. Jessie Bernard, *The Future of Marriage* (New York: Bantam Books, 1973), p. 65.
8. Jessie Bernard, *The Future of Motherhood* (New York: The Dial Press, 1974).
9. Ibid.
10. Elizabeth M. Whelan, *A Baby? . . . Maybe: A Guide to Making the Most Fateful Decision of Your Life* (New York: The Bobbs-Merrill Co., Inc., 1975), p. 185.

11. Lois Hoffman and Jean Manis, "The Value of Children: Why Couples Choose Parenthood," Institute for Social Research Newsletter, Autumn 1978.
12. Helen Rowland, "Quotable Quotes," *Reader's Digest,* November 1978, p. 185.
13. Fitzhugh Dodson, *How to Parent* (New York: The New American Library, Inc., 1971), p. 21.
14. James A. Levine, *Who Will Raise the Children? New Options for Fathers (and Mothers)* (Philadelphia: J. B. Lippincott Co., 1976).
15. Daniel Durso, "Where Are the Children?" *American Home,* January 1977, p. 14.
16. Susan Byrne, "Nobody Home: The Erosion of the American Family" (A Conversation with Urie Bronfenbrenner), *Psychology Today,* May 1977, p. 43.
17. Rhona and Robert N. Rapoport and Ziona Strelitz, *Fathers, Mothers and Society* (New York: Basic Books, Inc., 1977), p. 11.
18. Mel Roman, "How Do the Children Feel?" *Parents* magazine, April 1977, pp. 37, 72.
19. Rhona and Robert N. Rapoport and Ziona Strelitz, *Fathers, Mothers and Society* (New York: Basic Books, Inc., 1977).
20. Urie Bronfenbrenner, "The Origins of Alienation," *Scientific American,* August 1974, pp. 53–61.
21. Dennis Forney, "What Price Glory? For High-Level Aides in Washington, It Is All Work, No Family," *Wall Street Journal,* January 30, 1979, p. 1.
22. Mel Roman, "How Do the Children Feel?" *Parents* magazine, April 1977, p. 72.
23. Diane Gorak, "What the Books Don't Tell Working Mothers," *Redbook,* March 1977, p. 79.

Chapter V The Other-Than-Mother Dilemma: Choosing Child Care
(pages 92–135)

1. Earl C. Gottschalk, Jr., "Women at Work: Day Care Is

Booming, But Experts Are Split Over Its Effects on Kids,"
Wall Street Journal, September 15, 1978.

2. Ellen Goodman, in Jeanette Branin, "She Outlines the Realities for a Change," San Diego *Union*, June 29, 1977.

3. Ibid.

4. Margaret Mead, "Working Mothers and Their Children," *Manpower*, June 1970.

5. Jean Curtis, "How Child-Care Experts Fail the Working Mother," *Family Circle*, October 1976, p. 14.

6. Earl C. Gottschalk, Jr., "Women at Work: Day Care Is Booming, But Experts Are Split Over Its Effects on Kids," *Wall Street Journal*, September 15, 1978.

7. Beatrice M. Glickman and Nesha B. Springer, *Who Cares for the Baby? Choices in Child Care* (New York: Schocken Books, Inc., 1978), p. xi.

8. Ibid., p. 237.

9. Ellen R. Hock, in "Mom Out, Baby Fine, Study Says," San Diego *Evening Tribune*, April 29, 1975, p. D-3.

10. Colleen L. Johnson and Frank A. Johnson. "Attitudes Toward Parenting in Dual-Career Families," *American Journal of Psychiatry*, April 1977, p. 392.

11. Ellen R. Hock, in "Mom Out, Baby Fine, Study Says," San Diego *Evening Tribune*, April 29, 1975, p. D-3.

12. Sam Clark, "Maternal Employment," *Illinois Teacher*, May-June 1975, p. 270.

13. Mary C. Howell, "Effects of Maternal Employment on the Child," *Pediatrics*, September 1973, pp. 327-343.

14. Claire Etaugh, "Effects of Maternal Employment on Children," *Merrill-Palmer Quarterly*, April 1974, pp. 71-97.

15. Jessie Bernard, *The Future of Motherhood* (New York: The Dial Press, 1974).

16. Janet E. Harrell and Carl Ridley, "Substitute Child Care, Maternal Employment and the Quality of Mother-Child Interaction," *Journal of Marriage and the Family*, August 1975, pp. 556-564.

17. Claire Etaugh, "Effects of Maternal Employment on Children," *Merrill-Palmer Quarterly*, April 1974, pp. 71-97.

18. Ibid.

19. Ellen Goodman, in Jeanette Branin, "She Outlines the

Realities for a Change," San Diego *Union,* June 29, 1977.
20. Ann Blackman, "Problems of the Two-Paycheck Family," Los Angeles *Times,* March 10, 1978.
21. Alison Clarke-Stewart, *Child Care in the Family: A Review of Research and Some Propositions for Policy* (New York: Academic Press, 1977), p. 107.
22. David Robison, "Working Parents Choose Home-Based Child Care Arrangements," *World of Work Report,* February 1977.
23. Nathan B. Talbot, *Raising Children in Modern America: What Parents and Society Should Be Doing for Their Children* (Boston: Little, Brown and Co., 1976), p. 25.

Chapter VI   Dealing with Dollars
(pages 136–158)

1. *Webster's Seventh New Collegiate Dictionary* (Springfield: G. & C. Merriam Co., 1970).
2. "Costs for Car Operators Increased 10% This Year," *Wall Street Journal,* October 30, 1978, p. 22.

Chapter VII   Some Special Challenges: Launching, Role-Changing, New Opportunities, Similar Careers, and Successful Women   *(pages 159–213)*

1. Alan L. Otten, "Two-Career Couples," *Wall Street Journal,* July 29, 1976.
2. Patricia Light, in "Commuting: A Solution for Two-Career Couples," *Business Week,* April 3, 1978, p. 68.
3. "Commuting's Out," *Fortune,* July 17, 1978, p. 16.
4. Sharon K. Donegan, in Liz R. Gallese, "Women Managers Say Job Transfers Present a Growing Dilemma," *Wall Street Journal,* May 4, 1978.
5. Ibid.
6. Comment by a placement director, 1978 International MBA Placement and Recruitment Conference, Association of MBA Executives, Inc., New Orleans, November 29, 1978.
7. "Jacqueline Kennedy Onassis Talks About Working," *Ms.* magazine, March 1979, pp. 50–51.

8. Morton H. and Marjorie H. Shaevitz, "Changing Roles, Changing Relationships: Implications for the Mental Health Professional," *Psychiatric Annals,* February 1976, pp. 22–41.

9. Morton Hunt, "Making a Living Versus Making a Home," *Redbook,* April 1978, pp. 69–73.

10. Rhona and Robert N. Rapoport, *Dual Career Families Reexamined: New Integrations of Work and Family* (London: Martin Robertson & Co. Ltd., 1976).

11. Sharon L. Connelly, "Meeting the Challenge of Executive Stress," July 14, 1977, p. 38. Unpublished paper.

12. Roger Ricklefs, "Firms Become Willing—or Eager—to Hire Divorced Executives," *Wall Street Journal,* May 18, 1978, p. 1.

13. *Wall Street Journal,* February 27, 1979, p. 1.

14. Anthony Ramirez, "A Manager's Transfers Impose Heavy Burden on His Wife, Children," *Wall Street Journal,* February 28, 1978, p. 1.

15. Ibid.

16. Challenging Assumptions: Choosing Options Conference, Project: WILL, Barat College, Lake Forest, Illinois, April 8, 1978.

17. "A Study of Employee Relocation Policies Among Major U.S. Corporations," Merrill Lynch Relocation Management, Inc., 1978, p. 10.

18. "Employers 'Sensitive' to Dual Careers Gain Competitive Edge, Experts Say," *The Newsletter of the Association of the Association of Master of Business Administration Executives,* January 1979, pp. 10–11.

19. Christopher Hosford, "Roles . . . and Jobs: An Open Conflict," *Times-Union and Journal,* Jacksonville, Florida, June 25, 1978.

20. Arline L. Bronzaft, "College Women Want a Career, Marriage and Children," *Psychological Reports,* 1974, 35, pp. 1031–1034.

21. Thomas W. Martin, Kenneth J. Berry, and R. Brooke Jacobsen, "The Impact of Dual-Career Marriages on Female Professional Careers: An Empirical Test of a Par-

sonian Hypothesis," *Journal of Marriage and the Family*, November 1975, pp. 734–742.

22. Marlys Harris, "Couples Wedded to the Same Careers," *Money*, January 1978, p. 34.

23. Thomas W. Martin, Kenneth J. Berry, and R. Brooke Jacobsen. "The Impact of Dual-Career Marriages on Female Professional Careers: An Empirical Test of a Parsonian Hypothesis," *Journal of Marriage and the Family*, November 1975, pp. 734–742.

24. Ibid., p. 742.

25. Ibid., p. 742.

26. Rebecca B. Bryson, Jeff B. Bryson, Mark H. Licht, and Barbara G. Licht. "The Professional Pair: Husband and Wife Psychologists," *American Psychologist*, January 1976, p. 16.

27. Ibid., p. 14.

28. Cynthia F. Epstein, "Law Partners and Marital Partners," *Human Relations*, 1971, 24, p. 562.

29. Joann S. Lublin, "Working Couples Find an Increasing Chance of Conflicts in Jobs," *Wall Street Journal*, November 18, 1977.

30. Ibid.

31. Marlys Harris, "Couples Wedded to the Same Careers," *Money*, January 1978, p. 32.

32. Miriam H. Krohn, *Your Job Campaign* (New York: Catalyst, 1974).

33. Theodore Nadelson and Leon Eisenberg, "The Successful Professional Woman: On Being Married to One," *American Journal of Psychiatry*, 134, October 1977, p. 1071.

34. David P. Campbell, *Manual for the Strong-Campbell Interest Inventory* (Stanford: Stanford University Press, 1974).

35. Sally Koslow, "Working with the Man You Love," *Working Woman*, September 1978, p. 68.

36. Ibid., p. 76.

37. Constantina Safilios-Rothschild and Marcellinus Dijkers, "Handling Unconventional Asymmetries," in *Working*

Couples, eds. Rhona and Robert N. Rapoport, and Janice M. Bumstead (New York: Harper and Row, 1978).

38. Cynthia F. Epstein, "Bring Women In," in *Women and Success: The Anatomy of Achievement,* ed. Ruth B. Kundsin (New York: William Morrow and Co., 1974), p. 16.
39. Matina S. Horner and Mary R. Walsh, "Psychological Barriers to Success in Women," in *Women and Success: The Anatomy of Achievement,* ed. Ruth B. Kundsin (New York: William Morrow and Co., 1974), p. 139.
40. Marcille G. Williams, *The New Executive Woman: A Guide to Business Success* (Radnor: Chilton Book Co., 1977), p. 177.
41. Rhona and Robert N. Rapoport, *Dual Career Families Reexamined: New Integrations of Work and Family* (London: Martin Robertson & Co., Ltd., 1976), p. 16.

Chapter VIII   Choosing the "Right" Employer
(pages 214–229)

1. Rosabeth M. Kanter, in Noel Osment, "See Bill and Jane. See Them Work. They Set Their Time," San Diego *Union,* October 15, 1977.
2. Sharon L. Connelly, "Geographical Relocation of Dual Career Couples." Dissertation proposal, September 8, 1978, p. 4.
3. Jeremy Main, "Good Jobs Go Part Time," *Money,* October 1977, p. 86.
4. Allan R. Cohen and Herman Gadon, *Alternative Work Schedules: Integrating Individual and Organizational Needs* (Reading: Addison-Wesley Publishing Co., Inc.), 1978.
5. Jeremy Main, "Good Jobs Go Part Time," *Money,* October 1977, p. 86.
6. Ibid., p. 82.
7. Ibid., p. 84.
8. Sharon L. Connelly, "Geographical Relocation of Dual Career Couples." Dissertation proposal, September 8, 1978, p. 5.
9. James Robins, "Firms Give Employees All Kinds of Assist

ance to Get Them to Move," *Wall Street Journal,* May 2, 1979, p. 1.

10. B. Rosen and Thomas H. Jerdee, "Sex Stereotyping in the Executive Suite," *Harvard Business Review,* March–April 1974, pp. 45–58.

11. Women at Work Series, *Wall Street Journal,* August 28, 31, September 5, 8, 13, 22, 1978.

12. "Employers 'Sensitive' to Dual Careers Gain Competitive Edge, Experts Say," *Newsletter of the Association of Master of Business Administration Executives,* January 1979, p. 11.

Suggestions for Further Reading

Adult Development

Bardwick, Judith M. *In Transition: How Feminism, Sexual Liberation, and the Search for Self-Fulfillment Have Altered Our Lives.* New York: Holt, Rinehart and Winston, 1979, $8.95.

Levinson, Daniel J., with Charlotte N. Darrow, Edward B. Klein, Maria H. Levinson, and Braxton McKee. *The Seasons of a Man's Life.* New York: Alfred A. Knopf, 1978, $10.95.

Sheehy, Gail. *Passages: Predictable Crises of Adult Life.* New York: E.P. Dutton & Co., Inc., 1976. $10.95.

Child Care

Auerbach, Stevanne, and Linda Freedman. *Choosing Child Care: A Guide for Parents.* San Francisco: Parents and Child Care Resources, 1976. $3.00.

Glickman, Beatrice Marden, and Nesha Bass Springer. *Who Cares for the Baby? Choices in Child Care.* New York: Schocken Books, 1978. $9.95.

Communication Skills

Comfort, Alex, ed. *The Joy of Sex: A Cordon Bleu Guide to Lovemaking.* New York: Crown Publishers, Inc., 1972. $12.95.

Fromm, Eric. *The Art of Loving,* New York: Harper & Row, Inc., 1974. $1.50.

Masters, William H., et al. *Pleasure Bond: A New Look at Sexuality and Commitment.* Boston: Little, Brown and Co., 1976. $8.95.

Satir, Virginia. *Peoplemaking.* Palo Alto: Science and Behavior Books, Inc., 1972. $5.95.

Parenting

Bartz, Wayne R., and Richard A. Rasor. *Surviving with Kids: A Lifeline for Overwhelmed Parents.* San Luis Obispo: Impact Publishers, 1978. $3.95.

Bernard, Jessie. *The Future of Motherhood.* New York: The Dial Press, 1974. $10.00

Boston Women's Health Book Collective. *Our Bodies, Ourselves.* New York: Simon and Schuster, Inc., 1976. $4.95.

Boston Women's Health Book Collective. *Ourselves and Our Children: A Book by and for Parents.* New York: Random House, 1978. $2.09.

Dunn, Rita, and Kenneth Dunn. *How To Raise Independent and Professionally Successful Daughters.* Englewood Cliffs, New Jersey: Prentice-Hall, Inc., 1977. $10.00

Hoffman, L., and F. E. Nye, eds. *Working Mothers: An Evaluative Review of the Consequences for Wife, Husband and Child.* San Francisco: Jossey-Bass, 1974. $13.95.

Levine, James A. *Who Will Raise the Children? New Options for Fathers (and Mothers).* Philadelphia: J. B. Lippincott Co., 1976. $8.95.

Peck, Ellen. *The Baby Trap.* Los Angeles: Pinnacle Books, 1976. $5.95.

Peck, Ellen, and William Granzig. *The Parent Test: How to Measure and Develop Your Talent for Parenthood.* New York: G. P. Putnam & Sons, 1978. $9.95.

Price, Jane. *You're Not Too Old to Have a Baby.* New York: Penguin Books, Inc., 1978. $2.95.

Rapoport, Rhona, Robert N. Rapoport, and Ziona Strelitz. *Fathers, Mothers and Society.* New York: Basic Books, Inc., 1977. $15.00.

Talbot, Nathan B., ed. *Raising Children in Modern America: Problems and Prospective Solutions.* Boston: Little, Brown & Co., 1976. $17.50.

Whelan, Elizabeth M. *A Baby . . . Maybe? A Guide to Making the Most Fateful Decision of Your Life.* New York: The Bobbs-Merrill Co., Inc., 1975. $5.95.

Re-Entry Issues
Bolles, Richard N. *What Color Is Your Parachute? A Practical Manual for Job Hunters and Career Changers.* Berkeley: Ten Speed Press, 1977. $8.95.
Lenz, Elinor, and Marjorie Hansen Shaevitz. *So You Want to Go Back to School: Facing the Realities of Re-Entry.* New York: McGraw-Hill Book Co., 1977. $4.95.

Stress Management
Farquhar, John W. *The American Way of Life Need Not Be Hazardous to Your Health.* New York: W. W. Norton & Co., 1978. $9.95.
McQuade, Donald, and Ann Aikman. *Stress.* New York: Bantam Books, Inc., 1975. $1.95.
Lamott, Kenneth. *Escape from Stress.* New York: Berkeley Publishing Corporation, 1975. $1.95.
Pelletier, Kenneth. *Mind as Healer, Mind as Slayer.* New York: Dell Publishing Co., Inc., 1977. $4.95.
Selye, Hans. *The Stress of Life.* New York: McGraw-Hill Book Co., 1976. $4.95.
Selye, Hans. *Stress Without Distress.* Philadelphia: J. B. Lippincott Co., 1974. $7.50.

Time Management
Goldfein, Donna. *Everywoman's Guide to Time Management.* Millbrae: Les Femmes Publishing, 1977. $3.95.
Lakein, Alan. *How to Get Control of Your Time and Your Life.* New York: Signet Books, The New American Library, Inc., 1974. $1.75.
Reynolds, Helen, and Mary E. Tramel. *Executive Time Management.* Englewood Cliffs, New Jersey: Prentice-Hall, Inc., 1979. $4.95.

Working Couples
Bernard, Jessie. *The Future of Marriage.* New York: Bantam Books, 1973. $1.95.

Rapoport, Rhona and Robert N. *Dual-Career Families.* London: Penguin Books, 1971.

Rapoport, Rhona and Robert N. *Dual-Career Families Re-Examined: New Integrations of Work and Family.* New York: Harper Colophon Books, 1977. $3.45.

Rapoport, Robert and Rhona, with Janice Bumstead, eds. *Working Couples.* New York: Harper Colophon Books, 1978. $3.95.

Working Women (including books on successful women)

Bernard, Jessie. *Women, Wives, Mothers: Values and Options.* Chicago: Aldine Publishing Co., 1975. $5.95.

Kundsin, Ruth B., ed. *Women & Success: The Anatomy of Achievement.* New York: William Morrow & Co., 1974. $7.95.

Trahey, Jane. *On Women and Power: Who's Got It? How to Get It?* New York: Rawson Associates Publishers, Inc., 1977. $8.95.

Index

A Baby? . . . Maybe Services
(organization), 72
Accepting, art of, 248–49
Acting-out, by children,
132–33
Activities, planned: for
adolescents, 118; for
children on school
vacations, 119–20;
importance of, to effective
fatherhood, 87
Adam's Rib, 223
Adolescents, 116–17;
afterschool programs for,
117–18; lessons and other
planned activities for,
118
Advancement and
productivity, effect of
similar careers on, 197,
198–203
Afterschool programs, for
adolescents, 117–18
American Home, 83

Antinepotism. *See* Nepotism
Applauding, art of, 249
Aronson, Shephard G., 16
Association of MBA
Executives, 227
Au pair girls, 93–94, 99,
107–8
Availability, sexuality and,
252–53

Banking, 153–54, 155
Bart, Pauline, 46
Beckman, Linda, list of
rewards and costs of
parenthood developed by,
69–71
Bernard, Jessie, 13; *The
Future of Motherhood,* 71
Berry, Kenneth, 199
Big Brothers, 73
Big Sisters, 73
Bill-paying, 154–57
Birth control, widespread
use of, 2

Blaming and scapegoating,
overload and, 233–34
Bonding, 86–87, 88
Boston Women's Health
Book Collective: *Our
Bodies, Ourselves,* 71–72;
*Ourselves and Our
Children,* 72
Breneman, David, 88
Bronfenbrenner, Urie,
83–84, 85, 100–101
Bronzaft, Arline, 196
Brookings Institution, 88
Bulletin board, family, 90
Bureaucracy, effect of, on
families, 88
Business Week, 227

Calendars, yearly, used in
household management,
59
California, University of, at
Los Angeles, 69
Careers, challenges of
similar, 161, 195–97, 206–7;
and productivity and
advancement, 197,
198–203; and job
satisfaction, 197–98, 203–5;
and similar settings, 198,
205–6
Carnegie Council on
Children, 101
Catering services, 65
Cella, Barbara, 57
Change: difficulties of,
23–27; and inertia, 26–27;
and male/female identity

tension lines, 23–26; roots
of, 2–3; technological
versus social, 214–15
Chase Manhattan Bank, 228
Childbirth, 69
Child care, 50, 92–95; in
adolescence, 116–18;
behavior changes of
children in, 131–34;
changes in, 120–21, 134;
costs of, 121–22, 140–41;
day-care centers, 111–12;
dealing with negative
feedback about, 134–35;
family, 109–10; in home
(someone else's), 108–9; in
home (yours), 101–8; how
to find, 123–24; for ill
children, 118–19; industry-
or company-sponsored, 80,
112–13, 223; nursery and
preschools, 110–11; options,
99–100; out-of-home, what
to look for in, 127–31;
parental concerns about,
95–99; for parents
working part time,
100–101; persons,
qualifications of, 122–23;
planning of, for school
vacations, 119–20; for
school age to adolescence,
114–16; screening
candidates for, 124–27;
sharing of, with other
working couples, 113–14
Children: deciding timing
and number of, 75–78;

Children (cont.)
decision to have (or not to have), 66–75; fatherhood and, 84–88; making time for, 79–80; needs of, 83–84; quality versus quantity time with, 81–83; use of, in household management, 57
Chrysler, 217
Civil rights movement, 2
Classes, relating to parenting, 72–73
Clinging, children's, 132
Close, art of being, 250–53
Clothes, care of, 63
Cohen, Allan R., 216
Collister, Richard A., 228
Colorado State University, 199
Commitment, 12
Communication breakdown or failure, 21–22; overload and, 232
Commuting, career-choice and, 166–69, 184
Company- or industry-sponsored child care, 80, 112–13, 223
Conflicts of interest: company rules against, 223–24; in similar careers, 197, 198, 200–202
Connelly, Sharon, 7
Conner, Deborah D., 194, 228
Control Data, 112, 216

Cooperative child care, 113–14
Cornell University, 4, 83
Corporate insensitivity, 188–89
Costs, in earning second income, 140–42
Crying, children's, 132
Cummins Engine Company, Inc., 194, 228

Day Care and Child Development Council in America, 112
Day-care centers, 111–12; industry- or company-sponsored, 80, 112–13, 223. See also Child care
Denial, overload and, 233
Dentists and doctors, selection of, 60
Depression, overload and, 234–35
Divorce, no-fault, 8
Doctors and dentists, selection of, 60
Dodson, Fitzhugh, 78–79
"Do your own thing" era, 15–21
Dreams and waking up at night, children's, 133
Drive-ins, use of, to save time, 65

Effective Couples Communication, 22
Eisenberg, Leon, 36, 50
Employer: antinepotism and

Employer (cont.)
conflict-of-interest rules,
223–24, checklist of, 226;
child-care facilities, 223;
factors to consider in
choosing, 214–15, 227–29;
flexible hours (flextime),
215–17; leave options and
opportunities, 217–18;
part-time employment
opportunities, 218–20;
perquisites ("perks"),
224–25; sex-role policies,
222–23; transfer policies,
221; travel expectations,
220–21
Employment opportunities,
part-time, 80, 218–20
Epstein, Cynthia Fuchs, 208
Equal Employment
Opportunity Commission,
224
Equitable Life Assurance
Society, 219
Esalen, 15
Exxon, 216

Family: effect of
bureaucracy on, 88; effect
of "doing your own thing"
on, 16
Fathering, 84–85; rejection
of established attitudes
toward, 87–88; three steps
to effective, 85–87
Fatigue: overload and, 232;
sexuality and, 252–53
Feminist movement. See

Women's liberation
movement
Financial arrangements. See
Money
Financial planning,
long-term, 158
First National Bank of
Boston, 216
Flexible hours (flextime),
215–17
Forbes magazine, 217, 227
Fortune, 227; 500 list, 215,
225
Foster, Debbie, 201
Four-day week, 217
Frank, Harold, 8

Gadon, Herman, 216
General Mills, Inc., 195, 229
Glickman, B. M., Who Cares
for the Baby? Choices in
Child Care, 96–97
"Going crazy," overload
and, 237
Goldfein, Donna,
Everywoman's Guide to
Time Management, 58
Goodman, Ellen, 92–93, 100
Granzig, William, The
Parent Test (with Ellen
Peck), 72, 76

Harvard Business School,
166; Office of Career
Development at, 161
Harvard Medical School,
36

Harvard University, 96
Health, Education, and
  Welfare (HEW),
  Department of, 88, 97
Help, household: live-in,
  49–51; live-out, 51;
  part-time, 51
Helplessness, overload and
  sense of, 232
Hepburn, Katharine, 223
Hewlett-Packard, 216
H. J. Heinz Co., 201
Hock, Ellen Rozelle, 97–
  98
Hoffman, Lois, 78
Hopelessness, overload and
  sense of, 232
Horner, Matina, 209
Household management,
  32–36; care of clothes, 63;
  deciding on standards for,
  45–47; division of
  responsibility in, 47–53;
  efficiency in, 61–62;
  formula for, 53–57;
  managing time in, 58–61;
  man's dilemma about,
  41–42; miscellaneous tips
  for, 63–64; myth of versus
  media on, 36–40; saving
  time on meals, 62–63;
  spending money to save
  time and energy in,
  64–65; taking inventory
  in, 42–45; using children
  in, 57; woman's dilemma
  about, 40–41
"House-husband," 3

Identity tension lines,
  male/female, 23–26, 48
Illinois, University of,
  Medical School, 46
Illness, child care and:
  chronic, 118–19;
  intermittent, acute, 119
Including, art of, 246
Incomes, shrinking of, 4–5.
  See also Money
Industrial Revolution, 13, 14
Industry- or
  company-sponsored child
  care, 80, 112–13, 223
Inertia, 26–27
"Infectious exhaustion," 18
Inflation, 4–5
Information bank,
  household, 60
Interaction, parent-child,
  81–82
International Business
  Machines (IBM)
  Corporation, 187–88
Invitations, making mutual
  decisions on, 59–60
Iowa State University, 98
IUDs, 2

Jacobsen, R. Brooke, 199
Jealousy, 159
Job relocations. See
  Opportunities, challenges
  of new job
Job satisfaction, effect of
  similar careers on, 197–98,
  203–5
Job-sharing, 80

John Hancock, 216
Juvenile delinquency,
maternal deprivation and,
95, 97

Kagan, Jerome, 96
Koslow, Sally, 206

Lakein, Alan, *How to Get Control of Your Time and Your Life*, 58
Lamaze, 86
"Latch-key" children, 114–15, 171
"Launching" challenges, 160, 161–62; problem-solving strategies for, 162–69; questions to consider in, 169–70
Leaves of absence, 185; options and opportunities for, 217–18
Light, Patricia K., 161–62, 166
Live-in child care, 103, 107–8
Live-in help, 49–51
Live-out child care, 103–7
Live-out help, 51
Los Angeles *Times*, 227

Main, Jeremy, 217
Male/female dilemmas about household management, 40–42
Male/female feelings about success for women, 208–11
Male/female identity tension lines, 23–26
Manis, Jean, 78

Marriage, contemporary style of, 7–9
Martin, Thomas, 199
Maternal deprivation, juvenile delinquency and, 95, 97
Maternity leave, 217, 218
Mead, Margaret, 37, 73, 94
Meals, saving time on, 62–63
Media myths: about household management, 36–40; about two-career couples, 3–4
Meetings, weekly: importance of, to two-career parenting, 89–90; usefulness of, in household management, 59
Mental-health professionals, assistance from, in coping with overload, 242–43
Merrill Lynch Relocation Management, Inc., 187, 189, 221
Message center, household, 59
Midlife crisis, 5–7
Money: and banking, 153–54; and bill-paying, 154–57; and costs of earning second income, 140–42; "his" and "her," 143–44; issues about, 143–44; model, choosing suitable, 150–53; models for handling, 138–39, 144–50; as power, 137–38, 152; and savings, 157–58;

Money (cont.)
two-career conflicts over,
136–37; two-career
solutions to, 144–50;
unrealistic expectations
about, 139–40
Money magazine, 217
Ms. magazine, 5, 29, 80

Nadelson, Theodore, 36, 50
Nannies, British, 93, 94, 99,
107
Narcissism, 16
National Association for the
Education of Young
Children, 111
National Organization for
Non-Parents, 72
Needs, children's, 83–84
Nepotism: company rules
against, 223–24; in similar
careers, 197, 198, 199, 200,
202
Nestlé's, 216
New York Times, 227
New York University School
of Medicine, 16
Nursery schools, 110–11

Ohio State University School
of Home Economics, 97
Onassis, Jacqueline
Kennedy, 171
Opportunities, challenges of
new job, 160–61, 181–83;
and long-term changes,
187–90; possible solutions
to, 190–95; and short-term
changes, 183–87

Overload, 230; blaming and
scapegoating and, 233–34;
"calling" an, 238; defined,
231; denial and, 233;
depression and, 234–35;
diagnosis of, 238–39;
"going crazy" and, 237;
long-term strategies for
coping with, 242–44;
psychosomatic reactions
and, 235; reducing or
ending, 239–42; rigidity
and, 236–37; symptoms of,
231–32; withdrawal and,
236

Pacific Gas & Electric, 216
Parent Effectiveness
Training (PET), 79
Parenting: deciding timing
and number of children,
75–78; decision to have
(or not have) children,
66–75; definition of,
78–79; and fathering,
84–88; making time for
children, 79–80; and
needs of children, 83–84;
and quality versus
quantity time with
children, 81–83; rewards
and costs of, 69–71; style
of, 79; suggestions for
two-career, 88–91
Parenting by Choice
(organization), 72
Part-time employment
opportunities, 80, 218–20
Part-time help, 51

Paternity leave, 217, 218
Peck, Ellen: *The Baby Trap*,
72; *The Parent Test* (with
William Granzig), 72, 76
Perls, Fritz, 15
Perquisites ("perks"), 224–25
"Personhood," 3
"Pill," 2
Planned Parenthood
Federation of America, 72
Pleasing, art of, 250
Pondering Parenthood
(organization), 72
Power, money as, 137–38,
152
Prenuptial agreements, 7–8
Preschools, 110–11
Price, Jane, *You're Not Too
Old to Have a Baby*, 72
Pringle, Kellmer, 84
Productivity and
advancement, effect of
similar careers on, 197,
198–203
Professionals, use of, in
household management,
64–65
Profit-and-loss worksheet,
143
Psychosomatic reactions,
overload and, 235
"Punch-in" system, 216–17

Quality versus quantity time
with children, 81–83

Rapoport, Rhona and Robert
N., 24, 37, 211–12; *Fathers,*

Mothers and Society (with
Ziona Strelitz), 72
Reassignment, request for
temporary, 184–85
Responsibilities: division of,
in household manage-
ment, 47–53; re-examin-
ing distribution of, to cope
with overload, 242
Rewards: and costs of
parenting, 69–71; of
successful two-career
couples, 27–28
Rigidity, overload and,
236–37
Role-changing challenges,
160, 170–71; defined,
171–72; patterns emerging
in, 172–74; problems
caused by, 174–75; steps
for making successful,
176–81
Rosenblum, Constance, 67
Rowland, Helen, 78

Savings, 157–58
Scapegoating and blaming,
overload and, 233–34
School vacations, child care
and, 119–20
Separations, temporary, new
job opportunities and,
186–87
Service people, establishing
relationship with, 65
Settings, similar, effect on
similar careers of, 198,
205–6

Sex-role policies,
enlightened, 222–23
Sexuality, 251–53
Sick leave, 217, 218
Social versus technological
change, 214–15
Spock, Benjamin, 79
Springer, Nesha Bass, *Who
Cares for the Baby?
Choices in Child Care*,
96–97
Stanford University, 29, 161
Strelitz, Ziona, *Fathers,
Mothers and Society* (with
Rhona and Robert
Rapoport), 72
Stride Rite Corporation,
Children's Center of, 113
Success: challenges of, for
women, 161, 207–13;
historical association of,
with men, 207–8
Supporting, art of, 246–47
Synanon, 15

TA (Transactional Analysis),
79
Talbot, Nathan, 84, 114–15
Technological versus social
change, 214–15
Ten-hour-day system, 217
Therapists, assistance from,
in coping with overload,
242–43
Time: importance of early
and specific, to
fatherhood, 85–87;
making, for children,

79–80; quality versus
quantity, with children,
81–83
Time magazine, 3
Time-wasters, 60–61
Toffler, Alvin, *Future Shock,*
13
Tornabene, Lyn, 35–36
Touching, 251
Tracy, Spencer, 223
Trammel, Marvin, 195, 229
Transfer policies, company,
188–90, 221
Travel expectations,
realistic, 220–21
TRW, 112
Two-career relationships,
245, 253–54; accepting in,
248–49; applauding in,
249; categories of, 14–15;
closeness in, 250–53;
defined, 12–13; help for,
28–29; including in, 246;
planning in, 253; pleasing
in, 250; rewards of
successful, 27–28; sexuality
in, 251–53; supporting in,
246–47; touching in, 251

U.S. Bureau of Labor
Statistics, 4
U.S. Department of
Agriculture, 37
U.S. Department of Labor,
94
U.S. Geological Survey, 216
U.S. News & World Report,
227

Wall Street Journal, 188, 200, 227
Wellington, Sara, 101
Whelan, Elizabeth, *A Baby?
. . . Maybe,* 72
Withdrawal, overload and, 236
Woman's Day, 29
Women, challenges of success for, 161, 207–8; coping with, 212–13; difficulties with, 211–12; female feelings about, 208–10; male feelings about, 210–11
Women's liberation movement, 2, 36
Work in America Institute, Inc., 112
Working Woman, 29
World of Work Report, 112

Zero population growth, 3, 10, 11
Zero Population Growth (organization), 72